P.E. Buckland (handwritten)

A *Personnel* Book

SO-DXM-668

Human Resources Management: The Past Is Prologue

Edited by **Ernest C. Miller**

5 Phenomena (handwritten)
① Interact Between Capital & Consumer (handwritten)

amacom
A Division of American Management Associations

The articles in this collection have all been previously published in *Personnel,* AMACOM's periodical for professional human resources managers.

International standard book number: 0-8144-06802-0

Preface

SOME men at age 50 look back at how much they have done; others look ahead at how much they have yet to do. With its 50th Human Resources Conference . . . its Golden Anniversary Conference . . . AMA is looking back for wisdom and ahead for opportunity and challenge.

Young managers often ask their seniors, "What can you tell me that fits my problems of today?"

Mature managers often ask if the young can learn from the past.

This book looks ahead by looking back. By concentrating on five major areas—the fundamental philosophy of human resources management, the entry of the behavioral scientists, the nature of the function, ways to evaluate the performance of the function, and the importance of employee attitudes and work climate—this collection of articles from *Personnel* attempts to prepare you for the future. But by including articles from the 1930s, 1940s, and 1950s, it tries to highlight the wisdom that past practitioners brought to the function and the importance of historical perspective in reacting to present problems and in developing "new" solutions.

The "old" do have something to contribute to the young. And with application, the young can learn lessons for the future from the past. So the title of the collection: *Human Resources Management: The Past Is Prologue.*

All the articles in this collection are from *Personnel.* That wasn't the original concept of the book, but when we reviewed *Personnel* from 1922 through 1978, we were so impressed with the diversity and quality of its contents down through the years that we decided it would be only fitting to restrict our selections to this one source.

Our next problem was one of focus. *Personnel* has published much excellent material on almost every significant human resources management function. To have attempted to cover all these areas would have produced a hodge-podge of no depth and little value. Rather than do that, we decided to stay with the fundamental issues of philosophy, definition, and measurement. We also decided to emphasize how much what was said and done in the past fits today—and probably tomorrow. So, although you will recognize the names of many of the contributors, current fame was not a criterion for selection, usefulness was.

We would like to thank the members of the AMA's advisory councils who nominated authors for inclusion in this collection. Although we requested this help, the way the project developed we could make only limited use of it. The collection omits more of their nominees than it includes. We have nothing from Chester Barnard, Peter Drucker, Frederick Taylor, Abraham Maslow, Frederick Herzberg, Robert Blake, Jane Mouton, or Rensis Likert, individuals who were frequently identified as among the most significant contributors to the development of the human resources function. We do, however, have offerings from some of the others who were frequently nominated, such as Douglas McGregor, Elton Mayo, Robert Guest, and Charles Meyers. In any case, we were instructed by the comments of our council members, and we are in their debt. We were particularly stimulated by the suggestion that one of the outstanding human resources management books of recent years is Kenneth P. Williams's *Lincoln Finds a General* (Macmillan, 1949) and that another, of older origin, is *The Bible*.

Our thanks, then, to all those who have contributed to the development of human resources management over the past 50 years. Without your contributions this volume would not have been possible. Neither would we have the beginnings of a profession.

Ernest C. Miller
Editor

Contents

Part III   Defining the Function

Part IV   How're We Doing?

Part V   Employee Attitudes and Work Climate— The Critical Measure of Success

PART I

Attitudes to Build On

THE more things change, the more they remain the same. A hackneyed comment, perhaps, but still so true. Many managers think the problems they face today are new, without precedent, and the solutions they have proposed, novel. The five chapters in Part I may induce a change in perspective.

The fundamental attitudes that should underlie a modern human resources function are the same attitudes that professional human resources managers have known and used for more than 50 years. This should not be surprising, though. The nature of man has not changed during this tic of time. To emphasize the stability of these fundamentals, and to lend perspective to those who are encountering the challenges of human resources management for the first time, we have gone back to 1923 for the theme paper of Part I, "A Plea for the Man in the Ranks." If you read only one chapter in this collection, I hope it will be this one by E. K. Hall.

Hall's article was published in *Personnel* in November 1931, but it had been given first as a talk to the Illinois Manufacturers' Association in 1923. In 1931, when the speech was published, Hall was a special lecturer in the Amos Tuck School of Administration and Finance at Dartmouth College, but his comments were based on his extensive experience as vice-president in charge of personnel and public relations for the American Telephone and Telegraph Company. For him, human resources management is management—a view that is impressively modern. And his emphasis on teamwork and the four Cs of human resources management—contact, conference, confidence, and cooperation—would please the most ardent present-day organization development specialist. Hall's article demonstrates again that wisdom is "modern."

John H. Goss authored the second chapter, "The Employee's Challenge—A Right and an Obligation." At the time the article was published—May 1937—Goss was vice-president of Scovill Manufacturing Company. His special contribution was to lay down a tested and practical approach to developing and implementing policy. His approach rested on the same assumptions as Hall's: We proceed at risk if we ignore the knowledge and insights of our employees. With this philosophy as his basis, he described a program that centered on employees' right to challenge any new policy or procedure. Of similarly modern thrust was his recognition of the effects of the generation gap and of the special efforts needed to overcome it.

Elton Mayo also addressed the theme of building teamwork for increased employee satisfaction and productivity. By May 1941, the issue of *Personnel* in which his article "Research in Human Relations" was published, his work at the Hawthorne Plant of the Western Electric Company was completed and widely disseminated. That work started the revolution in human resources management practices that is still working itself out today. In addition to again focusing our attention on the influence of group membership on behavior, Mayo's article addressed the issues of executive authority and unemployment, matters of great current concern. If he were alive and still a professor of industrial relations at the Graduate School of Business Administration at Harvard, his comments would be as cogent today as in 1941.

The fourth chapter in the part also speaks to the matter of teamwork in terms of cooperation. In this case, the focus is on union–management relations. The authors, Irving Knickerbocker and Douglas McGregor, were both at the Industrial Relations Section at Massachusetts Institute of Technology at the time of publication in

November 1942. "Union–Management Cooperation: A Psychological Analysis," is a balanced, reasonable statement of what is required if two groups that might otherwise be in continual conflict are to learn to work together to their mutual advantage. Unfortunately, that is a problem that has not yet been solved. But those who follow current efforts to increase cooperation between unions and management will find that these authors anticipated and suggested the approaches that are now being rediscovered.

It somehow seems fitting to close Part I with an article by Lawrence A. Appley, written while he was a vice-president and director of Montgomery Ward & Company. Mr. Appley contributed much to the professionalization of the human resources function during his years as head of American Management Associations. In this May 1947 article, "Essentials of a Management Personnel Policy," he outlined an approach to the development of the function that can still serve as a model: In modern parlance, begin with the setting of general and specific objectives for the function.

I think you will find these articles interesting. Having read them, I am sure you will agree, the past is prologue.

1

A Plea for the
Man in the Ranks

E. K. Hall

WE do not need to look back 100 years in this country to find industry being carried on either by individuals or relatively small groups of individuals. The shoemaker owned his own tools, bought his own materials, completed his product, and marketed it. The factories were small. The employees and the management all lived in the same small town and were generally well acquainted.

Then came the invention of the steam engine, followed later by the discovery and development of electricity as motive power, and then followed the era of the rapid introduction of labor-saving machinery. The result was that the production of one man was doubled, trebled, and often multiplied even ten or twenty times. One after another came the big machines, the enormous plants and large industrial concerns, all of which resulted in tremendous increases in production.

As the cost of production decreased, the product became cheaper, and one after another new articles hitherto unknown appeared; and for all of them, at these lower prices, there seemed to be endless markets.

Civilization and industry were in the boom and men were now producing in large groups instead of as individuals.

It was literally an industrial evolution. Now what was the effect of all this on the artisan, the worker, or the man in the ranks? There were two very distinct effects. The first one was the way it affected him in the ability to secure and participate in the enjoyment of material things—things for which he could exchange the money that he found in his pay envelope. He was able to have a greater diversity of food upon his table, more and better clothing, broader opportunities for himself and family in the way of education, entertainment, and travel. Things that had been unknown or luxuries to his parents became commonplace or necessities with him, and he enjoyed many things that even the wealthy of the previous generation had not been able to secure.

Let me give you an incident in that connection, if you need any proof of that statement. I happened to be in Washington not long after the Armistice—when the Plumb Plan, so-called, was presented to Congress. I noticed by the paper that it was going to be presented to the House Committee that day; so I went over to the capitol and heard the Plumb Plan presented to Congress as a great and wonderful panacea for the industrial problem of the railroads. I sat there and pinched myself, to realize that such a scheme was soberly being presented to the United States Congress as a real, practical thing.

Material Welfare and Unrest

The chairman of that committee said to the speaker or one of the speakers, who happened to be Mr. Morrison, Secretary of the American Federation of Labor, "Mr. Morrison, I should like to ask you a question. I deem it a very important question. I consider its answer of great importance. The question is so important that I have reduced it to writing. After I have asked it, I wish you would deliberate before you reply, but when you answer, I should like, if possible, to get a categorical answer. I would rather have this answer from you than from almost any man in the United States."

This was the question he asked:

"Mr. Morrison, has there ever been a time in any nation at any time in history when the man who was working for wages was so well housed, so well fed, so well clothed, so well educated, so well entertained, as he is in the United States at this minute? I would like to have you answer yes or no."

After about twenty minutes, Mr. Morrison practically answered that there never had been any such time. And yet, do you remember the conditions that prevailed a few months after the Armistice? Although the material welfare of the man in the ranks had never been so good as at that moment, there never was a time in the history of the United States when the unrest was so acute and so widespread in industrial ranks as it was right then.

It would naturally be expected that as a result of all these material benefits we would have found the industrial wage earner contented and perhaps even enthusiastic over the improvement in his conditions and opportunities; but on the contrary, there had been developing for years an increasing unrest and dissatisfaction on his part with his relations with industry. It was obvious that there was something wrong with the industrial scheme that, although it was providing him with great material benefits, was at the same time changing his attitude toward his job and toward industry as a whole. This then was the second effect of this new industrial scheme on the worker, namely, the loss or partial loss of his morale and his satisfaction with the job.

This all became very apparent during the adjustment of industry to war and postwar conditions, and you and many other employers promptly undertook to diagnose the situation and find out what was the matter.

Human Factor Neglected

And when they came to diagnose the case, they found that in industry we had been overemphasizing machines, processes, and production. We had been underestimating or neglecting too much the prime or motive factor in industry—the human factor. We found that the executives had lost contact with the man in the ranks; that the man in the ranks, who used to be pretty close to the executive, now was a long distance away from him, and in between the executive and the man in the ranks there had been interpolated officials of different kinds and different names so that the man in the ranks never did get a chance to see or know much of anything about the responsible executives because the industry was too big.

We found that he was losing his interest in his job; he was indifferent; he was more inclined to think, not "How well can I do my job?" which the old craftsman used to think, but "How much do I get out of my job and how little can I do?"

We found that in cases he was even hostile, distinctly and definitely hostile, to the concern he was living with and making his bread and butter from, and we found that he was often going outside for the leadership that he wanted inside, but which in some way or other had disappeared, and that leadership outside was too often contrary to his interests, the interests of the industry, and therefore to the interests of society.

It is quite obvious that if that condition really existed, if that was a fair diagnosis, there was something wrong in the new scheme of things—this scheme of big production, which was benefiting the man in the ranks materially, but at this terrible price of taking his interest out of his daily work. If it had really deadened his interest, if it was threatening to alienate his loyalty to the industry, the outlook for industry was indeed serious.

Further study, I think, made it fairly clear how all this was a natural and logical result. These changes, this growth, these new processes, these new methods of big business, all came so fast, with such speed and with such a roar that he could not very well see what was going on. But he did know one thing, or he did feel one thing that was going on, and that was that somehow he was losing his status in industry. He was lost in the shuffle somewhere, so to speak. He felt that he was just one of many, just a cog in the machine, that nobody paid any particular attention to, or took any particular interest in him. His job, which had been originally a fairly broad job, had been narrowed, specialized, and routinized, until most of the life in it, as far as he was concerned, had been taken out.

Furthermore, his tools had been taken away from him. He did not own his own tools anymore. He could not buy his tools any more. The tools were big group tools or great machines and neither he nor any other workman had enough money by themselves to purchase such tools.

He found that he was losing pride in his craft; he found that many of his responsibilities had been taken away from him, and that the responsibilities that he did have seemed trifling. He did not even know whom he was working for. He did not know, in the great big corporation, just who the real boss was. One thing he did know, though, that whoever it was, he seldom, if ever, came around the shop where he was, and he missed that contact with the boss.

Lost Contact with the Real Boss

The straw boss was generally the only sample he had of the executives who were finally responsible, and too often he did not like the sample.

Demagogues and the yellow papers kept telling him that the real boss was someone who belonged to another class to which he could never hope to attain and assured him that this boss had no interest in him other than to make exorbitant profits out of his labors.

Although things did not seem to be going right, and although he had grievances which he felt were real, and although he thought his chances for advancement were being diminished all the time by the growing size of the concern, there was no opportunity for him to get at the real boss, the source of final responsibility and plead his own cause.

I am not arguing now whether or not he was justified in thinking all these things. If he thought them, that was enough to cause him to begin asking himself "What's the use?" and everything tended to make him indifferent, in extreme cases hostile and even bitter. Sometimes he even reached the point where he came to the conclusion that anything that could hurt the boss or the organization that employed the boss must in some way benefit him—the man in the ranks. Under these conditions it was simply natural that he should lose all interest in work itself as work. It was equally natural that his only interest should center in the pay envelope and what it was going to get for him after he got off his job. If there was no joy or interest in the job itself, the shorter the hours and the quicker he got to where he could spend some of his pay for entertainment or other things that interested him, the better.

If this attitude toward the job was fairly representative of any substantial part of the people who were working in the industries of the country, it meant that in industry the house was in danger of being divided against itself. Under such conditions, industry could not permanently succeed and civilization and our institutions were as good as doomed. It was quite clear that there was something wrong in spots, if not in fundamentals in the existing industrial scheme. It was equally clear that it was up to the leaders in industry to find out what was the matter and remedy it.

It was soon found that part of the root of the trouble lay in the nature of the industrial organization. Industry suddenly called on to organize large groups of people looked about for a precedent. Up to that time the only large groups of individuals in a single organization were to be found in the military, and this form of organization was adopted by industry. The big industrial corporation was organized like the army. Instead of generals, majors, colonels, captains, lieutenants, and so on, there were general managers, general superintendents, division superintendents, shop and floor superintendents, foremen, and so on, and a staff organization was built up to plan and advise the line organization.

But in too many cases, industry neglected to recall that the purpose of a military organization is to deal with emergencies where the lives of people and of nations are at stake. Therefore, its discipline must be rigid and unyielding. Action must be instantaneous and orders must be carried out. They may be stupid or fatal—it makes no difference. The soldier is forbidden to think—objectives cannot be disclosed or discussed. The men are not supposed even to speak to the officers. The whole spirit is one of blind obedience. "Their's not to reason why, their's but to do or die!"

A military organization is suitable for industry so far as form is concerned—the staff for planning, the line organization for administrative and executive duties, and the men in the ranks for carrying out the operations. But the spirit of the military organization and its methods are ill adapted to industry. Yet both were too often and too naturally adopted. In industry there is no great emergency. There are no big stakes like lives of individuals or of nations. No industrial organization stands between the nation and its annihilation, nor does it enforce law and order. An industrial organization is simply a corporate individual. It has only the rights of an individual; the right to produce for the benefit of society. It does not have and could not get the right to say, "Yours not to reason why, yours but to do or die."

The military has rendered a great service to industry in providing a suitable and practical form of industrial organization. But those industrial organizations that failed when they took the form to distinguish between war and industry, that failed to distinguish between the purposes and prerogatives of war as compared to those of industry, and that adopted the military discipline, the military spirit, the military caste, and the military theory, have fallen into grievous error—often unwittingly. In the natural consequences of this error we will find many of the sources of our difficulty—the indifferent or discontented attitude of the worker.

What is the answer? Let us see first if we can agree upon the true nature of an industrial organization and the worker's relation to it. First of all, his relation is voluntary. It having become impossible for him as an individual to discharge his responsibility of producing something for society, he joins with other workers and with people willing to supply the tools or the capital to buy the kind of tools required in modern industrial processes. They join together in a cooperative enterprise to produce something that society requires. The worker is to receive wages in proportion to the value of his services. The capital is to receive wages in proportion to its service and its risk.

Capital's Interest in Industry

If that is the way the organization is set up, who is going to run it? There is not very much question about who ought to run it. Obviously, the people who have taken their own savings and risked them in the enterprise are entitled to run it and to have the final and last word as to its management. They are entitled to appoint the men who shall manage and conduct the business for them. That sounds like good sense. It is equity. It is sound business. I never have seen a man in the ranks who questioned it. The man in the ranks admits that is a fair proposition.

But what the man in the ranks would like to do is to know something about the plans. He is willing to turn the proposition over to the other people to run, the people who bought the tools, but he would like to know where the job is headed. He would like to know something about the plans. He would like to know something about the results from time to time. He would like to make suggestions once in a while. He would like to discuss his relations with this joint enterprise. He would like to talk about his compensation and his reward from time to time. He would like to talk over and know something about the changes that are going on, whatever they are. He would like to have something to say about them, or he would like to ask about them.

If an order he gets looks to him from his point of view like a stupid order, one that is not in the interests of this joint enterprise, he would like to talk with somebody about it. If a practice seems wasteful, he would like to have it explained. In other words, he would like a chance to be heard, and he is right. He ought to have a chance to be heard. If he does not have a chance, he is bound to feel that he is out of it, that he does not belong, that he is in the wrong pew. He begins to believe that this is not the joint enterprise that he was led to believe it was. There is not the mutual interest, apparently, that he has heard talked about. Then, of course, he loses interest, and he feels that under those circumstances he is not getting a square deal; and he is not getting a square deal. He may be getting first-class bang-up good wages, but there is a whole heap of difference between a square meal and a square deal!

If we can agree that the industrial organization is really a voluntary organization for group effort, then it is not so much like an army, it is more like a team. The team has many members, often with widely diversified duties, but every one is supposed to perform his function at the right time, and in the right way, so that the team can reach the team objective, whatever that objective may be. And success in any large industrial organization, assuming reasonable ability of the men and women on the team, is going to be proportionate to the amount of real team play that there is in the organization.

You cannot have real team play without team spirit. What is team spirit? I do not know just exactly what team spirit is. I do not believe there is anybody who can define team spirit accurately. But there are probably few men who have not at some time or other felt it. We talk about a team, and originally we thought of a team of horses. We know approximately what a team of horses can do. The engineers can take their slide rules and tell us just how much horsepower we can figure on, and it is a definite, fixed amount, just so much horsepower, always figured in the same way. But that is not the way you measure man-power. Who has a formula that can say what manpower is per man? Nobody knows, because in addition to his muscle, he has two intangible elements of power—brainpower and willpower.

Elbow-to-Elbow Contact

In some magical way the elbow-to-elbow contact of men working together with a common purpose and toward a common objective stimulates these two intangible elements of manpower to a degree of joint accomplishment far beyond the aggregate of what the same men working separately could possibly attain. That indefinable something is team spirit. It is group morale. It defies defeat. It insists on success.

How are we going to get team spirit? Would it not be fine if we had it in industry? Would it not be fine if every man in the ranks were just straining, on edge, to get in and help the other fellows put the thing across, whatever it is that you are trying to put across? Well, how are you going to get it? You can only get team spirit in this way: Every man on the team must know that he is a member of the team and that the team is banking on him no matter how humble the position, no matter how seldom he carries the ball. He must realize, if he is going to get the team spirit, that he is a real member of the team. Now, he must know also what the team objective is; he must know whether it is going this way, or that way, or the other way. He must know something about his teammates. No man is going to give all he has, and then some more, unless the fellow right next to him, and the fellow over here, and the fellow over there, is giving all he has got, and more. Then is when you get team play.

But you have got to know the men on the team first. You have got to know them well enough to believe in them, and bank on them, and you have got to get into the frame of mind where you want the team to win, and you are going to make it win. Then you have got something approaching team spirit. Then, win or lose, you will get the thrill of joint accomplishment, the inspiration that comes from elbow-touch-elbow effort and that is one of the greatest of all incentives for human endeavor.

Here is the plea I want to make for the man in the ranks. Make him a member of the team, just a straight, honest-to-God member, and treat him like one till he realizes himself that he is a member. That will take time. It will take quite a lot of time. He does not think he is on the team now. He does not think that you think he is on the team now. He thinks that you consider that your team consists of the men whose names are listed on your organization chart—the chart showing your line and staff organization. He thinks that he is working for that team, and not on it.

Throw Away the Military Spirit

The first thing to do is to make him realize that he is a real, actual, recognized member of that team. This requires no change in organization. You can keep the form of organization you have, the staff, the line, and the men in the ranks. But it is time to throw away all of the military spirit, and all of the military theory. Keep the form, but do away with the military caste and the military theory. Then call in your line organization and just explain to them that there is something new; that you are going to play this game in a bigger way than you ever have before, and let them know what you are trying to do, that you are trying to take hold of the man in the ranks and bring him in, and make him a real member of the team, and make him understand that he is a member of the team. Explain it patiently and carefully to your line organization. They are the backbone of your business. They are the backbone of industry. They will make or break the whole proposition. Tip them off that it is all right to keep some of the discipline, for we have got to have law and order in industry just as we have got to have it in government, and just as we must have it in war. But just whisper to them that discipline, in order to be firm, does not have to be rough. Tell them that what you are doing is not making any change, but you are simply enlarging the responsibilities of the line organization; you are making them responsible for something new, and that is for giving the man in the ranks the opportunity to really get into the game, and get some fun out of it. You might tip them— the line organization—to let the man in the ranks carry the ball once in awhile.

The line organization is pretty likely to think that their chief and perhaps their only function is to direct. How would it be to tell them that from now on, they have an important additional function, and that is to interest, to stimulate, to inspire, and to humanize? Tip them off on this too, that instead of trying to have a team that is depending solely on a few stars, from now on you are going to have a star team, and then get out your Kipling and read "The Maltese Cat," and see what the difference is between a star team and a team that is staking its success on a few individual stars.

What next? How are we going to get this team play? What we are after is the sympathetic, earnest, honest, determined cooperation of the human factors in industry. How are we going to get that? There is no definite formula for it. There is no fixed, ready-to-use, ready-to-wear program. It is a question of dealing with all the human reactions and everything that that implies—human emotions, yearnings, discouragements, weaknesses, hopes, and ambitions. It is not an exact science and there is no exact formula, and the problems will differ in every industry and they will differ in a given industry, in every department, and in every department they will differ more or less according to the individual.

Contact, Conference, Confidence, Cooperation

In our companies, however, we adopted some years ago four guideposts. They have served us well. They never yet have led us off the trail. We have a good deal of confidence in them. I will tell you what they are, and recommend them for your consideration. It is not a formula, as I say. It is not a panacea. They are simply four guideposts, that have seemed to lead us toward where we are trying to go. We call them "the four Cs," and those Cs stand for four words: contact, conference, confidence and cooperation.

Let me explain them. Let us start first with this word *contact.* I will start with an illustration. Suppose, while we are sitting here, that door over in the corner opens, and we all look over there to see who is coming in. We see a woman with a shawl over her head and a baby in her arms. It is obvious as we look at her, that the baby is sick and suffering, and that the woman too has suffered for a long time. Somebody over in that corner of the room will say, "What is it, madam? What can we do for you?" And she will say, "I beg your pardon. I am all wrong here, apparently. What I am trying to do is to get to the hospital with my baby." Then somebody asks her, "What about the baby?" "Well, the baby has been sick, and the baby is not going to live if I cannot get it to the hospital. Its father is away hunting work, and we have not had any food in the home for two days." Now, what happens? Somebody at every table in this room gets up and says, "Come on, fellows. Loosen up. Dig deep. This family needs some help." Why is action so immediate and spontaneous? Simply because you have been in contact, and direct contact, with human suffering and human anguish and human need. But you do not have to actually see it to know that throughout this city there are thousands of cases of human suffering and human need right now; you know it, of course, in a way, but when you get into contact with it, then you feel it, then you really sense it.

In other words, we have to get close to the things that we really want to understand. We cannot get close to conditions or people at arm's length. We found that as we had grown, and grown, and grown, we had lost contact with the men and women in our industry, and they with us. That was their loss to some extent, but it was our loss most of all. We had lost these valuable contacts by getting so big. We must get them back in some way or other. The first thing is to start getting together again. That is *contact*—the first guidepost.

But just getting together in and by itself would not be very much more than a gesture. What we want to do is to get acquainted once more, to understand each other, and each other's job, and just where we each fit, and something about the other fellow's ideas and his purposes. Now, that means we must talk over things together. You cannot get acquainted with a man until you have talked with him. You simply say, "Mr. Smith, Mr. Jones—how do you do," shake hands and are gone. Smith does not know Jones yet. You have got to wait around and talk with him and then you begin to get acquainted.

Getting Acquainted with Each Other

So here comes along our next guidepost: *conference*. We have got to arrange in some way or other to work out some conference with our people, especially between the men in the ranks and the men in the line. Then we will get acquainted with each other, then we will get acquainted with each other's responsibilities and each other's ideas.

We are working on a theory that we believe is sound, and I know that many people are working on a very similar one in their industries. Our theory is this, that in our companies at least 95 percent of the men in the ranks, in the line organization, and on the staff are fair and square when they know the facts.

Well, if that is so, then when they get acquainted well enough, they will all come to realize it themselves and they will naturally begin to have confidence in each other. When they have talked long enough, this suspicion, this doubt, this distrust, and all of that sort of thing, is going to disappear. That is inevitable, if in these three groups 95 percent of the men are square, and that means that sooner or later they are going to come to have confidence in each other. So that is the third guidepost: *confidence.*

That means that they are going to begin to bank on each other, believe in each other, depend on each other, stand by each other, and see each other through. That is *cooperation.* That is what we started for—teamwork, through contact, conference, confidence, and cooperation. Perhaps it would be more accurate instead of speaking of four guideposts, to say three guideposts and a goal post, because the fourth one is really our goal—cooperation or teamwork.

If an organization is small, if it is not too large, if the groups are not too big, and are not too scattered, that line of three guideposts and a goal post lays out a very easy course to follow. It is simple. But the trouble is in most of the industrial organizations today, the groups are so big, and the organizations are so big, that it is a practical impossibility to get the whole bunch together. You cannot have universal contacts. Therefore, it must be done by having the big groups—that is, the men in the ranks—represented in some way.

Employees' Representation

We must work out the four Cs in part at least through representation. How are we going to do it? Obviously it is up to the management or the line organization to take the initiative. The next step is to invite the groups of the men in the ranks, the big groups, to get together and organize in some form and elect their representatives with whom the men in the line can join in establishing these contacts and conferences. But some executive will say—and I have often had it said to me—"Yes, but don't you see what you are doing? That is just about the same thing as organizing a union. If you have not already got one, do not go ahead and invite one."

I hold no brief against the unions. Many unions have accomplished a great deal for the material welfare of the men and women in industry. Some unions are fair and constructive. Other unions are destructive and have done great harm, to their own membership, to industry, and to society. I am not discussing unions at this time. I simply want to point this out, that you cannot deal with big groups of men in the ranks in industry, unless they are organized in some way.

I would like to mention also in passing, that it stands to reason that the spirit of an organization based on the cordial, hearty, man-to-man invitation of the management to organize for the purpose of getting together with the management for the mutual interest of both is bound to be quite different from the spirit of an organization that is based on an invitation from outsiders to get together, for the purpose of keeping the men in the ranks and the men in the line apart, and of stirring up distrust, suspicion, and hostility, and even hate, as has too often been the case.

I also would like to make this remark in that connection, that a loyal, earnest employee can join the former type of organization with his head in the air, without any loss of self-respect or standing, but he can join the latter organization only reluctantly, only with a sense of regret that has many a time nearly torn his heart out more because he knew he was losing something that he prized as one of his highest possessions.

Value of the Round Table

But to get back to the point. Once the organization is formed and the people in the ranks have effected their organization, what is the next move? It's up to them; not up to you. They will probably go ahead and elect their committees, but right here let me raise a hand of warning. Remember that they are their committees. It is their organization, and not the management's. You have your own line organization. Do not undertake to butt in and run theirs. It is theirs, it belongs to them, and it is right that it should. You do not need to be disturbed about what they may do. They may do things that might disturb you at first but pretty soon they will begin to invite you to their councils, just as you invite them to yours. Do not try to mix into their organization or try to tell them how to run it unless they ask for advice. It is their proposition.

Pretty soon, after these committees are elected, and the management has appointed its committees, they will get together for the first conference. You all know how it is. Everyone is ill at ease, the people on this side of the table, and the people on that side of the table. Of course, before very long there is not going to be any side to the table. The table is going to be a round table, and you are going to sit wherever you happen to come in. But the first time there are always two sides to the table, and the men from the ranks do not act like conferees. They take the attitude of advocates, and the men from the line do not act like conferees. They also take the attitude of advocates—only they seem to act more on the defensive. Very soon, however, this disappears and they all act more like conferees. Then in some way or other, after they talk it over long enough, the grievances that are the first things that are brought up, always, sort of get ironed out. The real ones get fixed up, and then the great multitude of fancied ones that are largely due to lack of information, knowledge, and understanding, just naturally clear up as the facts come out.

We have things pretty well cleared up. What are we going to do next? Do we stop here? Most certainly not. The man in the ranks has some more things that he wants to talk about. He wants to talk about wages, and wage schedules. He wants to know whether those wages are just. They may be, and they may not be. He does not know. He has been told that they were, but he would like to talk the matter over. He would like to talk about the working conditions. Most likely he has some ideas of his own about them. There are certain spots, very likely, where he would like to have the rough edges pared off, and a little change made here and there. There may be something dangerous in the shop, that keeps him a bit worried, that continually keeps the good wife at home a bit worried, and he would like to know if there is any way that could be made just a little safer. Then he would like to know what the prospects are of the job being steady, whether there are going to be any lay-offs within the next three months, six months, nine months, or a year. Those things in due time all get talked out, and the conferees come to a general agreement that things are about right, if in fact they are about right. If they were not, they have probably by this time been adjusted.

Now, the job is done, is it not? That is where so many people have made the mistake. This is not the place to stop. Why not? If the grievances are cleared away, if the wages are at the moment agreed to be all right, if the working conditions at the moment seem to be satisfactory, if dangerous conditions that may have existed seem to have been eliminated, if about everything that the man in the ranks wanted to discuss has been cleared up, why should we keep on? Why, this simply clears the decks, that is all. We have not really gotten anywhere yet. We have just been clearing the decks, and getting ready for business, that is all.

Common, Everyday, Decent Justice

Here is where constructive effort, constructive action really starts. So far, results have been essentially negative. They have been extremely gratifying to all the conferees. But it has only been a matter of doing what is common, everyday, decent justice; that is, letting the man in the ranks know, fully, frankly, and thoroughly, just where he stands and what his material relations to the business are.

But here is where I want to come back to my plea for the man in the ranks. Now is the time to put the man on the team and make him a member of the team. How are we going to do it? Well, first, make these conferences that you have been having more or less spasmodically and perhaps only when the men took the initiative, a permanent, regular part of the conduct of your business. Make them just as much a part of the organization of your business as the line organization chart that hangs on your wall. If you can, put some of their committees right on the organization chart itself.

What we want, what every executive wants, if he is entitled to it, is the unstinted confidence of all the men and the women in his organization. All right. How are we going to get it? Give them yours first. If you want theirs, it is your move. It is up to you. Give them yours first, and theirs will soon come back. Prove to them that you regard them as essential members of the team and propose to treat them as such. Prove to them that you are going to have unlimited confidence in them. Take a few chances on making a few mistakes. You will make some, but not very many. Give them all of the information about the business that they will absorb. They are entitled to it. Explain the policies of the business, explain the practices, tell them what is the foundation of the rules, and why the rules are necessary in the orderly conduct of the industry. Tell them why the routines that seem to be dry and deadening are necessary, and that routines are simply methods of fixing responsibilities, which they know have to be fixed, as well as you do.

Explain to them about the balance sheet, and what the balance sheet means. Put all of the cards on the table. Discuss the plans for the future. Tell them the obstacles that threaten the success of the industry. Tell them what your difficulties are. Tell them what the problems of the management are and what your own problems are. They do not realize that you have so many or such baffling ones. Tell them something about the business economics that lie at the foundation of your business. Ask for their suggestions. Let them know that you know they have got brains. Do not let them think that you think you have hogged all of the brains in the industry, because you are wrong. You haven't all of the brains, the men in the ranks haven't all of the brains, but among you all, you have all of the brains that there are in the industry. So why not pool them and get all the benefit of all the brains in the industry for the industry and the people in it. So ask for

their suggestions. Put up problems to them and ask for recommendations, and you will get some answers that will surprise and help you.

Share Responsibility with Workers

Let them figure out the costs of their individual or small group
jobs. Let them have all the responsibility they prove they can carry.
Share with them the traditions and the romance of your industry and
theirs.

I have had people say to me as some of you have had them say to
you, "But they will not understand it all." Their leaders will understand it. The live ones will understand it. The men who are going to
take your place and mine some day in our industries will understand
it, and they will all understand one thing about it, if they do not
understand another word or a single figure: They will understand
that what you are trying to do is to give them your confidence. They
will understand that, and when they do, you will have theirs.

Another remark that is sometimes heard is: "Yes, that sounds all
right; that sounds fine, but it simply won't work." It is too late to say
that. That time has gone by. Too many men can tell by the hour how it
has worked. That is the answer, as to whether it will work or not.

But we have heard this said: "What about this balance sheet business? You are not going to show them the balance sheet, are you?" I
did not say "show them the balance sheet." I said, "explain the balance
sheet." I do not mean to take the balance sheets, and broadcast them
when the men come out of the factory gates and say, "Here you are,
get the latest dope, right off the books." I am talking about explaining
the balance sheets.

Let me give you, in order that I may make myself perfectly clear,
two or three illustrations, and if you will pardon me for doing it, I will
take them from my own industry. The total assets in our group of
companies is about $2 billion. Of that, $1.7 billion is invested in plant.
We found out very early in talking with some of our people, how they
regarded these figures. They saw them in our annual reports. They
asked, "What do you do with all this money? Where do you keep it?"

They simply did not get the picture. Why not? Because no one had
ever taken the trouble to let them look at it. And the picture was so
easy to paint. Any amateur could paint it. It is this: Our business is so
big the company must furnish the tools. The telephone plant is the
tools. Every time a man or woman comes to work in our organization,
we have got to go out and get $6,000 to provide the tools for that

individual, the average investment for tools per employee being more than $6,000.

Explaining the Financial Surplus

Let me give you another illustration. One year the surplus for our group of companies, at the end of the year, was between $24 million and $25 million. That looks big to any man who is working for wages and who is not accustomed to analyzing figures. It is the perfectly natural thing for him to say, "If all this money was left over at the end of the year, what was the meaning of all this talk that we have been hearing all through the year, about the necessity of economizing, that we must save every scrap of copper wire, and that every minute during working hours must count? What do you mean that we have got to avoid waste of time, effort, and material all the time in order to be prosperous, when at the end of the year we have $25 million left?" What I said was, "Explain the balance sheet." It is explained very easily, and when you tell the man that if the expense of operating our business last year had been one cent per telephone instrument per day more than it actually was, there would not have been any $25 million, but the whole blooming surplus would have been wiped out and the dividends would have been cut in half. The balance sheet in respect to that item is explained. Then he is ready and anxious to get in and help to keep that one cent per day margin on each telephone instrument, because his job is at stake, his future is at stake, his company is at stake. When he knows that, and understands it, there is no one in the whole outfit who will go stronger or further to help preserve that margin of safety. That is what I was talking about. Not broadcasting the balance sheet but explaining the balance sheet.

I know perfectly well that there are gentlemen who think just as we do about this, but who are raising in their minds this question: "That is all right for you fellows in the public utility business, with no competition, you can put every card you have on the table. You can take all your figures and facts and put them right out on the table. They are open to the whole public now because they are subject to inspection of the public authorities all the time. But we are in private business, in competitive business. There are figures and there is other information that we cannot put on the table the way you fellows do because our competitors might get hold of them." I realize that, and you are perfectly right about it. We have the advantage of you there, but it is not so much of an advantage after all. But I will tell you what I think is the answer. You do not have to show to the men any of the facts about your business that it is necessary to keep in the executive offices for the protection of the industry. It is their industry just as it is yours. It is just as much in their interest to protect it as it is in yours. And just the minute that you inspire in the men confidence so that they are ready to bank on you 100 percent, all you have to do is to say, "Boys, this is about all we can let you have. We cannot tell you the rest of it. Some of these roughnecks here among our competitors might get wise and we have to tightwad the rest of it." And they will say, "All right. Lock it up. That's your part of the job, meeting this competition." Just once get the confidence of the men; earn it, and then get it, and they will take your word for it as to what is proper for them to see and what is not proper for them to see.

Wage Is Not the Only Thing

But we have all of us run across men who have said this to us, "That sounds all right, but you don't really believe it, do you? The men do not care anything about all this information about the company and its affairs and how their particular job fits in with the whole thing. Their only interest is in the pay envelope, in their wages, and in how long they have to work."

Well, all I have to say is, if that were true, God help the industries of the United States and the men who are dependent on them. It is true that wages are necessary and vital. The man in the ranks must have them, just as you and I must have them for our work. They are necessary and vital to society. But wages are only money, that is all they are, just money, and money is a long way from being the whole thing.

I would like to tell you a little incident, if you will pardon me for making it personal again. It is right plumb to the point. A good many years ago, when I started in business, I began in the practice of law. My mother, who lived up in the country, had saved a little money, being a thrifty New England woman. I was home one time for a visit; I had been practicing law then for a couple of years, and she thought I must be quite the real thing, and of course I never tried to disillusion her. So she said, "I have four hundred dollars that I would like to invest. I would like to have it earning something. You would know, being down there in the city in touch with business affairs, just what to invest it in. I don't. Will you take care of it for me?" Oh, yes, surely I would know. Well, to make a long story short, I took it back with me. I invested it, and inside of six months this particular stock had declined in market value by just 75 percent. Before it was all gone, I woke up, swallowed my pride, got what I could save out of the wreck, and sent it to her with a very humble and abject apology. Now, she could not afford to lose that money. It represented a substantial item in her savings. I got back a letter that had some very good dope in it. It has been good for me and I will pass it along to the rest of you. It may help in the study of this industrial relations problem. She said, "My dear boy, do not give it another thought. Don't you know that I have a thousand things that are infinitely more valuable to me than money?"

When the man in the ranks finds that the interest of the boss is not confined solely to the balance sheet, he soon ceases to center his own interest solely on the pay envelope. He knows just as well as anybody knows, that wages do not buy him and cannot buy him the thing that he wants above all else, and that is the pride and joy of work. Where do you people in this room get your real fun? You get it on the job, every day, working on your problems, working at the problems of your industry. There are men who could retire from business tomorrow. They have the money to retire, but they do not dare do it. Why? They are afraid they would shrivel up and blow away if deprived of joy of work—interesting work. That is their great big interest in life. Don't you suppose the fellow in the ranks wants to get a little taste of that? He wants it and needs it more even than he or anyone of us realizes.

He knows wages will not buy it, and he knows that wages alone will not buy him a real status in his industry but he wants to get into his industry and be a part of it. His industry is his only chance for contact with the world, and the big scheme of things, just as it is your big contact and my big contact. You say they do not care? You say that the men in the ranks do not care? I tell you, the man in the ranks is waiting right at the chalk line to grasp the hand of welcome the moment it is stretched out to him, the hand of brotherhood and friendship, the hand that is going to pull him over that chalk line, from being a water carrier for the team, to being an honest-to-God member of the team. That is where he is waiting.

When he comes across that line, he is going to come to cooperate, to team play, to get into the game and get the thrill of joint accomplishment that means as much to him as to you and me, to win or lose fighting shoulder to shoulder with his comrades in his industry.

I have had this said to me, just as doubtless many of you have, "That sounds all right, but it takes too much time, getting together in all these conferences and explaining everything. It takes too much time. Of course, it is fine to have the gang know something about the business, but we are too busy; we are busy executives."

All right. There are plenty of men waiting just outside of the factory gate who are not too busy. The labor parasite, the soap box orator, the yellow press—they will spend all of the time that is necessary to tell the man in the ranks all about your business. There may not be one single word of it true, but they are waiting there to tell him all about your business and about you, and they will call him brother and comrade while they are pouring their poisonous dope into his ears. They are not too busy.

When a man says to me, "I am too busy; this will take too much time," I think that what he really means is: "Will it pay for the time it takes?" I think that is the real thing that he has in his mind. Well, I dislike to discuss it from just that point of view, but I would like to answer that question. I will take three illustrations out of the hundreds that I could quote. Once more, if you will pardon me, I will take them from my own industry, my own experience, these illustrations as to whether it pays when the men have been taken over on the team and made actual members of the team.

The Habit of Paternalism

The telephone business is not in itself a hazardous business, but we have hundreds of thousands of miles of wire high in the air. Men have to work on those wires. Sometimes they have to work on wires that are in proximity to the wires of the high tension companies, which carry a dangerous current while ours do not. Furthermore, there is a certain amount of accident hazard in any ground or shop work. We used to get out semi-occasionally—not only specifications about how to build the plants, how to carry on the work, but along with that went safety rules, "Don't do this, don't do that. If you do this, do it this way; if you do that, do it that way," and so on. We had fallen into the habit of paternalism just as so many of you doubtless had. Our intentions were of the best, but the results were not especially satisfactory. The men kept on getting hurt. Finally someone had an inspiration. Who are making these safety rules? The ablest engineers in the profession, sitting in a room on the top floor somewhere, earnestly working out instructions to fellows out on the firing line as to how not to get hurt. It seemed just like when a youngster starts out for school: "When you cross the street, look both ways for automobiles. Be sure not to step on any banana peels, and don't climb any fences with nails sticking out." Why not put it up to the gang, and let them make their own safety rules? They know what causes these accidents. They know what protection they want for themselves and from a careless fellow worker.

Give them a chance to do it, and get some real rules. That was tried, and there were some safety rules that *were* safety rules—rules not made by the line or by the staff but made by the men in the ranks. In some of the companies, they analyzed every accident for the last five years to find exactly what caused it and how it could have been prevented.

I was trying to answer the question when I started out: Does it pay? The accidents decreased 10, 20, and even 30 percent in some companies—and in specific divisions and districts as much as 60 and 80 percent. That is the answer as to what happens, when the men in the ranks are really taken in and given the opportunity to do the kind of things they can do—often far better than the men in the staff or the line.

Putting up Prices

Let me give another illustration. We cannot do the way industries do to increase our revenues. When you want to increase your prices, you increase them over night. As I understand it, you get together, make a few figures, decide you need some more revenue and then add 10 percent to the price lists in effect the first of next month. I do not know whether that is exactly the process, but to us, who are under the public utility regulation, it looks just about that easy. Anyway, in our business, it is a long, painful, painstaking, patience-requiring process. It is a major operation, in other words.

The utilities were working on narrow margins before the war, and we are working on narrow ones now. We had to get our rates raised to get them adjusted to the dollar of today. In one of our states, not a long way from the middle of the United States, but not adjoining or touching Illinois, for some reason or other this process of adjustment functioned very slowly. I do not think you have such things in Illinois, but there are some states where politics seem to creep into some of these business questions. And in the particular state that I have in mind, politics had entered in. It was a long time before any adjustment was made and the result was that in that state the company was in the red.

Well, in line with the general practice I have been talking to you about, the men in the ranks all knew that. They knew exactly what the results were in that state. They knew that the company was running behind in that state, and that the other states for the moment were really carrying that state. One day without any of the management knowing anything about it, right out of the clear sky there came a communication, a letter. I wish I had it here. A copy of it was sent to me, and I read it, and it choked me up when I read it. It was from the men in the ranks, and they are a bunch of thoroughbreds. They said, "Whereas," and then they recited the conditions that I have described and they wound up by saying, "We want to do something to help." Now in that particular company the wage scale is set up on a basis of time and overtime. So the men went on to say, "If it will help any, we would like to give up our overtime for a period of six months, and if at the end of that time conditions are not better, then we would like to go along for six months or a year more if necessary, so that we can feel that we have done our full share."

Real Help from Friendly Employees

Let me tell you what the men in Chicago did in the Illinois Bell Company. We had a lot of what we call "held" orders; the kind of orders where we cannot install your additional telephones as quickly as you want them. I guess you call them the "Oh hell" orders. Well, they were piling up and up. The trouble was, you had not tipped us off a year or two before as to how much service Chicago was going to call for. There was an abnormal lot of orders waiting when the men in the plant organization realized the situation, and they saw that that was not a good thing for the company. They talked it over among themselves, and they came back with a suggestion. In Chicago the men work on a different form of wage schedule, one that does not ordinarily include extra payment for overtime. Those men came to the executives and this was their suggestion: "We have a proposition to make on this held-order business. The public does not like it. They don't understand it. It is not a good thing for the company. We will work extra time, overtime, until we reduce that number of held orders to normal. We will put in as many more hours each day as we can put in effectively to reduce the orders to normal and relieve this tension." That was their own suggestion. They gave of their own accord, on their own initiative, 60,000 working hours to remedy that situation. For whom? The company? For themselves? For the management? No. In order to protect the reputation and good name of their team—their company—with the public in the City of Chicago. That is what they gave it for, and they are proud of it and we are proud of them—proud to be members of the same team.

Now that question, "Does it pay?" seems kind of foolish. It seems foolish to ask, "Will it pay?" to give a man a man's chance, a chance for intelligent performance as against blind obedience, a chance to let him help protect his own job, his own future, his own industry.

But I would like to answer that question "Will it pay?" categorically. If that is what anyone wants to ask, I should like to answer. And I will say this, that in satisfaction to the executives of having given a thoroughly square deal, it will pay a hundred fold. In money, it will pay dollars for nickels, and the time will come in many cases where that one thing alone will spell the difference between success and failure, and I can tell you industries where it has spelled that, within the last two years.

In these difficult days of changing and uncertain conditions, local and worldwide conditions, is it worth anything to an executive or to the group of executives that carry the staggering responsibilities of modern industry for them to know that every man and woman in their organization are with them, because they know that the executives are with them? Is it worth anything for an executive to realize that the men and the women in the ranks have an unshaken confidence in him, because they know he is square, and is banking on them? Is it worth anything to him to know that they are ready to stand behind him through thick and thin, with every single ounce they've got, muscle and brain, heart and soul? Get out your pencils and your paper, and your slide rules, and figure out how much it is worth to an industry to know that the men and the women in it are right behind the leaders to the finish, win or lose. Find out how much it is worth to that industry, and that is the answer to the question of whether or not it will pay.

Normal, Human Relationships

The answer to this whole industrial relations question is so near to us, so close to us, and such an everyday thing, that the tendency is for us to overlook it. It is simply this. We must get back into industry the normal, human relationships that bigness in anything tends to squeeze out. Whether it is a city, or whether it is an industry, mere bigness tends to squeeze out the human understanding, the human sympathy, the human contacts, and the natural human relationships.

What are the right human relationships in a given industry? I would like to answer that question in a single statement. It is not my statement. It came from a man in the ranks. He said in one sentence all I have been trying to say to you all the evening, and he said it a good deal better than I have said it. This is what he said after this general program that I have been talking about to you had been going on for about 12 months:

"I have been in this company a little over seven years. I always felt until about a year ago that I was kind of a servant of the family. But now I am beginning to feel like I am a honest-to-God member of the family, just a real member, and believe me, it makes life look different." There is the story in a nutshell.

I used to be a lawyer before I came into the telephone business, and I have the greatest respect and admiration for the profession. But I am going to admit that I think the lawyers have unwittingly been very largely responsible for starting industry and the thinking of industrial executives up a wrong trail as to what the real human relationship is or ought to be in industry, and I think it came about in this way. When this great industrial expansion came along, some vehicle was necessary to carry it, and right ready at hand was the corporation, which could be made as big as the needs of a given industry demanded. Then the executives called in the lawyers and said, "We have questions here that we want answered. We want to know what is the relationship between this great big corporation and the men whom it employs. We want to know what are their mutual obligations." The lawyers turned to the common law that has come down to us through centuries of jurisprudence, and they came back with an answer and said, "It is the relationship of master and servant." Then the executive, being advised that that was the legal relationship between the corporation and the employees, apparently began to assume in too many cases that the relationship between himself and the man in the ranks was probably that of master and servant when, if he had consulted either his heart or his conscience, he would have satisfied himself that the man in the ranks was entitled to have that relationship become that of brother and brother. That is what the man in the ranks has been yearning for. But it was always the management's first move, and the management was being advised that this was a relationship of master and servant.

Too Much Blackstone

Right here lies the source of practically all our trouble in trying to work out what we call the industrial relations problem and in trying to find out what is the true, proper human relationship in industry, we have had too damned much Blackstone and not enough New Testament. That is one of the things that is the matter with industry.

I hope in my zeal in presenting the case for the man in the ranks you have not assumed that I feel that in all industries the man in the ranks needs any advocacy by me or by anybody else, or that I feel that great progress has not already been made along the very lines that I have been talking about. Hundreds of industries in this country have already gone a long way in working out this relationship on a cooperative, human basis, and have been bringing the men in and onto the team.

I have neither sympathy nor patience with the men who rant about capital and labor, and who either assume or argue that it is going to be an everlasting conflict between capital and labor, and that in some way or other, it is nothing but a fight to the finish. The executives who take that position, and refuse even to try to work the thing out on any other basis, are not in step with human progress, and in my judgment they are a menace to the industries for which they are responsible. The so-called labor leaders who preach the doctrine of hate and force, and the doctrine of forcing apart instead of getting together, are false to the people they claim to represent and are a menace to society.

I want to go on record as saying that there has been more progress in working out this industrial relations problem in the United States in the last five years than in this or any other country during any similar period in history.

We have shown the old world that the biggest single problem in government could be worked out by giving to every citizen a real place and a real part in the government. And we are going to show the world that the biggest single problem in industry can be worked out in the same way—by giving every man and woman in a given industry some real place and some real part in that industry.

In closing, I want to tell a little story. I have told it a good many times, and it may have come to your attention. However, it will bear repeating, because it seems to me it tells the whole story in a nutshell. There were three men cutting stone, stonecutters, working inside an enclosure, and back of them, up on a little eminence, there was a cathedral, about three-fourths completed. A stranger came along and said to the first man, "My friend, what are you doing?" "Me? What am I doing? I am working for eight dollars a day." He went along to the next man and he said, "My friend, what are you doing?" "Me? What am I doing? I am squaring this stone. See? I have got to make it just like this; see, right there. I have to make it absolutely straight, an absolutely straight edge right down there, on that part of the corner, and square it right off here. Look, I'll put the straight edge on it for you. Isn't that a perfect edge! You see this little niche that I have cut, that little niche right there? The other fellow working down there is cutting a niche just like this, only the other way. His fits right into mine. If we get them just right, they lock together tight, and they are just as solid as if it was one stone." The stranger walked along to the next man and said, "What are you doing, my friend?" "Me? What am I doing? You see that cathedral up there? I am helping to build that. Isn't it great! Isn't it grand!" There is the answer. There, I submit, is the whole answer.

If we in industry can only all realize that working toward the pay envelope alone is a sordid job, that it isn't worthwhile, that it isn't living, that it isn't life, we will have accomplished much. We should of course, in every possible way instill and inspire the interest of all our comrades in doing each his own job right so that it will fit into the next fellow's and make the whole thing strong. The more interest and the more pride we can each find in our own individual jobs, the better citizens we will be. But we will all find our greatest incentive and our keenest pleasure in the job that we all share together—share and share alike—the man on the staff, the man in the line, and the man in the ranks, and that is the job of building up a great industry that has its recognized place in the community, in the state, or in the nation. One that we can all be proud of, for it is the product of our joint effort. We have contributed each his humble part. We have felt the joy of joint accomplishment. We have felt the thrill of the team play—the exhilaration of the team spirit. And above all we have had the supreme satisfaction of having played the man's part—working shoulder to shoulder with other men giving every ounce they've got. And there is no higher incentive nor richer reward for human endeavor.

The Employee's Challenge– A Right and an Obligation

John H. Goss

MY message (in any formal sense) is so simple that I should need less than the balance of this page to deliver it. But if I did furnish so succinct a statement, it would be likely to fail of its informative purpose. For any such statement tends to assume the characteristics of a formula, and a formula is in the nature of the case only a symbol—a rule, a routine procedure. And no rule, no routine procedure, is an adequate answer to anything. So I shall venture to stretch out my discussion to cover considerably more than a page, with the succinct part of my statement given as a summary at the end.

Why is there dissatisfaction? Why, for example, should there be any question as to the interpretation that workers may place on company policies or orders? So far as that goes, why are company officials concerned about it, one way or the other?

Of course, the obvious way to arrive at an answer to the first two questions is (it's not a new idea) to put yourself in the other fellow's place. How would *you* react in the circumstances? And let me suggest

right here that you can't answer that question until you assure yourself of just what these circumstances are. One of the first duties of
anybody is to take the trouble to *know,* so far as he can, what he is
talking about, and I don't think that company officials are exempted
from that obligation. Well, if they do it, they may reasonably expect to
find various things to disturb them—things they didn't realize existed,
things they find appearing in action very differently from what they
anticipated when they originally put them in motion. And, finding
this, they will be dissatisfied themselves—whether their workers are or
not. And that, I think, is at bottom the answer to the third question in
the paragraph above. It is part of management's job to know how its
policies and orders do actually operate.

Three Influential Factors

Back of this question lie, as I see it, three influential factors, and
important ones, because they are so influential that they may be determining:
   –One is the general purpose or intention behind the order or
     policy adopted.
   –Another is the character of policy or order drawn to realize the
     intention.
   –And the third is the actual operation of the order so issued.
I hope I do not appear to be undertaking to outline "the whole
duty of man" in discussing, however briefly, these three points. My
purpose in doing so is simply to present the point of view from which
the policies of my company are drawn with respect to the employee
relations issue which has been raised.

General Purpose

The general purpose of plant employee relations policies is in no
way different from that of all other plant policies. It is to effect efficient and economical operation of the plant business. Of all the many
and various elements in this complicated problem, the "employee
relations" element is one of the most important. It always has been,
from the beginning of our organized industrial life. If there has been
any tendency to overlook this, it may be attributable to the growth in
mechanization of productive processes, the necessary development of
standardization as prerequisite for large scale production, the increasing size of our plant units and personnel, and the trend (which I
consider unfortunate) toward absentee ownership and control.

As a matter of fact, I am willing to support the statement that employee relations are and of right should be the most important single factor in the whole managerial problem; that is to say, for efficient and economical operation, a plant must have a happy, hopeful, and cooperative personnel. There are, of course, a number of essentials for this, but the important thing is that no single one of them—wages, hours, or other conditions of employment—is of such predominant importance that the successful establishment of it alone will solve the problem.

One's philosophy of management must be broader than check accounting, or factory accounting, or any other factor of purely statistical evaluation. On the other hand, it should be the easier for just that reason. The problem is human, and in that field every executive should be able to avail himself of his birthright of sound experience and information.

Character of the Order

What, then, of the character of policy or order that will effect our intention? Here, of course, the problem becomes difficult. We enter the field of difference, of disputation, of experiment, and of good and evil, of trial and error. But some cardinal points stand out. Of them all, I regard as holding first place this primary question, respecting any industrial policy and any factory order: What will be the human or emotional reaction among the people who are affected by it? I never issue an order in the plant without first thinking over for quite a time what the probable reaction of the employees of one sort or another is going to be to that order.

If you cannot get a program accepted, you cannot do anything with it, and whatever work you have done in connection with it is thrown away. But if you compromise or modify to the extent necessary—not give the economist fully what he would like to have but give him only as much as he should have in the program—not give the scientist or technically trained man (in whatever field he may be) all that he wants, but what seems to be all the program will carry and be accepted—then you will probably receive reasonable acceptance of your program. This accomplished, you can start to perfect it and in time give the economist and the scientist more of what they would like to see in the picture, but only to the extent that it will be acceptable.

I think our government can profitably consider this. I think all social agencies and administrators should consider it. There are two lines of thinking: one, let me call, the "economic," and one, the "social"; that is, one, the impersonal generalization, and one, the essentially personal application. Perhaps in the broadest summary, I may express one as the "rationalistic" and one, the "emotional." They are both necessary, but each must be qualified and tempered by the other.

We use in the brass industry an expression which I think is *apropos* here. Phosphorus is used in limited quantities in many of our alloys to improve them, and we say about that phosphorus to the men who are using it, in order to impress them, "Phosphorus is a mighty good servant, but it is a damn bad master!" And that is true. If you get too much of it in, everything goes haywire, all your alloys with it, and it takes a long time to readjust them.

That is also true when we get too much religion, economics, science, and so on, in our social programs. Church programs are prone to be too emotional to be acceptable. They are not practical; they expect too much of human nature. On the other hand, the programs of the economist are likely to be not sufficiently emotional. The political economist (I prefer that old title) must be really a sociologist, because his proposals must be adapted to receive acceptance of the masses. Thus political economy becomes practical economics. Religion must be practical ethics. These professions have been brought about, developed, and perfected by human effort, human desire, and human ambition. But they must try to deliver their programs not as masters but rather as servants of the social order. Such a method will be a masterly rather than a masterful application and development of programs that will operate for the benefit of mankind.

Here, I think, I shall have the support not only of successful executives but of theoretical psychologists. A policy, a plant rule, is not a mechanism, a foundation stone placed positively and definitely once for all. One cannot state it, say "that's that," and go off and forget it. A policy, a plant rule, is an *approach to an objective;* it is not the objective in itself. And every approach is in the nature of an effort of salesmanship. A good salesman must be a practical psychologist. He must, of course, also be honest. He does not tell his customer, "*You* want this." He puts before his customer the considerations that will cause his customer to say, "*I* want this." It is the fundamental difference between the methods of democracy and dictatorship, between peace and war.

I am failing of my purpose if, in writing this, I am giving any suggestion of weak will, lack of positive authority, or vacillation in procedure. An administrator is a leader or he is nothing. And a leader sees clearly his end, plans generally the means to that end, and follows a program. In this, he may appear "hard boiled," but in such case it will be found that hard boiled really describes his recognition of the necessities of a situation and his readiness to accept and deal with uncomfortable facts. But back of all that, there must be the "philosopher." There must be the rounded and formulated basis of one's thinking, to which one may ever go back, as a starting point for his approach to any problem that comes before him. With that, one may hope for reasonable consistency in his decisions and, so, for substantial justice in his relations and gradual progress toward his objectives or ideals or whatever he pleases to call them.

Actual Operation of the Order

In an earlier paragraph, I referred not only to the character of order adopted to realize a plant policy but also to "the actual operation of the order so issued." Here may be the breaking point of the entire fabric of the managerial philosophy. The issuing of orders is easy. The drafting—that is, the shaping and forming of them—is not so easy. But ensuring that they will be interpreted and administered by others, in the spirit and for the purpose intended, is by far the most difficult of all. The larger the enterprise, the greater the difficulty.

The difficulty arises out of two facts: first, the weakness of the medium of communication. We use the English language; no matter how carefully the senior executive may prepare what he has to say, or write, connected with orders that go out into the enterprise for interpretation and administration by the junior executives, the weakness of language is such that he cannot be sure that those who read or hear what he has to say are going to understand it and carry on as he intended.

Second, and worse than the first, there is the common human characteristic known as "the wish being father to the thought," under the influence of which few of us can help trying through rationalization to *make* what we read or what we hear mean what we would like to have it mean. That is a great danger. It is the cause of a vast amount of the labor trouble in industry. When there is any option in the interpretation of an order by a junior executive who has certain duties connected with that order, he is pretty sure not to elect an interpretation on the order that is going to hurt *him*. If he thinks it will, he goes to headquarters and gets an explanation. But if he puts an interpretation on it that may result in injury not to him but to some fellow down the line—the man out on a machine or at a bench in the factory—he is likely to be careless; and *he* doesn't know, often *nobody* knows except the man injured, what injury is done.

How, then, can I find out when such injuries are done to the men out on the machine and at the bench in my plant through misinterpretation and, based thereon, maladministration of executive orders, programs, and planning in the plant? It is the greatest worry I have as an executive, because all the orders in the plant are prepared by me and go out through my office. I can discuss these matters with the junior executives and many of the senior executives below me in rank, but that penetrates about so deep and then its effect is lost. We can train a group of men competent to audit conditions in departments at random times unknown to the foremen or other executives, to see whether the regulations are being followed out. Thus we pick up some of the errors, but only a small proportion.

The Right to Challenge

More than 20 years ago, realizing this, we instituted at our plant what we call the "right to challenge," which accrues to any employee or any group of employees with respect to any condition in the plant that affects him and he thinks should be corrected, or that affects a fellow-worker, or that he doesn't think is in the best interests of the business. The word challenge is understood to be not in its militant sense but in its inspirational sense. It is a challenge to the executive to sit down across the table and discuss that particular case with the challenger.

This plan has proved most effective in perfecting many of the professions, particularly in the medical and legal professions. It is known as the "case system" because you have definite cases called to attention at the time they arise, at the place they arise, and by the individuals affected. Why should not industrial management avail itself of a like opportunity to improve itself as a profession?

By this method we have a process of training from the bottom up. Many hundreds of our employees have made those challenges. They have been very helpful. They are voluntary—but we call attention to the fact that this *right* to challenge involves also an *obligation* to make the challenge when the employee finds a situation which calls for it.

When Section 7-A came into the picture under the National Industrial Recovery Act it made no difficulty for us because that was simply, from our point of view, properly and appropriately interpreted, calling the attention of employees to the fact that they had the right to challenge. The difficulty throughout the country was that so many groups misinterpreted the situation and made their challenges in a spirit not of obligation and cooperation but of militancy. And there—since we are living in a fine American world of red-blooded men—the fat pretty often fell into the fire. When the approach was properly made, I think there usually was a successful outcome. When the approach was made in the wrong spirit, there was an unsuccessful outcome.

We've had success in our plant. At least two groups of our employees affiliated themselves with the Federation of Labor. We run a strictly open shop plant. We do not care who belongs to a union so long as he does not interfere, through propaganda or otherwise, with the efficiency of the plant during working hours. It is none of our business what he does outside. When I was approached by a letter from the International vice-president of the unions in question, it was a courteous approach. He wanted simply a chance to meet me on a certain day, at a certain time, with a committee of my employees, naming them, to tell me about certain conditions in the plant they thought I ought to know about. Of course, I met them and we got along tremendously well, and have ever since. I knew they could tell me "plenty"—and they did.

Youth and Age

There is a physiological factor that enters into this picture. I am coming to realize it more and more. It is the matter of youth and age, youth and age not only as contrasted in management but as it develops in the plant.

Management has become a technique, and I have endeavored to present in this article some of the exacting problems of that technique. They are problems that, up till now anyway, have found their solution in the years of experience that managerial officers have accumulated before arriving at their present responsibilities. An invaluable element in that experience has been the old contacts and friendships of the early days in the plant. I knew what my co-workers were thinking; they knew what I was thinking. Always there could be a meeting of minds. But the years that carried the managerial worker out of the old arena were taking those other fine fellows out of the arena too. It is almost appalling to think how few of them are left. And in their place—indeed, in our larger units of organization, replacing them three or five or ten for one—have come a new and younger group with whom the managerial officer has only the rarest opportunity to establish a relationship of anything like the old personal understanding.

But it is not merely the difference between youth and age. Rather, it is a question of proportion. I am impressed by the fact that conditions wholly beyond industry itself are affecting this change. The span of life is notably increasing, not so much that people are living to be older, but that many more people are living to be old. The trend is to recognize this approach toward superannuation and to provide for it by release from industrial service. Very marked advances have been made, as we know, in recent months, but they are child's play to what the problem will be in another decade or two. Meantime, the juniors are coming in, in continually greater proportion of the total, and the managing official finds himself to be more and more isolated, more and more lonely, in the sense of his old-time comfort and security of personal contact. It seems to me that this also indicates the need of a new technique—of a new approach to the problem of management as an effective art.

The Heritage of Management

We hear a great deal about cycles of different things. We heard about a lot of them in the depression—business cycles, prosperity cycles, depression cycles; statisticians of all kinds are busying themselves trying to determine the causes and the frequency. *But the most important cycle of all is the cycle of life.* It does not need any statistical research to determine that there is such a cycle and that it has a very definite frequency. The fact is that approximately every 25 years an entirely new group is at the helm of affairs; a new group of leaders has developed with, of course, their own ideas as to their responsibilities.

The fortunate thing is that this cycle develops not by a *revolutionary* but by an *evolutionary process.* The influence of one generation *may* leave its impress upon its succeeding generation. After all, our best hope is to leave a favorable impress upon our successors. But this can only be accomplished by presenting to them an example of high character. Therefore, I submit that the best heritage that a management, as well as an individual, can leave is a philosophy of life that has become improved under its stewardship and is confirmed by the honest and sincere practice of its tenets.

3

Research
in Human Relations

Elton Mayo

THE course followed by the inquiry at the Hawthorne Plant of the Western Electric Company and the results obtained have been described in a recently published book, *Management and the Worker.*[1] It is an interesting fact that an edition of one thousand copies was issued in October 1939, and that by the end of February 1940, it was completely sold out. It is significant, too, that the book has attracted the attention not only of management but also of intelligent organizers of the CIO. It would seem that both these groups, management and the CIO, are willing to accept the findings as representative of the actual situation on the working line in industry.

Industrial and Social Relations

Just one word as to what these findings are. First, the inquiry began with intensive studies of the individual worker—physiological, psychological, psychopathological. Step by step over a period of six

[1] By F. J. Roethlisberger and W. J. Dickson, Harvard University Press, 1939.

years, as Mr. Stuart Chase describes it,[2] the inquiry was diverted from an intensive study of the individual worker to a study of the individual as related to the informally ordered group of workers about him. The psychoanalytic method of probing deeper and deeper into the particular individual's condition, though exceedingly interesting, and in a few cases relevant, proved entirely fruitless for the main inquiry. The whole investigation, and the manner of its conduct owe a heavy debt to Asklepios and to psychopathology. Nevertheless, the study finally turned to the relations between individuals and away from study of the individual himself.

The science of economics tends to adhere to assumptions made in eighteenth century France and nineteenth century United States, the assumptions being, first, that society consists of individuals and that their organization is predominantly economic; second, that the individual is motivated mainly by his material interests; third, that the individual thinks logically in the service of these interests. But we have found that in industry it is almost invariably true that the individual is actuated chiefly by a passionate desire for an intimate and routine relation with his fellows at work. It is our general finding that in the service of this passionate desire he will sacrifice not only what seems to be his own material interest but also his right to independent and logical thinking. It is, in other words, the chief character of the human scene that the individual adapts himself to his work by subordinating his own sentiments to the sentiments demanded by a routine association with his fellows and that, as adequately as may be, he adopts their ways of thinking and living as his own. This, indeed, is society as we find it in industry.

Now, it is the habit of industry and economists and psychologists and psychiatrists to ignore this very real informal group organization and to behave as if one exercised control over the mass by relating the control directly to the separate individuals in it. This is not true, and it leads to grave misdirection of research. It leads, in fact, to what I call a psychological "rat hunt." First, the psychologist is trained to search for IQs and particular vocational "sets." I am not denying that such inquiries have great value, but in effect this may deteriorate into a search for a structure (traceable possibly to the biological genes) that does not inquire into, or take account of, the balanced relation between individuals in an organization. Yet it is this balanced relation that is the important fact for the administrator. In other words, the inquiry is directed at the structural and neglects the dynamic com-

2 *The Reader's Digest,* February, 1941.

pletely. Since at the moment our modern problems all relate to the dynamics of social control, these studies, however interesting in themselves, become irrelevant to certain important problems of the day.

Defect of Psychiatric Approach

Second, psychiatry. Here also is another instance of the same technical error. In his ordinary practice there are brought to the psychiatrist those persons who quite obviously have failed to establish a harmonious and happy relationship with other people about them. Frequently, though not always, the failure is serious, because if any ordinary adjustment will serve to aid the individual it is contrived for him before he drifts into the hands of the psychiatrist. By reason of the work he is required to do, the psychiatrist is therefore in part disqualified for actual social study. Indeed, the ordinary practitioner of medicine is in this respect better qualified because he is required to handle many milder cases of maladjustment and does so admirably; he does this work so well that he stops many individuals on their way to the psychiatrist and contrives for them a happy solution of their troubles. The psychiatrist therefore is by his work conditioned to expect that behind the social ineptitude that he studies there will be a structural defect in which the unbalance originates. When therefore his attention is turned toward industrial or social inquiry, he charges into action with this as a guiding idea—the idea, namely, that it is his business to discover those persons who are not readily adaptable and to make special provision for them. One would have expected that psychoanalysis, with its close study of infancy and adolescence, would have effectively changed this point of view. Curiously enough, the psychoanalysts are no better in this respect than are the psychiatrists. For them, the structural defect is traceable to an infantile trauma or to a distortion of attitude due to a defect of infantile environment. But once they have established this as their main tenet, their attitude becomes in other respects identical with that of the ordinary psychiatrist. In other words, their main idea resembles far too closely the "rat-hunt" principle of looking for individuals with structural defects in order to throw them on the ash heap.

I am happy to say that I know exceptions to this rule. Dr. J. S. Plant, in Essex County, New Jersey, has conducted for many years an inquiry into delinquent children that, if one makes allowances for differences in situations studied, moves step by step very closely with direct studies of the actual balanced relation between persons organized in groups, which is the main character of our industrial and social life.

Third, economics. I can illustrate an identical point of view by quoting briefly from a book entitled *An Essay on the Nature and Significance of Economic Science,* by Lionel Robbins, professor of economics at the University of London.[3] On page 98, he states that from the point of view of pure economics the demand for commodities is conditioned on the one side by "individual valuations" and on the other side by the technical facts of the given situation. He goes on to discuss whether one can scientifically investigate individual valuations, and in this regard he at once makes the statement, ". . . we are here entering upon a field of investigation *where there is no reason to suppose that uniformities are to be discovered."* The reply to this observation is twofold. In the first place, I do not suppose that in any scientific investigation is there ever certainty before the investigation begins that uniformities can be discovered. Science has always assumed that there are such uniformities if an inquiry is rightly conducted, and the assumption has not yet been disappointed. Second, these uniformities have been discovered, though not by the economists. It is these uniformities, *imposed by informal groups upon members conditioned to a particular way of living,* that the Western Electric Company has been studying for 14 years. It is true that Mr. Robbins and the economists have not discovered the uniformities that actually exist, but this fact implies nothing but preoccupation with the individual on their part.

Executive Authority

This subject has been discussed admirably by Mr. Chester I. Barnard in his book, *The Functions of the Executive.*[4] This study is based on his experiences as president of the New Jersey Bell Telephone Company. But although I regard knowledge of Mr. Barnard's work as a necessary preparation for the research required, I do not regard his book as doing more than mapping out the country and indicating where exploration is gravely needed. In this connection I should like to point out that every department of government or political science in the universities of this country discusses the exercise of executive authority, whether politically or in industry, as if government were a one-phase system, capable of being set out thus as a blueprint plan. This inadequacy to the actual facts of democracy and executive control puts our political theorists into a very awkward position with

[3] Macmillan & Company, Ltd., London, 1932.
[4] Harvard University Press, 1938.

respect to the exponents of authoritarian systems, such as fascism and communism, for it makes it appear that the only difference between democratic and fascist authority is the inferiority both of intelligence and action of democratic systems. In other words, there is no university government department in the country that has even begun the appropriate research into the superiority of democracy to absolutist systems.

Two-Phase Aspect of Democracy

The fact is that democracy is a two-phase (perhaps multi-phase) system. In any society, authority originates mainly in the spontaneous cooperation of the people who constitute the society. That is to say, it originates in the informal group associations to which I have referred. In a complex society, no matter where, this spontaneous cooperation still originates in the informal associations at the working bench, but the formal, logical and purposive authority, the organization plan and control, originates at the executive head. This, then, gives the two-phase aspect of democracy logical and critical control from above, spontaneous and cooperative control from below. Democracy, therefore, is at least a two-phase system. In ordinary times it is important that any authoritative reordering of the group should proceed from the lower level of spontaneous cooperation. In exceptional times, in times of emergency, it is necessary that the central authority should assume an almost absolute control for the period of the emergency. Democracy, then, is a two-phase system in that in times of emergency the central control is strengthened; when the emergency is past, the control is automatically passed again in some degree to the peripheral organizations. This fact has not been adequately studied or documented. It is, nevertheless, crudely represented in the elective system of the great democracies. The periodic election is at least symbolic of the passing of the control to the peripheral organizations. The period between elections is symbolic of the vesting of control in the logical and purposive executive.

Unemployment

The usual method of studying unemployment, which can be exemplified either here or in England, is first to find out and express statistically, as accurately as may be, the number of unemployed. Second, a study is made of so-called depressed areas and of the morale of individuals in them. Third, an attempt is made by means of civilian camps or resettlement or training in new trades to start some of the unemployed again in work. I should like to point out that, excellent as this is, it is no more than the intensive study of a symptom and includes no attempt whatever to diagnose the illness. Yet it is possible to take account of work done many years ago in France (and some work here) and to see, however dimly, the nature of the illness that so urgently demands diagnosis. First, one must study the people who are employed rather than merely the unemployed. Palliatives are excellent, but the disease demands specific treatment. In the last century, Durkheim pointed out that during prosperity the informally organized ways of living that had developed historically in a society were apt to be adversely affected by civilized development. And he showed that this is specially true of modern industrial societies. It is not only the rapid movement from place to place that disrupts the ordered way of living; it is also the rapid change in the type of home and the type of relationship between families in a neighborhood. Whereas in simpler times a neighborhood unit was a real entity in the modern industrial center, it is nowadays largely inhabited by a floating population that has no time or opportunity to develop a common and neighborhood way of living. The effect of this upon the standard of living is disastrous. Economists are accustomed to consider the phrase "standard of living" as if it were satisfactorily accounted for by examining the amount of money spent, or available for spending, by individuals. While this does give actual expenditures and may be of interest to those who study demand, it gives practically no information about *standard* of living. A standard of living is (once again) a group determination. There is stability of demand for those commodities that an informal group has nonlogically decided are necessary to the social group life. Such a group, even when its income is gravely diminished, will not willingly abandon the purchase of those commodities that to them are necessary for the maintenance of social relationships with their acquaintances and friends. Now, as Durkheim has pointed out, in times of rapid social movement, in times of chaos and social disintegration, these standards suffer severe damage. If people cease to be members of a group, they no longer have actual need of those material possessions that are necessary to the group amenities. Consequently, those material goods that formerly were necessities for a people become merely luxuries, the purchase of which can be instantly abandoned in any period of depression. For example, when we lived in small communities, a marriage at almost any level required of those marrying that they should possess household linen and household silverware of some kind. In these recent times of rapid movement and social impoverishment of living, the demand for these goods has fallen rapidly. They have ceased to be necessities and have become luxuries that few people can afford. All that a marriage requires in these days is a single apartment and a few cocktail glasses. This is social impoverishment of the most serious kind and a definite degradation of the standard of living that infallibly shows itself in a diminished stability of demand for almost all civilized commodities.

Capitalism and Living Standards

If one reads such a book as Schumpeter's *Business Cycles*,[5] one sees much justification for what is termed American capitalism. Only American capitalism can claim to be a system that has in fact progressively raised the standard of living of the working group; this is indeed the chief character of North American civilization. It is, however, unfortunately true that in the process of continuously raising the standard of living, American civilization has unwittingly destroyed all *standards* of living. The resulting ills are an incredible instability of demand for almost anything, with embarrassingly wide fluctuations according to the popular estimate of the present and future and, as a consequence very largely of this fluctuation, unemployment.

So far as I know, this study, which is cardinal to the diagnosis of the social disequilibrium we call unemployment, is not actually in process anywhere. Here again it is perfectly obvious that the implicit claim made by psychologists, psychiatrists, and economists, that society is no more than a horde of individuals, must be thrown overboard, and as speedily as possible a case study of informal group organization substituted for the gratuitous and unwarranted assumption.

[5] McGraw-Hill Book Company, Inc., New York, 1939, 2 vols.

4

Union–Management Cooperation: A Psychological Analysis

Irving Knickerbocker and Douglas McGregor

SINCE the campaign of the War Production Board a few months ago, many plants throughout the country have been experimenting with labor–management production drive committees. The results achieved have varied tremendously. Some of these committees have been dismal failures. Many have been mildly successful. A few have been so successful that the participants themselves have been startled.

The idea that cooperation between management and union might be a powerful force to increase productive efficiency is not a new one. It has been the subject of experimentation for many years in a few industries, notably the railroads, certain branches of the men's clothing and the needle trades, and more recently steel.[1] However, this

[1] Cf. Slichter, S. H., *Union Policies and Industrial Management*, The Brookings Institution, Washington, D. C., 1941, Chaps. XIV-XIX; and Golden, C. S., and Ruttenberg, H. J., *The Dynamics of Industrial Democracy*, Harper & Brothers, New York, 1942, Chaps. VIII and IX.

campaign of the War Production Board has been the first attempt to promote such cooperation on a large scale.

The literature contains a number of case studies of union–management cooperation as well as many partisan arguments on the subject,[2] but there have been few attempts to analyze union–management cooperation from a psychological point of view. Nevertheless, cooperation is a relationship between people. It is, therefore, a psychological phenomenon. The purpose of this article is to present an analysis in terms of some of the important psychological factors that influence the success or failure of cooperation between management and union.

The emphasis in this analysis will be on the relationship between management and union *within* the company. We shall be concerned with the thinking and behavior of workers, union leaders, and management in an industrial organization. We shall discuss attitudes, points of view, personality traits, habits of thought, and action as important psychological factors determining the nature of the relationship.

Without in any sense denying their importance, we shall ignore external, social, and economic factors such as the impact of the business cycle. While the details of the relationships will undoubtedly differ as these external factors change, it is nevertheless true that all forms of union–management relations are to be found under almost any given set of external circumstances. This is an analysis of the psychological determinants of labor–management relations *within* the plant.

Union–Management Relations As a Process of Psychological Growth

It has frequently been noted that union–management relations follow a fairly typical course of historical change. When a union is first organized in a plant, the relationship is likely to involve a high degree of suspicion and conflict. Usually this "fighting stage" gradually disappears and is followed by a relatively neutral stage characterized by a decrease of suspicion, a growth in mutual understanding, and in general a mildly friendly atmosphere. This is the stage of successful collective bargaining. Where circumstances have been favorable, a third

[2] For references, cf. "Union–Management Cooperation with Special Reference to the War Production Drive," Industrial Relations Section, Princeton University, Princeton, N. J., May 1942.

stage in union–management relations emerges. This is a stage in which suspicion and conflict have disappeared and in which the atmosphere is one not alone of acceptance but of constructive joint efforts to solve mutual problems. The term *union–management cooperation* has been applied to this third stage of the historical process.

This transition from stage to stage becomes more meaningful if it is viewed, not merely as a process of historical change, but as a process of psychological growth and development similar to that experienced by the individual as he passes from infancy through childhood and adolescence to maturity. The transition becomes even more meaningful if the emphasis is laid on the emotional aspects of the developmental process rather than on the intellectual aspects alone.

There are four important characteristics of psychological growth that apply equally to the individual and to union–management relations. In the first place, psychological growth is a slow and arduous process. It involves a myriad of small changes in thinking and behavior, which normally occur imperceptibly day by day. While the rate of growth may vary somewhat, depending on circumstances, sudden jumps occur rarely and then only as a consequence of rather severe crises. Thus some cooperative plans have emerged suddenly as a result of the very real threat of the complete bankruptcy of the company. This is not normal growth, but an abnormal "spurt" brought about by a crisis.

In the second place, psychological growth is not an all-or-nothing process. Even the emotionally mature adult retains some childish habits. On the other hand, the child can in some ways be startlingly mature. The same thing is true of union–management relations. The growth process is uneven. Maturity is achieved in one small way today and in another tomorrow. Many "childish" habits and ways of thinking are retained long after their usefulness has apparently disappeared. The differences between one stage of union–management relations and another can be viewed only in the overall sense. Detailed analysis reveals elements of every stage at any given time. Each individual participant possesses some habits and attitudes that are childish and others that are mature, and the interacting individuals differ among themselves in their overall maturity.

The third characteristic of growth is that it may be arrested at any stage. Just as some individuals of 40 are still at an adolescent level of emotional development, so do some union–management relationships remain in the fighting stage for long periods of time. This characteristic of being arrested in the course of development is so common that real emotional maturity is rare among individuals. Likewise genuine cooperation between union and management is rare. When one recognizes how complex are the necessary emotional adjustments between individuals and groups in union–management relations, it is not surprising that only a small proportion of union–management combinations have succeeded in reaching a fair degree of maturity.

Finally, psychological growth, unlike physical growth, is a two-way process. Retrogression is not at all unusual. Occasionally, in a critical situation, mature habits and ways of thinking that have been acquired painfully and slowly will suddenly disappear, to be supplanted by childish ones that have been presumed to be long since dead. In an extreme sense this phenomenon may be observed when civilized people become barbarians under the stress of strong emotions (for example, in a lynching mob). The same phenomenon may be observed in a milder form when, in a cooperative meeting between union and management, someone inadvertently brings up a point that strikes at the heart of an emotional "blind spot" of one or more of the participants. Sometimes the results of the retrogression last not for minutes or hours but for months or even years.

In the end, the psychological growth of union–management relations is no more than the growth of the participating individuals. The situation in any given organization is exceedingly complex because of the varying extent to which one individual or another dominates the picture and because a number of different individuals are participating in the relationship.

The process of psychological growth in labor–management relations takes place through the interaction of the participants. The interaction occurs in face-to-face meetings between representatives of the two groups and in the day-to-day contacts between individuals on the job. A change in management's ways of acting or thinking influences the union and results in a change (not necessarily the same one, to be sure) on the part of the union. This alteration in the union's thought or action in turn reacts on management, and through the circular interaction the relationship develops.

In the past there was very little interaction because management dominated the relationship almost completely. During the past decade, the development of the union movement has changed the picture from one of *action* by management on the workers to one of *interaction* between them. Interaction is the means by which the relationship grows.

The Difference Between Collective Bargaining and Cooperation

The use of two different terms may imply mutually exclusive phenomena, but in this case that is not intended. Collective bargaining and cooperation are terms that refer to overlapping stages of development in union–management relations. Just as a relatively mature adolescent may be more like an adult than like the average adolescent, so may collective bargaining in a mature relationship resemble cooperation more than it resembles typical collective bargaining. In the discussion that follows we shall describe an arbitrarily selected point in each of two wide ranges of phenomena. Our descriptions are intended to throw into relief the differences between the two processes, and therefore the selected points are well separated. Many individual instances of collective bargaining or cooperation are more or less mature than those that would be fitted exactly by our definitions.

Collective bargaining is essentially a competitive process. It arose historically by carrying over to the relationship between union and management certain practices that were at one time habitual in the relationship between competing firms. The bargainer tries to outguess the other fellow, to hide his own motives, to play up the concessions that he grants his opponent, and to play down those that he receives. The process is reasonably well characterized by the metaphor of "playing one's cards close to the chest."

Genuine cooperation, on the other hand, is a mutual effort on the part of individuals or groups to achieve jointly desired goals. It is not a bargaining process, even though it may develop from bargaining practices. Effective cooperation can occur only when the "cards are face up on the table." Regardless of appearances and "stage dressing," real collective bargaining is essentially characterized by conflict, cooperation by mutual aid.

We are not attempting to criticize collective bargaining or to praise cooperation. Both procedures have important roles in union–management relations. Collective bargaining does not disappear when cooperation emerges. There are some problems, notably wage negotiation, which are likely to remain matters for collective bargaining regardless of the degree of cooperation that exists between a union and management.

There is nevertheless some shift as the developmental process takes place. Some of the things that were originally dealt with through collective bargaining come in time to be dealt with cooperatively. For example, a great many grievances come to be handled in time by cooperative means. As the union and management deal with each other, and as mutual trust and confidence begin to develop, there comes a gradual recognition that the real aim of a grievance proce- dure is the solution of common problems to the mutual satisfaction of all concerned. This recognition leads to a tendency to look behind the immediate, apparently conflicting demands presented with any par- ticular grievance to the really basic desires that are present but unex- pressed. In many cases the basic desires of the two parties are found not to be incompatible.[3] When this occurs, the settling of a grievance becomes a cooperative procedure in which both sides attempt to find a solution that is mutually satisfying. To the extent that this happens, the grievance procedure becomes a cooperative process rather than one of collective bargaining. There are some grievances, of course, that involve a genuine conflict of interest or desire, and these cannot be handled cooperatively.

It is perfectly possible for union and management to cooperate on some things and to compete on others. What is not possible is for them to compete and to cooperate at once with respect to the same problem. Matters for collective bargaining (involving conflict) cannot at one and the same time be matters for cooperation (involving mutual aid). This point is fundamental and must be realized by both parties before genuine cooperation becomes possible. It is for this reason that companies setting up joint production drive committees were urged by the War Production Board not to permit matters con- nected with collective bargaining to be discussed in the meetings of the production committees.

Recently a member of management in a discussion with union leaders raised a question that is pertinent here. He asked the union leaders: "When you fellows go on to the point where you have organized practically all of industry, and when you have gotten prac- tically all you can get from management without forcing it into bank- ruptcy, what then?" This question points to the fundamental distinc- tion between collective bargaining and cooperation. If the returns from a business enterprise are considered to be a pie, there are two ways for the union to get more pie. One way is to fight for as big a piece as can be obtained. That is collective bargaining. If the union has gotten as big a piece as possible by this means, there remains another way: to strive to increase the size of the pie so that there will be more for everyone who partakes of it. The concept of union– management cooperation springs from the latter point of view.

There is one more point to be considered in connection with the distinction between collective bargaining and cooperation. We have

[3] Cf. Follett, Mary, *Creative Experience*, Longmans, Green & Co., New York, 1924.

already indicated that some problems are likely to remain matters of collective bargaining indefinitely. What, then, are the problems that lend themselves most readily to cooperative effort? One thinks first of the problems of productive efficiency. Through cooperative effort it is possible to increase output and reduce waste, thus increasing the size of the pie.

Many companies have experimented with cooperative procedures for dealing with other problems. For example, although the establishment of the general level of wages is accomplished through collective bargaining, problems connected with the internal wage structure may be handled with considerable success on a cooperative basis. Job evaluation plans are rather widely administered today on a joint basis.[4] A few firms have had some success in the joint administration of wage incentive systems.[5] Many problems connected with the formulation of a general labor policy such as would be printed in a booklet for new employees can be successfully handled cooperatively.[6] As suggested above, the grievance procedure is in part amenable to a cooperative approach. There have even been instances where the union has cooperated with the company on problems connected with merchandising and selling.[7]

Union–management cooperation may encompass a variety of phenomena. It begins to appear in rudimentary form during the neutral, or collective bargaining, stage of the relationship. Its further development is often unnecessarily delayed because of a failure of the participants to recognize clearly the essential differences between collective bargaining and cooperation.

Basic Differences in Union and Management Organization

We have pointed out above that growth in union–management relations takes place through the medium of the interaction of representatives of the two groups. Certain basic differences between the management organization and the union organization materially affect the nature of the interaction that takes place and thus influence

[4] Cf. Bergen, H. B., "Union Participation in Job Evaluation," PERSONNEL, March 1942, pp. 261–268.

[5] The Murray Corporation, Detroit, is an outstanding example.

[6] Decker, D. D., "A Practical Supervisory Training Program," PERSONNEL, November 1939, pp. 62–68.

[7] Hochman, Jules, *Industry Planning Through Collective Bargaining*. A program for modernizing the New York Dress Industry as presented in conference with employers on behalf of the Joint Board of the Dressmakers' Union. International Ladies' Garment Workers Union, New York, 1941.

the growth of union–management relations. The most important difference, and the only one that we shall discuss, is in the way in which authority and responsibility are handled by the management organization and the union organization.

Industrial management is so organized that control is from the top down, with authority and responsibility delegated by the few to the many. Those at the top who have final authority are presumably the most capable and the most skilled of the whole management group.

The control by those at the top is exerted over the management organization through the formulation of a policy that sets limits within which action may be taken by the rest of the group. This policy is usually a fairly general one, and emphasizes long-range achievements. It may be written down, or it may exist only in the minds of those at the top. It may be implemented by few or many rules and regulations.

Top-management policy is aimed at the promotion of a profitable enterprise.[8] This is essentially the reason for the existence of the management organization. In promoting a profitable enterprise, management is likely to stress in its policy the necessity for freedom of action, and to feel that without it control of the business (purchasing, manufacturing, sales) is lost. Restrictions are placed on the authority and responsibility of subordinates so that they will not through their actions interfere with top management's control.

Top management also exerts a fundamental control on the rest of the management organization through its methods of selecting and training subordinates. A certain degree of conformity with top-management policy is required of all subordinates. Those who do not conform are dropped from the organization. A conscious control is exerted in this manner. However, men are selected as a result of unconscious influences that are even more important. A member of management chooses his subordinates, not only to fill the logical requirements of his organization, but also to satisfy certain unconscious demands of his own personality. A commonly recognized example is the executive who surrounds himself with "yes men."

Finally, top management exerts control by issuing orders. These may be broad or specific, and may be called by a variety of names, but essentially they are orders that must be followed within certain limits of tolerance by subordinates within the organization. Even the most

---

[8] There are, of course, top managements whose policies are aimed actually at the achievement of purely personal goals (money, power, and so forth). These are not under discussion in the present article.

liberal top management, using the consultative methods that are popular today, retains a veto power over the actions and decisions of its subordinates.

In union organizations, on the other hand, control is ultimately from the bottom upward, with authority and responsibility delegated by the many to the few.[9] The many who control are usually less skilled and less capable than the leaders whom they control.

The aims of the rank and file are likely to be relatively opportunistic and short range. They are further likely to be very specific rather than general in nature: Get this wage increase, settle that grievance to our satisfaction, prevent management from carrying out this course of action, and so on.

In the early stages of union–management relations, one of the chief aims of the union membership may be revenge.[10] This depends, of course, on the past behavior of management. Where this desire for revenge exists, it is usually found that the provision of an opportunity for the open expression of accumulated dissatisfactions removes the necessity for other forms of revengeful behavior. When management has a sincere desire to eliminate past sources of frustration to its workers, there is little need to fear a long continuance of the revenge theme.

The union membership will also try to obtain specific improvements in working conditions and changes in procedural rules such as those of promotion and transfer. Finally, it will be their aim to obtain more money. The important needs for social recognition, security, and recognition of personal worth are difficult for the worker to put into words. The demand for money is tangible. It is therefore an excellent medium for the expression of these needs.

Other aims of a different nature will emerge only after a slow educational process by which first the leaders and then the membership of the union have been brought to the point of thinking in long-range terms.

The authority of the union membership is exerted ultimately through their elected leaders. There is a vast difference between the elective process and the carefully controlled selective and training processes utilized by top management. In addition, at least during the early period of the union's existence, the union demands greater

[9] While it is true that there are many "boss-ridden" unions, these, like the racketeer managements mentioned in the previous footnote, are arbitrarily eliminated from this discussion. Even among boss-ridden *international* unions there are many "boss-free" union *locals*.

[10] Cf. Golden and Ruttenberg, *op. cit.*, Chap. I, esp. pp. 15, 16.

conformity from its leaders than does management from its subordinates.

Members of management sometimes fail to recognize the consequences of these facts about the union organization. They display a kind of impatience that suggests that they expect to deal with the union in the same way that they would deal with the management of another firm. However, in the early stages of union–management relations, union leaders are specifically instructed delegates. They come to management with explicit instructions to obtain certain definite things. They are not carrying on negotiations within the framework of a policy, expressed or unexpressed.

As time passes and the union attains a greater stability and security, the control over its leaders is somewhat looser. Management's education of the union leaders begins to bear fruit. They can begin to operate within the framework of a policy. Nevertheless, because a union local is basically a democratic organization, union leaders must constantly check the opinions of their constituents to see whether the decisions they are reaching in their negotiations with management are consistent with the aims of the membership. The rank and file always lag behind their leaders in understanding and in willingness to accept broad policies and long-range aims.[11]

There is sometimes an interesting consequence of this "lag." A management that has been dealing with union leaders who have developed and broadened remarkably in perspective may be surprised to find them replaced at election time by a group of suspicious and antagonistic "fighters." What has happened is this: The old leaders, effectively educated by management, have failed in turn to educate the membership of the union, and the "lag" has become too great. *From the point of view of the members,* the leaders have "sold out" to management. They are suspicious not only of their leaders but of the management that has "betrayed" them, and they proceed to elect a new leadership that will "show management where to get off."

Union leaders are not alone in being restricted by the attitudes and capacities of their followers. Management is also restricted to some extent by the capacities and attitudes of its subordinates. Many firms have faced a real problem in the re-education of a group of "unenlightened" old-line foremen after a union has been organized in

[11] Management's employment policies will in the long run materially affect the growth of union–management relations by determining the quality of workers who are employed. Marginal firms, hiring from the lower fringes of the labor market, cannot expect the education of the rank and file of the membership to proceed as rapidly as that of firms that select their workers from the "cream of the crop."

the plant. After facing this problem, management will have a much clearer conception of what a union is up against.

We have indicated certain differences in the handling of authority and responsibility by the management organization and the union organization. These differences materially affect the nature of the interaction between management representatives and union representatives. All the discussion that follows must be seen against this background of the difference in nature of the two organizations. The requirements for effective cooperation would be entirely different if the management organization and the union organization handled authority and responsibility in identical ways.

The Influence of the Personalities of Management

It is obvious that the nature of the interaction between management and union will be influenced by the personalities of the participants.[12] Considering management first, we shall discuss one broad characteristic of personality that has a vital influence on the rate of growth of union–management relations.

The growth will be exceedingly slow, and may cease altogether at an early stage of development, unless the key members of management who regularly·deal with the union have a genuine, secure confidence in themselves and in their ability to perform the functions of management.

This self-confidence will reflect itself in a variety of ways. The men who possess it are quietly sure of themselves. They know (but they probably do not say so) that whatever happens, they will be able to land on their feet. They are able to take criticism, even from their inferiors. They are tolerant—able to see and to face the limitations placed on union leaders by the nature of the union organization. Since they have a secure confidence in themselves, they can face critical problems in human relations objectively. Their own inferiorities do not become involved in the situation. Consequently, they are able to take a long-range view of the union–management relationship, and their decisions will stand the test of time.

This basic self-confidence is not as common as might be supposed.

[12] This is a complex subject. There are a great many ways in which the personalities of the participants influence union–management relations. Within the scope of this paper we can present only a grossly oversimplified discussion of one or two aspects of the problem. For a more detailed discussion of the influences of personality on social interaction, see for example: Maslow, A. H., and Mittelmann, B., *Principles of Abnormal Psychology*, Harper & Brothers, New York, 1941, esp. Chaps. IV, XIV–XVI.

Many able managers lack it. Many who are not so able exhibit its absence by an overbearing manner.

A lack of self-confidence among the key members of management retards union–management cooperation by slowing up the growth of the relationship in several important ways. The member of management who is lacking in self-confidence cannot treat union representatives as equals. The relationship will be that of the master accepting somewhat warily the help of the slave, with fear and trembling lest the slave overpower him and assume the role of master. Under such conditions the growth process is fixated at a relatively early stage, because genuine cooperation involves at least a measure of equality between the participants.

The individual who lacks self-confidence fears and suspects those with whom he deals, particularly if they are somewhat antagonistic and aggressive. As a result of this fear and suspicion, he will be unwilling to take the *necessary* chances involved in the early stages of union–management cooperation. It is inevitable that the first attempt at cooperation will be harried by hangovers of past competitive habits. Particularly when the past experience of both parties has been one involving a fair amount of conflict, they are likely to "stub their toes" frequently when they begin to attempt to cooperate. It requires real confidence to accept these slips and to go on without the feeling that there has been a "dirty deal."

In summary, then, a vital factor influencing the growth of industrial relations will be the presence or absence of a genuine, secure confidence on the part of the key members of management who deal with the union.[13] If this is absent, union–management relations are likely to be arrested at an early stage of the process. Only in the presence of this factor will management have the courage to take the inevitable risks involved in making a transition from the neutral to the cooperative stage of union–management relations.

The Influence of the Personalities of Union Leaders

The man who has rebelled violently against authority is rarely tolerated in management. He is, however, frequently found among

---

[13] It may appear that we are more tolerant of weaknesses in unions than in management. We are, and for a definite reason: The weaknesses of the union movement have been amply criticized in the press, in literature, and from the lecture platform. Constructive criticism of management is far less frequent. The union movement today is a powerful force. We believe that management has much to gain by understanding it, and by learning how to live with it. Hence our emphasis on the ways in which management can change in order to influence the growth of the relationship.

those union leaders who are in power during the fighting stage of union–management relations. He is elected to his office because he possesses exactly the characteristics that the new and insecure union requires if it is to achieve the things its members desire of it at that time. His first appearance across the table from management may cause a good deal of consternation. Such a man is likely to be resentful toward management and completely unwilling to bury the past in order to build a new relationship. Consequently, the growth of industrial relations is arrested as long as he is in power.

In the normal course of events, however, the union achieves some of its purposes, and with this achievement comes a measure of security. When this happens, there is likely to be a change in union leadership. Men get tired of fighting (particularly when it is unnecessary), of fiery oratory, of being whipped into a frenzy at every union meeting. They want someone who will lead them and protect their interests without creating such a fuss about it. They are ready to elect to office intelligent leaders who are quietly confident and who possess skill in dealing with men. It is not until such men are elected to office by the union that the transition to later stages of union–management relations becomes possible.

The Quality of Foremanship

Interaction between management and union occurs chiefly in two ways: (1) through meetings between middle or top management and union leaders, and (2) through the daily contact between foreman and union members. The union *leader* acquires an understanding of management's problems, learns the why and the wherefore of company policy, and forms his opinions of "the company" by means of his contact with the higher levels of management. The union *member* acquires his understanding and forms his opinions about "the company": (1) from what he is told by the leaders of his union, and (2) from his experience with his foreman. When there are discrepancies between (1) and (2), the union member (as would most of us) accepts the evidence of experience. As a result, discrepancies between the "teachings" of top management and of the foremen will either forestall management's attempts to broaden and develop the union leaders, or undermine the union leadership by widening the gap between leaders and members.

It is obvious, therefore, that the foreman's methods of handling his men, his attitudes, and his personality are important factors influencing the growth of union–management relations.[14] The most progressive and well-intentioned top management may find that its efforts to promote better relations are not achieving the desired results because the foremen resent the union and show their resentment in their treatment of the workers. The situation is further aggravated if management (as is often the case) fails to recognize the effect of the behavior of the foremen on the workers. Failing to perceive the real cause, top management may feel that the union members are unreasonable and recalcitrant. Then the fighting stage of the relationship may be prolonged until the union educates the foremen or succeeds in "running out" the worst of them.

Thus the poor foreman may prevent the execution of the most carefully laid plans for improving union–management relations. He may even provide the reason for the belief that better relations are impossible. Too often he does both, and management—unaware of the real circumstances—unjustly accuses the union of bad faith.

The good foreman, on the other hand, provides a daily proof of management's real intentions. From his behavior the union members may obtain the substantiating evidence that their leaders need to sell them an enlightened, long-range program.

It is apparent, then, that the growth of union–management relations is vitally dependent upon the quality of men selected to be foremen, upon their training, and upon the degree to which they are made an integral part of management. Cooperation between management and union cannot occur until there is cooperation within the ranks of management.

A Recognition of the Ability of the Average Worker

The union and the management must each expect the other to contribute something worthwhile to the solution of their joint problems if there is to be any point in cooperating. This means each group must recognize in the other an ability that if utilized will contribute importantly to their cooperative effort.

Workers in general respect management's ability, even though they may not respect management's philosophy and motives. Management, on the other hand, has a tendency to underestimate those abilities of workers that may be utilized for cooperative efforts. Aware of the long period of apprenticeship they themselves have served,

[14] Cf. Hersey, R. B., "Labor Relations of 1941: Cooperation vs. Dictation," PERSONNEL, May 1941, pp. 270–288.

many members of management are likely to feel it is absurd to assume that workers could be of material help in promoting more efficient production. So long as the worker is regarded as a mere "quantum of labor," the idea of union–management cooperation is preposterous.

This underevaluation of the worker's potential contribution is especially prevalent where management lacks real self-confidence. When an individual lacks confidence in his own ability, he does not readily recognize it in others. He is likely to protect his opinion of himself by underestimating the ability of the other fellow, particularly if the other fellow occupies a lower position on the social scale.

The abilities of the worker that may be tapped for the cooperative effort differ from those of management. That is the main reason why they are valuable. Management typically has a generalized knowledge of engineering principles and of the production problems and processes in the plant. The worker, on the other hand, has a highly specific knowledge, drawn from his intimate daily contact with the process on which he is working and the machine he operates. As a result, he can often assist management materially in discovering ways of improving the process, of reducing waste, of increasing the efficiency of a machine.

Because he is quite unfettered by a knowledge of the principles of physics, chemistry, and engineering, he is frequently able to view the process on which he is working with a perspective that would be impossible for management. A great many important contributions in science and engineering have come about because the inventor was able to take an absolutely fresh slant on the problem. This, above all else, the worker can do. Out of his fresh perspective sometimes emerge suggestions and ideas which, although they may appear initially to be foolish, have real merit. The literature of union–management cooperation contains example after example of suggestions submitted by workers that have proved practical after management has overcome its initial skepticism sufficiently to experiment with them.[15]

Since the worker is likely to be overawed by management's knowledge and ability, he is likely to keep his mouth shut for fear of criticism and ridicule. Management must have a genuine and evident respect for his ability before he will feel free to express himself.

We are not suggesting that management must be prepared to put

[15] Cf. Golden, C. S., and Ruttenberg, H. J., *op. cit.*, Chaps. VIII and IX.

into practice every idea suggested by its workers if cooperation is to be effective. We are suggesting that the cooperation will be fruitless unless management has learned to deal with these suggestions in a way that does not injure the worker's rather shaky belief in his own ability along these lines. Also, management must be flexible enough intellectually to recognize potential merit in a fresh point of view and to experiment with ideas that may seem revolutionary in the light of accepted engineering principles. The history of science is full of examples of great discoveries that were ridiculed merely because they were somewhat unusual.

The member of management who lacks faith in the worker's ability will demonstrate it readily in his reaction to the idea of union–management cooperation. He will feel and say that it is a waste of time. Although he will not be so apt to say it, he will also feel that it is insulting to him to have to accept the help of workers in solving his problems. He believes he is on top of the heap because of his own ability and that workers are on the bottom because they lack it.

The existence of the ability denied the worker by management is often demonstrated when it is utilized to defeat management's purposes. It is the boast of many workers that they can "beat" any incentive system that management can devise, and the evidence tends to support this contention. The longer union–management relations remain in the fighting stage, the more strongly are union members motivated to utilize their abilities in order to outsmart management. It is only when the relationship has gone beyond the neutral stage that these abilities can be harnessed for the solution of common problems.

This respect for the ability of the worker has a corollary—a realization of the potentialities of the worker for learning. Workers are likely to be humble concerning their own potentialities for development and learning, but they are ordinarily eager to learn if properly motivated. The fruits of union–management cooperation will not be realized unless management takes advantage of these potentialities.

A Willingness to Share Equitably the Gains from Cooperation

Neither management nor union will ever seriously consider the possibility of cooperation unless they expect to gain from it. It is probably unwise to depend too much on the purely philanthropic motives of man. Even the patriotic motives appealed to by the War Production Board in its campaign for production drive committees are likely to operate only to the extent that management and workers alike view the war as something very close to home. If the present crisis really is a crisis in their eyes—if they honestly believe that their own efforts can help prevent a catastrophe—only then will this appeal be an effective one in promoting their joint efforts to cooperate. As of August 1942 one may be permitted to doubt whether this kind of motivation is as yet very widespread.

There are a number of possible gains from union–management cooperation that the worker will recognize as important to *him*. The motives involved can be harnessed to the cooperative effort, however, only if there is a genuine willingness to share the resulting gains equitably.

The first of these gains is the economic one. There is plenty of evidence to suggest that the economic gains can be sizable, but there is not so much evidence of a willingness on management's part to share them equitably. Many suggestion schemes have been set up as a means of stimulating the worker's ideas for the promotion of greater productive efficiency. Even the more liberal of these plans seldom grant the worker an equitable share in the results obtained from his suggestions. Many of them have a top award of $50 or $100, while savings effected through the suggestions submitted sometimes total thousands of dollars per year.

The traditional American philosophy has been individualistic. Consequently, it has been natural for management to seek ways of motivating individuals to be more productive and to reward the individual for his efforts. During the past decade, however, there has been an increasing emphasis on collective goals. Social security, "share the work" plans, union organization, wage and hour legislation—all are *group* rather than individual phenomena. It is actually just as possible to harness motives to group effort as it is to individual effort,[16] although we have only recently begun to recognize the fact in industry.

Union–management cooperation is a group effort. Although effective cooperation is unlikely if the contributions of the individual to the collective effort are ignored entirely, the economic gains can best be shared on a group basis. The economic gains of cooperation do not go to individual members of management. There is no reason for them to go to individual members of the union. Some of the other gains can be shared in a way that rewards the contributions of the individual.

[16] The recent writings of the social anthropologists provide ample evidence. Cf., for example, Mead, Margaret, *Cooperation and Competition Among Primitive Peoples*, McGraw-Hill Book Company, Inc., New York, 1937.

There is a growing realization today that the possibility of economic gain is only one of many reasons that keep the worker (as well as management) on the job. A second highly important motive is the desire for prestige and social recognition. Properly handled, this motive becomes a powerful asset to union–management cooperation. The efforts of both the individual and the group may be rewarded by proper recognition.

Investigators of the War Production Board, reporting on the experiences of companies that have installed production drive committees, point out that one of the major obstacles to successful cooperation has been the unwillingness of management to give the union proper credit for its contribution to the joint effort. There is something ironic in the fact that management, traditionally motivated *solely* by the desire for profits, is sometimes loath to share prestige with its own workers. Nevertheless, this unwillingness on the part of management has proved a stumbling block to successful cooperation many times in the past.

Once more we refer to the factor of management's confidence in its own ability, which was discussed above. The member of management who is not genuinely confident of himself feels that he loses face when his workers gain prestige for having contributed importantly to an increase in productive efficiency. He feels that, since the management of the productive processes is his concern and responsibility, any improvement in them that he has not instituted is essentially a criticism of his own skill. Naturally, then, he is unwilling to see others obtain praise, since he regards that praise as criticism of himself.

One of the outstanding examples of union–management cooperation in the country has been plagued recently by this bugaboo. The remarkable success of this venture has resulted in considerable publicity. Because of the man-bites-dog feature of the situation, the publicity has stessed the contributions of the union to the cooperative effort. In the recent past, management has begun to play down the contributions of the union when discussing the situation with visitors. In this particular instance the problem is probably not a serious one, because the relationship between management and union has become so mature that the issue will undoubtedly be discussed openly and cleared up by both sides before it becomes critical. The example is significant because it illustrates the fact that, even though the economic issue is settled, the problem of sharing the further results of cooperation (prestige, in this case) can be a real one, even though union–management relations have reached a remarkable degree of maturity.

It is likely to be a much more critical problem in the early stages of cooperation.

The gains from union–management cooperation can be shared with the workers in another important way—in terms of job security. When the Baltimore and Ohio Railroad began union–management cooperation back in 1923, the guarantee by the company that induced the union to try out the plan was one of job security. Certainly, if cooperation is effective, it will strengthen the position of the company competitively, and to that extent make possible a greater stabilization of employment and greater guarantees of job security. With the experiences of the past decade still fresh in their minds, this is a matter of considerable importance to workers.

Some well-known instances of union–management cooperation in the steel industry and in the needle trades were begun as a last resort in companies that were about to go out of existence because of financial insecurity. Job security was obviously a fundamental motive in these cases. It has been suggested by some critics that effective union–management cooperation can occur only under such extreme circumstances. It is more probable that these cases represent examples of a sudden maturing of union–management relations brought about by the necessity for surviving a real crisis. The growth process was speeded up materially in these instances. Had the course of development been normal, the stage of union–management cooperation might well have been delayed for several years.

There are other potential gains from union–management cooperation that are somewhat intangible. Chief among these is the interest in the "game" of running the company successfully. There is little doubt that this is a basic motive of management. It can be shared with workers. When it is shared, some of the workers at least will begin to display the same loyalty to the company that is expected of management. The sharing of this interest inevitably narrows the gap between management and union.

Economic gains, prestige, increased job security, and interest in "the game" are all potential consequences of union–management cooperation. Unless there is a genuine willingness to share the results equitably, there will be not only a lack of motivation for the cooperative effort, but a real dissatisfaction with the whole relationship. Without a plan for the equitable sharing of results, the idea of cooperation will probably be viewed as an attempt on management's part to bring about a speed-up. The consequence of such suspicion is not cooperation but its antithesis.

Union Security

When a union is fighting with management for its existence, union–management cooperation is impossible. Its leaders are motivated primarily to get more and more from management through collective bargaining so that they will remain in office and the workers will remain in the union. When the union has achieved some form of security (for example, a maintenance-of-membership clause, a union shop, or a closed shop), its leaders will no longer have to weigh every move in terms of what their constituents will have to say about it. They can weigh the problems they discuss with management in terms of their real merit, rather than in terms of their political significance for the union membership. They can count on time in which to educate their followers and in which to demonstrate the value of long-range rather than short-range goals.

This issue is a difficult one to discuss because the arguments that are usually advanced contain far more heat than light.[17] Regardless of the merits of the case, there is very little doubt that some form of union security is essential if union–management relations are to develop to full maturity. It may well be that a new formula for union security will be discovered that will be superior to any of those commonly used today. One formula that seems to have been almost entirely ignored is to share the gains of union–management cooperation between the groups that are cooperating, namely, the management (or the owners) and the membership of the union. Thus a genuine motivation is provided for joining the union, and the problems of coercion and freedom of contract are not involved.[18] Union members may be unwilling to expend the effort involved in union–management cooperation if the fruits are to be shared alike with members and nonmembers.

In general it may be pointed out that union security is normally an issue only during the early stages of the growth of union–management relations. When these relations have reached the stage where cooperation is being seriously considered, and where a fair proportion of the factors mentioned above are present, the question of union security is likely to be settled with very little argument.

[17] For a well-documented, objective analysis of the issue, cf. Toner, J. L., *The Closed Shop*, American Council on Public Affairs, Washington, D.C., 1942.

[18] The fact that management is ordinarily unfavorably disposed toward this arrangement indicates that the reasons usually advanced against the union shop are not the basic ones.

Mutual Understanding

If the reader will look back over the whole list of factors we have discussed, it will be apparent to him that one that has not yet been mentioned specifically runs through all of them as a common thread. This factor is a genuine mutual understanding on the part of the participants in the union–management relationship. Only when this understanding is present is it possible for growth to occur.

Unless management understands the problems of the union leaders that arise as a result of the nature of a union organization, the behavior of the leaders will be viewed with suspicion, and sometimes even contempt. Unless the union leaders can acquire a genuine understanding of the authoritative relationships of management, and their consequences, they will remain suspicious and antagonistic.

Unless management understands the worker's desires for security, social satisfactions, prestige, and the recognition of personal worth, union–management cooperation will appear to be a utopian idea entirely outside the realm of practicality.

On the other hand, unless the union can acquire a genuine understanding of management's desire for a productive enterprise, many of management's suggestions for improving efficiency and reducing waste will be viewed with suspicion. Unless the union members can acquire an understanding of cost reduction through a knowledge of the problems of their company, there is little point in cooperative effort to improve productive efficiency.

This mutual understanding—so essential to the development of labor–management relations—is not a mere intellectual phenomenon. If someone says to you, "I want to explain how this machine works," and then proceeds to show you blueprints and demonstrations of the operations of the machine in question, you will end (if he is competent) with an "understanding" of what he is talking about.

On the other hand, suppose someone says to you, "I want you to understand how I felt when I asked the boss for a raise the other day," and then goes on to describe his feelings as he approached the boss, his reaction when he discovered that the boss was in a bad temper because he had just lost a large order to his chief competitor, and his crushing disappointment when the request for a raise was indignantly refused. Whether or not you "understand" in this case depends not on a mere knowledge of the facts, but on your ability to put yourself into the other fellow's shoes emotionally. This ability to put yourself in the place of the other fellow and to feel as he does is an important means by which tolerance and trust are developed in people who deal with each other day by day.

Union–management meetings are often carried on in an atmosphere of "being logical" or "sticking to the hard facts." When this atmosphere exists, a barrier is raised against the expression of feelings and emotions. The man who insists on logic and facts will almost certainly fail to get "out on the table" the nonlogical opinions and feelings that are important to real understanding. Cooperation under these circumstances is an impossibility.

*   *   *

We have aimed high in this discussion, but we do not believe we have been unrealistic. None of these requirements for union–management cooperation is impractical, although some of them may be difficult to achieve in particular situations at particular times. Instances of really successful cooperations are indeed rare, partly because union–management relations in this country are still generally in the early stages of growth and partly because most people do not realize the requirements for genuine cooperation. The existence of even a few remarkably mature relationships gives the lie to those who insist that union–management cooperation is but an idealist's pipedream.

There are many union–management combinations that are today, after a normal, healthy growth, enjoying a collective bargaining relationship that they would have thought fantastic a few years ago. If they have the patience to accept the inevitable slowness and unevenness of psychological growth, if each side has enough self-confidence to permit a belief in the ability and honesty of the other, and if they have a real understanding not only of the factual but also of the emotional problems involved, they will over the next few years make the transition to a relationship whose potentialities have been only dimly perceived: genuine union–management cooperation.

5

May 1947

Essentials of a Management Personnel Policy

Lawrence A. Appley

BEFORE discussing the essentials of a personnel policy, it is necessary to have a clear concept of what a policy is and what constitutes a well-constructed policy. The dictionary tells us that a policy is a plan of action and that a plan is a policy. Policymaking and planning are therefore synonymous. A policy and a plan of action are the same.

A specific and clear-cut plan of action is basic to the accomplishment of a given task and to the attainment of any objective. Planning is a major function of management. Since management is the achievement of results through the efforts of other people, the most important activity of management is the direction of human effort. Human effort can be directed most effectively through the guiding influence of a plan of action known to all concerned.

Definiteness of policy reveals the caliber of an executive. It is an indication of the moral fiber of which he is made. It reflects his clarity of thinking, depth of conviction, and willingness to commit himself to a course of action guided by basic principle. Readiness to commit oneself to a written policy indicates bigness. Readiness to alter policy with changing conditions in favor of a wiser course of action is indicative of greatness.

Essential Parts of Policy

A policy, or a plan of action, that is to be made effective by others is of little use unless it is in writing. When put in writing, it should contain three basic parts: (a) the objectives; (b) the procedure for the attainment of the objectives; and (c) definite assignment of various parts of the procedure to individuals as specific responsibility.

Despite the vividness with which you may visualize a house you would like to build, despite your enthusiasm and determination to erect that house, you will never accomplish your aim without an architect's drawing of the finished house (the objective); without a blueprint (procedure) showing exactly what has to be done to build a house resembling the drawing; and without indicating the various parts of the blueprint that are the responsibility of different workers, such as the carpenter, electrician, plumber, mason, painter (assignment of responsibility).

Joint participation in its development is another essential of sound policy. Many minds are better than one. If individuals who are to work on a given project have a voice in the determination of the policies to be followed, the policies will be more complete, practical, and applicable. Many a policy has ended on the rocks because of flaws that could have been detected immediately had it been exposed before adoption to those who had to implement the policy and follow it.

Personnel Objectives—General

In applying this general thinking concerning policy to the essentials of a management personnel policy, let us first consider the question of objectives. A management personnel policy should have two types of objectives: general and specific.

The statement of general objectives should express top management's basic philosophy toward human resources and reflect its deep and underlying conviction as to the importance of people in an organization and of that management activity that deals with people— personnel administration.

Top management has too long been silent as to its views on labor. It has too long allowed outside interests to misrepresent, misinterpret, smear, and condemn its attitudes and to attribute to it views that, in many cases, have been nonexistent. The time has arrived for top management to formulate and adopt a basic creed and to make that creed known to employees and public. Such a creed would contain a clear-cut statement of the company's general objective with respect to personnel management's major responsibility.

If the people of this country actually knew what most industrial and business managements stand for, and what constructive steps they are taking with respect to the human element, the economic and political thinking and action of this nation would be profoundly altered.

Personnel Objectives—Specific

The statement of specific objectives should refer to the various activities of personnel administration. In most instances, management has the following specific objectives in relation to human resources:

1. Finding and selecting the right caliber and number of people required to perform the operations of the organization involved.
2. Proper orientation and introduction of new employees to the company and to the job.
3. Fair, sound, and effective salary and wage administration.
4. Establishment of incentives that will result in the highest possible productivity of workers.
5. Establishment and maintenance of personnel inventories based on periodic appraisals of the productivity, methods, qualifications, and potential of employees in all categories.
6. Well-organized and specific training for better job performance and for other jobs.
7. Continuing personal research that keeps management supplied with facts and with the knowledge of trends essential to the making of sound management personnel decisions.
8. The kind of first-line supervision that improves knowledge, increases skill, and develops a high degree of willingness to work on the part of those supervised.
9. Employee benefits that create the kind of an organization and work situation in which people want to work (these include safety and health programs, medical benefits, group insur-

ance, pensions, vacation plans, leaves of absence, and other
· such benefits, the objective of which is to hold competent and
qualified people in the organization).

10. Full and fair consideration of an employee at time of separation from the payroll.

11. Relations with organized labor based on mutual confidence
and respect.

Personnel Procedure

Top-management personnel policy must provide for the development of specific procedures and programs for the accomplishment of the objectives just outlined. Some of these are as follows:

1. The policies and basic principles guiding top-management
thinking must be fully understood by the entire executive and
supervisory force. This can only be accomplished by a well-
planned and well-organized system of *executive and supervisory
education and training.* Such a system would cover not only
employees already in managerial positions, but also those who
are potential supervisors. No individual should be permitted
to take on supervisory responsibility for the first time without
thorough and formal training in the basic principles and techniques of management, as well as in the policies of management. Such a program should be worked out in detail and
identified as an executive and supervisory training program.

   It is essential that individuals in managerial positions
realize clearly that their major responsibility is the personnel
under their direction and that they exert the strongest influence upon the character and caliber of that personnel. The
basic concept that must be instilled in the minds of supervisory
people is the idea that their job is to develop those under their
supervision, to increase their skills, to improve their knowledge, to change their habits and attitudes, and continually to
raise their individual productivity.

2. *Placement* procedures would incorporate programs for recruiting, the use of various advertising media, interviewing,
employee records, personnel testing, standards for employment office layout and procedure, and so on.

3. If it is the objective of the management that a new employee
shall be properly oriented and introduced to the company and
to a new job, that objective will be attained only through the

establishment of a specifically prepared program of *orientation training.*

4. Fair and sound *wage and salary administration* requires the setting up of procedures for job evaluation and for the making of wage and salary surveys. It also requires the establishment of proper procedures for the administration of wage and salary adjustments.

5. Incentives should be simply worked out and easily understandable. The suggestion system is one commonly accepted form of incentive. Bonuses, merit rating, and piecework are all well-known procedures with numerous advantages to specific situations. They are inherent in the private enterprise system but are attacked and opposed because of the way in which they have been complicated and loaded with technicalities.

6. If management is to be provided with comprehensive *personnel inventories,* a procedure must be developed and put into effect that calls for a careful appraisal of each individual on the payroll. Various tools and machinery are well known and essential to its success. There are many techniques, such as the use of "multiple evaluation" and "open appraisals," that have been successful enough to justify much broader application.

7. The old idea of master–learner methods for training is fairly well outmoded. There are those who were not convinced of this before the war. There are many thousands of executives in this country who became converted during the war. *Training* does not result from the statement of an objective or from wishful thinking. It results only from well-established procedure and program. The simplest of training devices quickly justify themselves because of the immediate and noticeable improvement in the productiveness of those who are the recipients.

8. *Personnel research* exists in name only when it is irregular, scattered, and incidental. This activity must be integrated under a single leadership. Research projects must be specifically outlined and listed in order of priority. There are single studies needed from time to time and continuing studies required at all times. As a part of personnel research, a clearly identified procedure must be established for the maintenance of measurements of the effectiveness of the activities of personnel administration. Just as much needs to be known, and should be known, about the human resources under our direction

as is known about the physical resources with which we deal.

9. *Vacation plans, medical and health insurance, leaves of absence, profit-sharing systems, pensions, safety and health programs* are all specific procedures that are a part of top management's personnel policies. They must be clearly related to each other, must supplement each other, and no one of them can be expected to accomplish more than a part of the overall objective in relation to human resources.

10. Fair and adequate handling of *separations* from the payroll requires procedures for warning interviews, exit interviews, and assistance in finding jobs elsewhere or in adjusting to a life of retirement.

11. *Labor relations* represent a highly developed field of activity. There is still great variance in practice. The procedures to be followed by management in its relationship with organized labor must be carefully worked out and well applied if the objective is to be realized. The result otherwise is misunderstanding and chaos.

Clarifying procedure, of course, requires the making of many basic decisions. Frequently these are decisions that management has avoided and with which, in many cases, it has compromised. Illustrations of some of the decisions essential to the establishment of a labor relations policy follow:

What is top management's attitude toward labor organizations?

What about the closed shop, the check-off, seniority, and compulsory arbitration? These are not questions of expediency; they are questions of basic principle. They involve issues that can be settled only by top management. The sooner they are faced squarely, the better will be the management–labor relationship that exists. Groveling in the dust and hiding under the table on these issues gains no one's respect and contributes little, if anything, to industrial peace.

Responsibility for Personnel

The third section of a policy calls for clarification of responsibility in relation to the policy. This is particularly essential in a management personnel policy. Without going into detail about each of the various personnel activities, we might start with some general responsibility designations.

First, let us differentiate between the character of line and staff management. Line management consists of those executives and supervisors responsible for attaining the objectives of the organization. The staff executives are those who provide the guidance, assistance, and tools required by the line in the performance of its tasks. Line and staff are equally essential to the success of any organization. There is a distinct difference, however, in the nature of their relationships, and this must be clarified.

The responsibility for personnel administration rests squarely upon the shoulders of line management. Nothing must ever be said or done to dilute this concept, or to permit that responsibility to be taken away from the line, or to permit the line to sidestep that responsibility. The quality of the people on the job, the way in which they perform on the job, as well as all related activities in connection with them, are the full responsibility of their immediate supervisors.

The responsibility of the personnel executive, wherever he may be located in the organization, is to help the line executive and supervisor do the personnel task. He works toward the adoption and clarification of policies; he develops the tools and the machinery; he guides, directs, and evaluates the effectiveness of the use of the tools in the application of policy.

There are instances where the personnel executive actually performs certain line personnel functions. When he does so, it must be remembered that the responsibility is delegated to him by the line and that the only justification for this is that such functions can be more effectively and economically administered on a centralized basis than decentralized among the line supervisors. Illustrations are provided by employment offices, medical departments, orientation training courses, and so forth.

The Ideal Personnel Man

The ideal personnel manager is always endeavoring to work himself out of a job. That means he is continually influencing and training the line supervisors and executives to do a better personnel job. Human inadequacy and executive and supervisory turnover leave such a man with no fear of being out of work but with his objective unchanged. Frequently, a personnel executive falls for the temptation to gather unto himself greater and greater authority and responsibility for human relations. The more he does so, the closer and closer he gets to the end of the limb.

The very core of all personnel administration is the kind of relationship that exists between the workman and his immediate supervisor. All sound personnel administration is directed toward the strengthening of that relationship. The personnel officer who permits any weakening of that relationship, or any wedge to form between the worker and his boss, is doing a great disservice to the organization of which he is a part.

There are practical executives who readily agree that the responsibility for personnel administration rests with line management but who, at the same time, are too quick to carry the concept to extremes. Such executives would say, "Well, if personnel is the responsibility of the line, let's make the line executive do the personnel job. When you do that, there is no need for a personnel executive or a personnel staff." If that is sound logic, then it goes for the comptroller, the treasurer, the general counsel, the sales promotion manager, the engineer, the advertising executive, and all the other staff activities that are set up for the purpose of assisting the line executive in doing his job. Misconceptions of this sort are usually due to a lack of the kind of responsibility clarification which is proposed here.

Carpenters need tools to do their job. They do not know how to manufacture the tools, and most of them would use the same tools generation after generation if there were not specialists who manufactured better tools for them and trained them in their use. The carpenter hasn't the time or the special technical knowledge required to manufacture or perfect these tools, but he can supply the manufacturer with plenty of practical suggestions.

The effectiveness of personnel administration in any organization is basically dependent upon the clarity of policy formation—the development of plans of action in relation to personnel activities. The effectiveness of personnel administration in any organization may be quickly evaluated by the importance top management attaches to it. This is reflected in the time, effort, and consideration that same top management gives to human resources. This, in turn, is reflected in soundness and clarity of policy.

In Conclusion

The federal government itself is largely to blame for this country's present state of management–labor chaos. A basic reason for this is the government's lack of a definite labor policy. Possibly that statement should be amplified by saying that that element of the labor policy of our government that seems clear cannot be judged as sound, since it is directed by political expediency.

What are the objectives of the federal government in relation to labor? Is it the objective of government to establish the rules and to protect the people of the country against infractions of those rules, or is it government's purpose to foster the organization of labor and actually to conduct negotiations between management and labor? Whatever its objectives, are they related only to organized labor, or are they related to all the workers in the country?

The government should decide what its objectives are, should set up clearly established procedures for the attainment of those objectives, and should indicate definitely the responsibility of management, labor, government, and the consumer. There must be further clarification of responsibility in regard to the respective government agencies and facilities. The absence of such government policy and the existing conditions are proof of the need for a "top government personnel policy."

The essentials of a management or government personnel policy are the same as those of any policy: (a) a clear statement of overall objectives; (b) a detailed statement of specific objectives; (c) the preparation of workable programs and plans for the attainment of the objectives; (d) clear differentiation of responsibility in relation to the application of the policy. Meeting these essentials takes time, effort, and thought. There is no one top-management personnel policy that will apply to all organizations. Each must work out its own. The more clearly we think, the more specifically we express ourselves, the more effective will be our efforts in the field of personnel administration.

PART II

The Behavioral Scientists Step In

FIRST came industrial engineers with job study and methods improvements. Next, industrial psychologists offered selection tests and rating scales. Then in the late 1920s Elton Mayo and his team of researchers at Hawthorne applied behavioral science techniques to broader issues of industrial organization and management. The Depression and the rise of unions diverted attention from such matters during the 1930s, but World War II and the human problems involved in producing for the war gave impetus to increased use of behavioral scientists in a problem-solving mode.

The first article in Part II is by Stuart Chase. A distinguished writer and student of human relations, his books and articles helped disseminate important findings of the social sciences to "practical" men. "Social Science: Friend of Management," originally presented as one of a series of Bernays lectures on management's social responsibilities at New York University, summarizes many of the concepts developed by anthropologists, sociologists, psychologists, and other social scientists that had by 1951 already demonstrated their usefulness in practical affairs. It is still stimulating. It is still instructive.

In the second chapter of Part II, Robert H. Guest demonstrates the insights that can emerge from field research. At the time he wrote "Men and Machines: An Assembly-Line Worker Looks at His Job," Guest was on the faculty of the Institute of Human Relations at Yale University. The paper, first published in 1955, was adapted from an address he gave at the McGill University Industrial Relations Centre in Montreal. In the words of men on the assembly line, it describes the effects of mechanization. Precursor of Lordstown? Has anyone been listening?

If Robert Guest set the stage, Louis E. Davis suggested an answer—job design. His article "Job Design and Productivity: A New Approach," although written in 1957, while he was at the University of California, Berkeley, still describes a "new" approach. Job enrichment, job enlargement, job redesign, are as much in the news today and as much matters of management concern as they were matters of concern to behavioral scientists of the 1950s. There is a *necessary* time lag in getting helpful new ideas tested and put into practice. But should it be this long?

"Human Factors in Production" is a unique article because it was written by a company president who was also a professionally trained industrial psychologist. Alfred J. Marrow was president of Harwood Manufacturing Company when he published this article in 1949. It is an unusual article because it shows the productivity of the scientist and the manager collaborating in a research mode to find answers to significant practical problems. And answers they found—some still "new."

One of the results of the behavioral scientists' research has been a better understanding of the attitudes, needs, and reactions of people who work. Building on these findings, many managers evolved better ways of working with their people. One new style was—and is— consultative management, and H. H. Carey set it down in "Consultative Supervision and Management" in a way that makes it a revelation still. Here is one of the pillars of modern human resources management, as fresh today as in 1942, when it was first published. Here is an employee on strike making it all so real when he explains the strike against his paternalistic employer by saying: "But *he* done it all. We didn't have anything to do with it. I don't want anybody to be good to me. I want to be good to myself."

Leland P. Bradford and Ronald Lippitt take the question of how a supervisor should relate to his or her people one step further. In "Building a Democratic Work Group" they described typical supervisory styles and employee reactions to these styles. They went beyond this, though. They also analyzed why each of these styles—the hardboiled autocrat, the benevolent autocrat, the laissez faire leader, and the democratic leader—has the effect it does on people. Bradford, at the time director of adult education service with the National Education Association, and Lippitt, at the time acting chief of training for the Federal Security Agency, demonstrated clearly the value of behavioral science insights.

Where have the behavioral scientists taken us? To the executive chambers of some of the world's largest corporations, that's where, and Howard C. Carlson, assistant director of organizational research and development at General Motors Corporation, tells us what is going on in these cells of influence. GM's top management has evolved a philosophy and a strategy of organizational development, which Dr. Carlson presented in his 1977 article, "Organizational Research and Organizational Change: GM's Approach." The article is interesting in every regard, but the important place given to measurement—the domain of the scientist—in GM's approach is particularly noteworthy. In the company's programs you will also see the present-day application of the early findings of the behavioral scientists. The past *is* prologue.

6

Social Science:
Friend of Management

Stuart Chase

TACKED on the door of my study in Connecticut is a cartoon that David Lilienthal sent me long ago when he was with the T.V.A. Mr. Lilienthal said that this cartoon helped him to keep going over the rough places, and I find a glance at it does the same for me. It is a picture of a man who has isolated himself in a small box, cramped and scowling. The old curmudgeon who is making himself so miserable would be surprised to find how much warmer and more comfortable it would be to trust people a little.

The encouraging part is that social science can now prove him wrong. The cumulative findings to date go far to vindicate the lesson of this cartoon. People are all right, but some of us have crabbed and distorted ideas about them. We see through a cake of ice, darkly. What we see may be not in the space-time world at all, but in our minds—images created by past conditioning.

Abraham Lincoln once put it this way: "Why should there not be a patient confidence in the ultimate justice of the people? Is there any better or equal hope in the world?" He sensed intuitively what scientists later have been able to demonstrate.

Not long after Lincoln made this statement, Lewis H. Morgan began to lay the foundation for the science of cultural anthropology (which deals with group behavior, not with measuring skulls) by studying the family system of Seneca Indians in upstate New York.

I want to talk about some of the contributions that have been or are being added by this new science to the old one of business management. I think that what I have to say on this subject falls into four groups:

First, two central concepts social scientists have introduced.

Second, some common ideas about people that have been shown to be incorrect.

Third, items from work in progress that promise some useful results to management.

Fourth, the problem of the relation of executive and scientist.

Two Central Concepts

Following Morgan's modest beginnings, other brilliant men, Sumner, Boas, Malinowski, and a galaxy of famous names, developed the "culture concept," the central finding in the whole field of the social sciences. The Social Science Research Council, which is a kind of clearinghouse of the seven learned societies, sent out a questionnaire to representative social scientists throughout the country and asked them, among other questions, what they considered the outstanding accomplishments of social science. And not only anthropologists but psychologists, sociologists, economists, political scientists, and historians came back with the culture concept as the greatest accomplishment.

The assumption that "people are no damn good" cannot be fitted into the culture concept. A culture comprehends all the people in a given society. It is a set of patterns in which every individual grows and matures. It is the basic datum for the study of man.

The second concept is something that I will discuss again later in connection with the Hawthorne experiment. It concerns what happens whenever a group of people is together long enough to generate a common, if unwritten, set of rules and ways of conduct.

Studies are clustering around this and allied phenomena under the somewhat formidable title of "group dynamics," which you are going to hear more and more about. No manager can afford to neglect them. They are beginning to show not only the negative power of groups, but the enormous reservoirs of positive action that can be

released when conditions are, as the experts say, "correctly structured."

A Case in Point

Man is a social animal, as well as a working one, but we are still
learning how much he can sometimes surpass himself under the
stimulation of his fellows. One way to think of it is the energy released
in a fire panic, but in reverse—plus, instead of minus. Let us look at a
concrete example:

In the January issue of *Fortune* of last year, Russell Davenport tells
the story of one of Joe Scanlon's demonstrations in union–
management participation to increase production in a Massachusetts
machine-tool plant employing about 500 men.

As many of you doubtless know, Mr. Scanlon used to be an official
of the Steel Workers' Union and is now a full professor at Massachusetts Institute of Technology. He is perhaps the most dynamic
social engineer in the field of labor relations today and thus eminently
fitted to work with the concept of group dynamics. He knows very
well how to set up joint committees that can take output right through
the roof by releasing energy and intelligence in the rank and file that
hitherto had been bottled up. He can release it in management, too.

The plan that Russell Davenport describes in *Fortune* is only one of
about forty that Scanlon has set up. He told me about his first plan
when I was in Cambridge the other day

There was a steel mill near Pittsburgh heavily in the red, with
about 2,000 employees, at the bottom of a depression. Scanlon was a
cost accountant as well as a social engineer, and he knew, through his
accounting experience, that the mill was about done for. At the same
time he became interested in the new Steel Workers' Union, resigned
his place as cost accountant, went into manual work, and became the
president of the union local.

He examined the books and found that the trouble was just as bad
as the management said it was. He then called a meeting of the union,
locked the doors, and kept the men there practically all night until he
had hammered into their heads that the company was going broke,
that they would lose their jobs, and that they had to take a 25 percent
wage cut for six months if they wanted to keep going.

Well, they demurred. They said, "How about those Cadillacs, how
about those big limousines?" and Joe laid it on the line, as a cost
accountant. Finally they agreed, the company was saved, and it is still
operating efficiently.

Findings Refute
Some Common Misconceptions

Suppose we look now at a few findings of social scientists that are contrary to current assumptions and thus relatively newsworthy. Nothing so startling, of course, as "Man bites dog"; more on the order of "Man doesn't have to bite Man."

"People are no damned good" is one of these assumptions, and it is a more common belief in our democracy than one likes to think. The culture concept, based on observations in many different societies, refutes it, as we have seen. A more widely held doctrine is that most people are inherently lazy. They will not work unless they have to. They never would work dependably unless bribed or intimidated into it. The social scientists, the physiologists, the biologists cannot find any solid evidence for this assumption. Man, the scientists tell us, is a working animal. Unless he keeps his mind and his muscles active, he tends to degenerate rapidly. But people naturally prefer certain types of activity to others. Nobody seems to like coal mining very well, while preferences vary, of course, between individuals. Some cannot take an assembly line. Others can; they indulge in pleasant daydreams while fitting on the left front fender and never need to consult the company psychiatrist.

I was recently invited to analyze the pension system of one of our great industrial companies. I found that a very serious problem is developing there due to the human desire to work and be active. The plan of this company provides compulsory retirement at the age of 65. Many of the pensioners, though free of financial worry for the rest of their lives, do not know what to do with their freedom. Some of them are cracking up mentally. Said a man of 60 in this company:

> It's really tragic, you know. So many of the fellows don't want to think about the future. They'll have to go sometime, and they'll miss their jobs and the companionship of the men they've worked with so long. . . . For 20, 30, 40 years they've followed a routine, getting up at a certain time, going to work, coming home, relaxing, reading the paper. All of a sudden, it stops. They get up in the morning and they have nowhere to go, nothing to do.

To meet this problem, the company now gives passes to pensioners so that they can go back to the old shop and watch others doing what they are no longer permitted to do. It is also hiring social scientists as "old-age counselors" to start helping people five years before retirement to develop new interests and new hobbies preliminary to the ordeal of idleness.

And, of course, all this ties in with a problem we have known for a long time. I had a chapter about it in my *Men and Machines,* published 20 years ago—the problem of leisure time. As working hours dropped from 60, to 50, to 40 and are now headed toward 30 a week, this leisure-time problem has become really important.

People Are Not Innately Lazy

Dr. Alexander Leighton, about whom we will have quite a lot to say later, notes that much thinking at policymaking levels follows the line that man is innately lazy and prone to do nothing unless prodded by the threat of punishment, or lured by rewards, a little like the donkey with the carrot in front of his nose.

"Yet," says Leighton, "the weight of evidence, from careful study, is on the side of assuming that work is one of the enjoyed and rewarding human activities, and that most people, under normal conditions, actively seek it."

If people won't work—and sometimes they will not—it probably indicates that the conditions of work are abnormal. There is something wrong with the job, not with the man. Management, instead of cussing the help, would do better to concentrate on finding out what the abnormal conditions are and remedying them.

The Doctrine of "Economic Man"

We had a very interesting seminar on this whole question of what makes workers work last summer at the Y.M.C.A. Conference on Management Problems. Allied to the assumption that people are lazy is the well-worn doctrine of "economic man." This concept colors not only classic economics, but a good deal of managerial thinking as well. It is the assumption that "money makes the mare go," that economic gain is the only incentive that makes people work and gets things done. It follows that the more money you can offer, the harder people will strive and, per contra, if no gain is offered, the whole economy is likely to collapse.

The late Dr. Elton Mayo of the Harvard School of Business Administration was one of the first to use controlled experiments in testing this assumption. They were carried out in the Hawthorne plant of the Western Electric Company some 20 years ago, and have become social science classics, especially the story of the girls assembling telephone relays, a little gadget that looks like a pocket whistle.

I do not need to repeat anything but the conclusions, as we all know the story. It was found that the incentive which, above all others, affected the girls' production rate was the sense of being recognized, of being consulted, of feeling important. Remember that after almost two years of experimentation with various types of wage rates, hours, rest pauses, and working conditions, they went back to the base period of 48 hours, no Saturdays off, no rest pauses, no hot lunch at the company expense, no piecework incentive, nothing. They gave that test a good long time: they gave it 12 weeks. And when they came to examine the automatic counters through which the gi ls dropped the relays, they found that output had jumped to an all-time high, meaning, of course, that all these various new conditions they introduced had no effect compared with certain other factors—the factors of being recognized, of being consulted, of feeling important.

Economic man or woman seems to be made mostly of straw. Modern managers are increasing output and morale by putting this assumption in its proper place as only one of many incentives, and, under certain conditions, only a minor incentive.

The 14 men in the bank-wiring room at the Hawthorne plant provided an equally startling lesson. These men had formed an unofficial team, complete with leaders, for regulating production. Bonus plans and work-incentive schemes of management collapsed in impotence before this well-knit organization that nobody was ever conscious of organizing. And yet, woe betide any individual in a shop or an office who defies the unwritten regulations of such an informal group, which now functions or is potentially ready to function, wherever two or more people are working.

This is the second, and more negative, example of the functioning of "group dynamics," which I cited as one of the two central concepts social science has formulated.

"Let the Boss Decide"

Another widely held assumption is that workers have no place in management problems. It is for the boss to decide and for the worker to do what he is told. On the other hand, social scientists are finding that full participation by unions in top decisions creates an impossible administrative situation. The Russians experimented with that in the factories in 1920 when the unions took over. They found that production dropped to about 10 percent of the prewar total. Again, complete company dictatorship, no matter how benevolent, stifles the normal desire of a human being to contribute ideas to his work and blocks off his interest and his energy.

Somewhere between these two extremes lie maximum morale and efficiency. At certain levels it has been repeatedly demonstrated that the worker can make helpful and important contributions to management problems. Scanlon's work, the history of the Amalgamated Clothing Workers, some of the labor–management production committees of the war, suggestion-box results, the training-within-industry programs of the War Manpower Commission—all show this trend. Its vast possibilities are just beginning to be opened up.

The "Class Struggle" Concept

The class struggle is as cardinal in the Marxian hypothesis as "economic man" in the Manchester school hypothesis. According to the Marxists, as you know, there are only two dynamic classes in any society, the owners and the workers, the exploiters and the exploited. History is supposed to be nothing but the story of their timeless and unending warfare. Now there is just enough truth in the concept of the class struggle to make a powerful appeal to many people. Workers readily grasp at it when they feel that the future is hopeless. Labor leaders often base their strategy on it, even though they have never read *Das Kapital.* It will come out as a set stereotype in some of the speeches of labor leaders. Witness the perorations about the wicked bosses and the downtrodden workers.

It is possible, furthermore, that many managers accept the class struggle as a fact without, of course, embracing the Marxian proposals for solving it. They sense antagonism in their employees and generalize it into an inevitable condition, two classes always opposed. In Europe, veneration for the doctrine is widespread on all levels, from employers to workers, not forgetting Mr. George Bernard Shaw.

But anthropologists and social psychologists report no such animal! You will not find the class struggle as a human universal in the Cross Cultural Index at Yale, in the sense that monogamy, for instance, is a universal.

That Cross Cultural Index is a very interesting storehouse of social science in which the various societies, tribes, or races, analyzed by competent anthropologists, are cataloged under their various habits and mores. Monogamy is found to be a human universal. In every society studied, the rank and file has been found to practice monogamy. In some societies you may find some polygamy or some polyandry on the side, indulged in by those who can either afford it or stand it. But by and large the mass of the people practice monogamy; it is a universal.

In *The Proper' Study of Mankind,* I list 33 universals. Up at Yale you will find many more—but not class struggle.

Dr. Ralph Linton documents the way in which class struggles may appear in certain societies, or sections of societies, at certain times, especially in times of rapid cultural change. Down the ages, however, the typical society is one where each individual enjoys a particular status in his total culture pattern, is satisfied with it, and shows profound inertia about leaving it.

The chief motive that made the girls in the relay room at Hawthorne work so industriously was recovery of a sense of status, a sense of belonging.

Since the industrial revolution began, class struggles have been breaking out here and there—Harlan County, for instance—but they are temporary local outbreaks, a product of our factory system rather than of human nature.

If Linton and the social scientists are right, Marx is wrong. Lenin, Stalin, and the Kremlin are off in a blind alley. Human nature does not react the way they assume it does.

Mobility of the American Class Structure

We do have social classes in America—six of them, according to Dr. Lloyd Warner and his co-workers—but the important thing that Warner and many other competent scientists point out is the mobility of the American class structure. The lower groups are constantly being upgraded while the upper groups come crashing down, as thousands of them did in the depression.

In Warner's six-volume study, which he calls *Yankee City* (actually Newburyport, Massachusetts), and upon which John Marquand based *Point of No Return,* you will find that the upper groups were dominated for a long period by the old-line Yankees; and then the French-Canadians, and then the Irish, and then the Jews began to come into town. They moved right up the class ladder until they were ousting many of the old-line Yankees, who did a tremendous nose dive down onto—what does Marquand call it?—Fish Street, or Clam Street.

The class-struggle doctrine lists all working farmers as "downtrodden peasants." The Kremlin leaders today wring their hands about the dreadful poverty of our American "serfs and peasants." Now it is perfectly true that there are pockets of dire poverty in American agriculture. But I was also told, while lecturing in Pullman, Washington, last month, that the average income after taxes of the "peasants" working the rich wheatlands in that county, in which the State Agricultural College is situated, was $28,000!

No, one cannot clamp the straitjacket of the class struggle on actual conditions in America, or Europe for that matter. It is a useless concept for predicting human behavior.

We have now taken a brief look at five assumptions widely held by Americans, including some managers:

First, people in the mass are not much good.

Second, man is inherently lazy—it's in the genes.

Third, pecuniary gain is the only real incentive, the doctrine of Economic Man.

Fourth, workers have no concern with the problems of management—"Let the boss decide."

Fifth, the doctrine of class struggle.

Social scientists in recent years have been taking these assumptions, and others as well, through a sort of wind tunnel to test their validity, and the results are mostly negative. The contraptions do not fly.

Toward Improved Human Relations

Scientists have not been engaged only in knocking down popular concepts. They also offer managers valuable knowledge on how to improve human relations, how to increase both morale and output in the shop. Indeed, a whole new concept of the function of management is beginning to emerge from the work of social scientists in the last generation. Dr. F. J. Roethlisberger, coauthor of that classic describing the Hawthorne experiments, *Management and the Worker*, puts it this way in the *Harvard Business Review:*

> I should like to suggest that the manager is neither managing men, nor managing work, but that he is managing a coordinated set of activities; he is administering a social system. This is the human relations approach, as contrasted with any approach which implies that people at work can be considered separately from their work.

When Joe Doakes goes through the factory gates and rings up his time, he takes his whole cultural background right along with him. The factory is not something sternly apart from the community, subject to more logical rules. It is inseparable from the community. It is as much the community as the house and lot, Main Street, the church, the school, the ball field, and the Elks. Joe will bring his misunderstanding with his wife at the breakfast table right through the factory gates to aggravate his none-too-happy relations with his supervisor.

Culture is a seamless web. All useful conclusions about human relations, the behavior of groups, and social psychology are relevant to the factory, the office, and the profession of management. That came out very clearly when I took the job-relations course in the training-within-industry program with Remington Arms in Bridgeport during the war.

I was not being trained for supervisory activities—I was there to gather material to write an article—but I sat with supervisors and foremen and took the course and listened to their human-interest stories about the men working for them, and how trouble was cleared up, time after time, by going outside the factory into the home and remedying the situation there.

Some Relevant Research

Let us look briefly at a sampling of some relevant research, of use and benefit to managers, that the social scientists are carrying on now.

For instance, there is aptitude testing. That is useful in all fields. It was particularly useful for selecting pilots during the war. We would probably still be fighting the war if it had not been for Flanagan's work on selecting pilots, and it has a great future in industry. Maybe it is not too much to hope that some day aptitude testing might be applied to candidates for Congress.

It may be interesting to note that Dr. Flanagan is now back at the University of Pittsburgh working on the characteristics that make a man or woman a good executive and a good manager.

And there is public-opinion research. This technique is proving very helpful in giving both management and union officials a knowledge of how the rank and file feel about the shop.

When I was called in by the Standard Oil Company of New Jersey to take a look at their labor relations, I could go around and interview shop stewards, supervisors, top management, representatives of all divisions of the plant and come to a general conclusion. But I was only one individual, and not too wise a one either. Then along comes Elmo Roper, who goes down to Baton Rouge and gets the opinion of *everybody* in the plant. Thus I was able to check some of my one-man conclusions with these public-opinion surveys. Some of them fortified what I had come to believe, and other conclusions of mine had to be thrown out the window. They just would not stand up.

Then there is the work being done on two-way communication. A healthy shop needs two open communication lines, from workers up to management and from management down to workers. Grievance machinery, suggestion boxes, application of some elementary principles of semantics, shop bulletins, and joint conferences are all being used in experiments to clear these communication lines.

I have mentioned social scientists as old-age counselors in one large company with an ambitious pension plan. The Hawthorne experiments have demonstrated that interviews by experts provide a valuable release of tensions and grievances for workers. Some companies are experimenting with skilled counselors for emotional disturbances. Counseling has a great future in industry.

Next, there is a very interesting new development that we might call a "vertical round table." Dr. Francis Bradshaw, an eminent psychologist, has started an interesting experiment in group dynamics at a large New Jersey plant. Its purpose is to improve communication and understanding between the seven levels of management in that plant, from the junior supervisors up to the plant manager. They are meeting under the principles of group dynamics with Dr. Bradshaw as the leader and getting some very interesting results, which may have a wide application in industry.

The technique of "role playing" is making some headway in industry, too. A union using it can put labor men in the shoes of company officials, prior to negotiating a contract. The management group, using role playing, can have a corresponding experience. A better plan for achieving mutual understanding is difficult to imagine. It ties in very closely with group dynamics. I first heard about it from Dr. Douglas McGregor who was at M.I.T. The unions he was working with were pretending, in a preliminary session, that two or three of them represented the management and that the others represented the workers. Then they went to work and negotiated the contract in advance. This gave them a good idea of the other fellow's point of view.

The social scientists have a world of sound information on race and religious discrimination both in pure and applied science. Dr. Louis Wirth at the University of Chicago has done some outstanding work in the field of application. Perhaps you saw, in the magazine section of *The New York Times* one Sunday, a leading story about a five-volume study on discrimination in race and religion throughout

American society as something that could be applied directly to management's problems.

Then there is the whole broad field of "conditions of industrial peace"—not struggle, but peace. You should take a look at the comparative studies now being published by the National Planning Association where a score of companies with good labor relations over the years are being intensively analyzed to find those factors that tend to make good labor relations. We have had a lot of studies in bad labor relations, but this is something new.

Pension systems, we mentioned earlier. Economist Sumner Schlichter and statistician Louis I. Dublin, vice-president of the Metropolitan Life Insurance Company, can be very helpful in analyzing the whole broad pension picture.

Labor unrest baffles a lot of us, and it baffles a lot of managers. But take a look at Volume IV of Warner's "Yankee City Series" to which we referred earlier. It contains a masterly account of the change that occurred in the shoe industry from a handicraft culture, where the worker was an independent craftsman, to mass production and mass distribution and mass finance, where he is just a cog in a vast, impersonal machine. You will get a much clearer picture than you ever had before of the psychological reasons for industrial unrest. Nobody can read this story without greatly broadening his understanding of the labor problem. I gave a whole chapter to it in the *Proper Study of Mankind*.

Now, the above is very far from a complete list of current research, but it gives us, I think, a fair sample of the kinds of findings that have helped and can help management in establishing social responsibility in the fifth year of the Atomic Age.

The Policymaker and the Social Scientist

Let us turn to a new and, I believe, very important consideration of our thesis. In his latest book, *Human Relations in a Changing World,*[1] Dr. Alexander Leighton, psychiatrist and anthropologist, devotes some chapters to the personal relations between the policymaker, the executive, and the social scientist, based on his own experiences in the Pacific theater during the war.

Once and again, a slight tinge of unprofessional bitterness creeps into the discussion, perhaps because Dr. Leighton's team, which included Clyde Kluckhohn and Ruth Benedict among others, took quite

[1] E. P. Dutton & Co., Inc., New York, 1947.

a beating from the high brass. But by and large, it is an objective account, making points of central significance to both policymakers and social scientists.

"The policymaker," says Leighton, in one of his disillusioned moments, "tends to use social science the way a drunk uses a lamp post, for support, not illumination." The high command in the Pacific tended to look on scientists, and especially social scientists, as long-haired, impractical visionaries, stuffed with theories.

Now this is not too far from the usual view by top management in industry until recently. If the conclusions of Leighton's team, out there in the Pacific, coincided with those of the high command, which were arrived at more or less intuitively, the generals and the admirals were complimentary. But if Leighton's conclusions did not support their own, then the "impractical visionary" stereotype was forthcoming, and the report was buried in the files.

A Highly Significant Case Study

Dr. Leighton first gives us a careful account of what his team did and the techniques it employed. I do not know where else you can find a detailed case study of technique of a good, modern team of social scientists.

A major problem for the generals and the admirals was whether Japanese morale could be cracked and, if so, how. The morale of the fighting forces was known to be high, and it seemed likely that civilian morale on the home islands was equally strong. The high command was faced with decisions that involved human psychology, social behavior, the culture pattern of the Japanese people—problems not concerned with ballistics and logistics, but with social science. Let me give you a short quotation from Leighton regarding the attitude of the high command:

> There were many in the top command . . . who felt that the Japanese morale was a solid wall of uniform strength which nothing could destroy except the actual killing of the men who displayed it. Every Japanese soldier was regarded as an ideal fighting machine—fearless, fanatic, obeying instantly—something not quite human that looked only for an opportunity to die for the Emperor. . . . Prisoners of war would be exceedingly rare and would be of no value as sources of information. . . . Psychological warfare would be useless, both for softening resistance, and for securing the surrender of soldiers.

You can see what a formidable task the executives had lined up for themselves by these assumptions: take no prisoners, fight for every foot of ground, prepare for a practically endless war!

Some Working Principles

Dr. Leighton's division went to work testing these concepts as their first task. To begin with, the team set up a list of 14 basic statements about human nature, such as:

There exist psychological uniformities common to all the tribes, nations, and "races" of human beings.

All people, everywhere, are disturbed by threats to life and health, by discomfort from pain, cold, heat, fatigue, and bad food, by threats to children and family, by enforced idleness (there's idleness again), restriction of movement, insecurity.

When the threshold for stress is exceeded, all people, everywhere, respond with known physiological patterns.

Gathering the Facts

The division then constructed an information-screening machine that fed facts daily into the hopper, to be matched against the basic assumptions, in the way reports come into a central weather bureau to be mapped. The facts came from prisoner-of-war interviews, from captured diaries, captured letters—especially from Japanese officers, and captured official documents. They came from reports and from neutral observers in Japan, from translations of Japanese newspapers and magazines, from monitored Japanese broadcasts.

The team also collected background descriptions based on novels, histories, travel books, motion pictures, plays, and anthropological studies. Ruth Benedict prepared her analysis of Japanese culture, later published as *The Chrysanthemum and the Sword,* which many of you have read, or should read.

Conclusion of the Study

Despite the passions of war, Leighton's division kept their scientific objectivity. They knew that the Japanese were human, like anybody else, but equally important, they learned to understand the unique behavior patterns of the Japanese culture. As a result they could reconstruct, with high probability, what was going on in the minds of Japanese soldiers. They told the American top command that under certain conditions the Japanese would surrender and give useful information, that they were neither supermen nor apes.

This conclusion was amply confirmed, later in the war, as Japanese units, both in the Philippines and Okinawa, surrendered first by the hundreds and then by the thousands and, as prisoners, cheerfully gave valuable information.

The predictions of the generals and the admirals about fighting for every foot of ground, about taking no prisoners, turned out to be completely wrong. Some of those predictions, as a matter of fact, would have fitted Germany better than Japan, for, although more Germans than Japanese surrendered in combat, Germany as a nation fought until it was dismembered. Japan quit while still a relatively whole and functioning country.

It would be hard to find a more dramatic and conclusive case of wrong judgment leading to wrong decisions that involved countless human lives. Fortunately, some of the military were sufficiently impressed by Leighton's reports to modify a few of their earlier decisions.

Far-Reaching Implications

This example can form a starting point for a few observations about how policymakers and social scientists arrive at conclusions. Although the average executive tends to discount "theorists," thinking himself a very practical fellow, it was the scientists in the Pacific who tried to be objective, fact-conscious, shy of hasty generalizations, and the executives who indulged in some high and lofty theorizing. By and large, the high command tended to underestimate the Japanese strength before the war and to overestimate it during the war. We can discount for Leighton's frequent rebuffs, but enough still remains to make an arresting point.

The typical executive has his own private psychological theories about human behavior. He does not call them theories, but that, of course, is what they are. Everybody has theories, built up from childhood, about the behavior of other people. We could not deal with our fellow men without having theories about them.

Executives often show shrewdness, wisdom, tolerance, but they also tend to exhibit prejudices, sentiments, stereotyped responses, and current fashions in executive thinking. Compare, for example, the excitement about the term "free enterprise" today with the attitude of 20 years ago when the phrase was rarely mentioned. Common sense is highly prized by many executives, perhaps overprized.

Common sense tells us, among other things, that the world is flat and that it is impossible for men to fly.

What the Policymaker Can Learn from the Social Scientist

The social science approach to human relations, says Leighton, differs from that of the executive in that neither the experience of one individual nor the popularity of an idea is accepted as a warrant for its truth. The scientist tries to build his concepts on a foundation of systematic observations by competent men, with many checks and no preconceptions. As a result, his conclusions, while not final, are often closer to reality than are those of the average manager. Remember, we are not talking about the cost system in the drop-forge department, but about human relations. Remember, too, that the most important policies and decisions of the manager lie in the field of human relations.

Both managers and social scientists use definitions, categories, facts, and logic to arrive at their conclusions. But in social science today, facts play the dominant role. Leighton pictures logic as a kind of bridge to tie facts together. Reasoning that has very long spans between the piers of supporting facts must be suspect to a scientist.

The conclusions of the policymaker, however, are often reached by a bridge of logic with dangerously long spans between the piers of fact, or so it seemed in the Pacific theater. Sometimes the facts were not piers at all, but statistical festoons, unrelated to the foundation. Said a "big shot" to Leighton: "We are pressed for time this morning and must decide this matter at once. Tomorrow, we can figure out the reasons."

Dr. Leighton's team clashed repeatedly with the "big shots" and felt that they were not able to make their full contribution. But even with the differences between their modes of thought, the team helped save many lives, both American and Japanese, by showing that the Japanese soldiers were only human. They might, indeed, have saved us the eternal shame of Hiroshima if their reports, submitted early in 1945 and demonstrating the collapse of morale on the home islands, had been read and acted upon by the high command. The team knew, nine months in advance, that Japan was going to collapse in the fall of 1945.

The Job of the Social Scientist

Leighton is convinced, however—and this is a very important point—that the social scientist, as such, should not make decisions. That is the executive's function. Scientists should lay the facts and the probabilities before the manager just as other experts, accountants, engineers, or lawyers do.

There are, of course, emergencies when the executive must decide hurriedly, as undoubtedly that chap whom we just quoted had to do. There is no time to marshal the piers of fact and build a careful structure of logic upon them. "Snap!" as Uncle Ponderevo used to say in H. G. Wells's novel when he bought a new company.

The social scientist well understands the occasional necessity for such drastic action, but he cannot afford to prejudice his professional reputation by being responsible for it. The good scientist must deal in probabilities rather than absolutes. He must beware of becoming too closely identified with policy and of acquiring an emotional vested interest in it. He must keep his scientific detachment. It is far better for the executive to fire the social scientist, however wise, than to surrender the power of making decisions to him, for a surrender would corrupt both men.

Social Science: Friend of Management

The real solution is for managers, generally, to acquire a better understanding of modern social science and the way in which a scientist arrays facts and logic to reach conclusions. The manager himself needs to become something of a social scientist to get the most out of the new findings now pouring in. He especially needs to know more about checking his intuition against the growing body of dependable knowledge about human behavior. He needs, I think, a good, elementary grip on two new mental tools, the culture concept and semantics, using semantics as a means of clearing communication lines between people.

After all, this is not an especially advanced proposal. Most American top executives today are college men. More and more colleges are giving students large draughts of modern social science. I went down to the Case Institute of Technology in Cleveland the other day to help the faculty set up a course in social science, a compulsory course for all the freshmen. The Harvard School of Business Administration, which is staffed with very competent scientists skilled in these tools, has, as you know, considerable prestige in executive circles. Dr. Leighton is now at Cornell. Even the Foreign Service Institute of our State Department is drilling career men, our future diplomats, in the culture concept.

The leader must lead, keeping the "long hairs" out of the front office. It is exciting and hopeful, however, to think of a future where leader and professional scientist not only cooperate, but where the leader himself becomes a kind of amateur scientist.

7

May 1955

Men and Machines:
An Assembly-Line Worker
Looks at His Job

Robert H. Guest

WHEN future historians get around to appraising our present mid-century industrial era, they will, of course, note the enormous developments in our technology, and they will note, too, our popular preoccupation with the so-called science of human relations in industry. I should like to comment on this preoccupation and this science, and to suggest some ideas about technology and human relations that have been somewhat neglected.

Just as the designer and engineer drew upon the physical sciences to meet the technical problems of modern production, so today we find the administrator turning to the social sciences to meet the "human" problems of management. Industry is coming to accept the contributions of the psychologist in such a range of activities as interviewing, testing, counseling, placement, and training—to mention only a few. Consciously or otherwise, it is absorbing many of the findings of the sociologist and anthropologist in its efforts to understand the problems of conflict, group relations, communications, and the structure of organization.

We are constantly seeking to perfect our engineering skills and our human relations skills, but the curious fact is that we *have somehow failed to recognize the interdependence of the two fields.* The Technology Project at Yale is one attempt to meet this challenge.

Our research work and our practical experience in industry have convinced us that a full understanding of the behavior of "men at work"—the dynamics of human relations in industry—cannot be achieved until this behavior is placed in its proper technological perspective. What the engineer does to change the machine environment is as crucially important to human relations as what the administrator, the foreman, the personnel manager, or the shop steward does in the nontechnical sphere. In other words, we must know what is happening to machines before we can interpret what is happening to man. It is perfectly proper to interpret labor disputes as struggles for political power, to analyze foreman–worker relations as sociological, wages as economic, and attitudes as psychological phenomena. But let's make sure that we first understand the technological factors that impinge on these other aspects of the total situation.

The Typical Assembly Line

To develop this central theme I should like to describe the effects on workers of a specific technological environment, the automobile assembly line.

A few years back, the Yale Technology Project undertook to study the relationship between technology and human relations in a few industrial plants in the United States, with particular reference to attitudes and behavior of workers in mass-production industries. For years, there has been a great deal of speculation about the effects of highly repetitive and routinized tasks on workers. The British were perhaps the first to begin serious research in this direction. Many years ago, Wyatt and Frazer concerned themselves with the problems of fatigue and boredom. Elton Mayo, acquainted with the work of the British Medical Research Council, wrote a penetrating little essay called "Monotony." But perhaps the one person who did most to popularize the effects of mass-production work on people was Charlie Chaplin in his film classic, *Modern Times.*

Of all occupations in modern industry none has aroused such controversial comment as has that of the assembly worker, and especially the auto assembly worker on the "final line." The extraordinary ingenuity that has gone into the construction of automobile assembly lines, their perfected synchronization, the "all but human" or "more than human" character of the machines, the miracle of a car rolling off the conveyor each minute under its own power—all this has caught and held the world's imagination for a quarter of a century. On the other hand, the extreme subdivision of labor (the man who puts a nut on a bolt is the symbol) conjoined with the "endlessly moving belt" has made the assembly line the classic symbol of the subjection of man to the machine in our industrial age.

General Characteristics of the Mass-Production Method

But before considering man in relation to the machine, it would be advisable to define the general characteristics of the mass-production method.

Utilizing the two basic principles of standardization and inter-changeability, Ford was able to work out and apply the three following additional "principles" of progressive manufacture:

1. The orderly progression of the product through the shop in a series of planned operations so arranged that the right part always arrives at the right place at the right time.
2. The mechanical delivery of these parts to the operators and the mechanical delivery of the product from the operators, as it is assembled.
3. A breakdown of operations into their simple constituent motions.

The Mass-Production Job

Let us now look at these familiar principles or techniques as they are translated into the work experience of individual men and women in mass-production factories. The characteristics of the average mass-production job may be summarized in the following manner:

1. Mechanical pacing of work.
2. Repetitiveness.
3. Minimum skill requirement.
4. Predetermination in the use of tools and techniques.
5. Minute subdivision of product worked on.
6. Surface mental attention.

For the engineer, all the above characteristics are brought into focus in what is known as the *job cycle*. Each worker must perform a prescribed number of operations within a set time limit and, in the case of those working on moving conveyors, within a given distance along the assembly line.

How a Typical Assembly-Line Worker Feels

With these characteristics in mind, let us go right to a man on the assembly line and see how they affect him, but instead of a statistical summary of the findings from interviews with more than 400 assembly-line workers in two plants, excerpts from a single interview will be given here and commented upon insofar as they hold true for the total sample.

The worker whose actual words are quoted below is, like many others, a graduate of a public vocational school in the United States. He is 36 years old and married; he has a couple of children, is buying his own home, and "takes home" just under $80 a week. Here, he is talking to me in his home:

> In 1940 I heard that they were hiring people for the assembly plant. Must have been thousands of fellows lined up for the job. The word got around that they were paying real good money. It was a big outfit, too. No fly-by-night affair.
>
> Figured I'd get any job and then, with a little electrician experience I had in vocational school, I could work my way up to a good job. And the idea of making automobiles sounded like something. Lucky for me, I got a job and was made a spot welder on the front cowling. There wasn't much to the job itself. Picked it up in about a week. Later I was drafted into the Army, and then 1946 I came back. I tried to get into the Maintenance Department as an electrician, but there was no opening, so I went back to the line—we call it the iron horse. They made me a welder again, and that's what I have been doing ever since.

What His Job Is Like

The worker then went on to describe his job:

> My job is to weld the cowl to the metal underbody. I take a jig off the bench, put it in place and weld the parts together. The jig is all made up and the welds are made in set places along the metal. Exactly twenty-five spots. The line runs according to schedule. Takes me one

minute and fifty-two seconds for each job. I walk along the line as it moves. Then I snap the jig off, walk back down the line, throw it on the bench, grab another just in time to start on the next car. The cars differ, but it's practically the same thing. Finish one—then have another one staring me in the face.

I don't like to work on the line—no man likes to work on a moving line. You can't beat the machine. Sure, maybe I can keep it up for an hour, but it's rugged doing it eight hours a day, every day in the week all year long.

During each day I get a chance for a breather ten minutes in the morning, then a half-hour for lunch, then a few minutes in the afternoon. When I'm working there is not much chance to get a breather. Sometimes the line breaks down. When it does we all yell "Whoopee!" As long as the line keeps moving I've got to keep up with it. On a few jobs I know, some fellows can work like hell up the line, then coast. Most jobs you can't do that. If I get ahead maybe ten seconds, the next model has more welds to it, so it takes ten seconds extra. You hardly break even. You're always behind. When you get too far behind, you get in a hole—that's what we call it. All hell breaks loose. I get in the next guy's way. The foreman gets sore and they have to rush in a relief man to bail you out.

It's easy for them time-study fellows to come down there with a stopwatch and figure out just how much you can do in a minute and fifty-two seconds. There are some things they can see and record with their stopwatch. But they can't clock how a man feels from one day to the next. Those guys ought to work on the line for a few weeks and maybe they'll feel some things that they never pick up on the stopwatch.

I like a job where you feel like you're accomplishing something and doing it right. When everything's laid out for you and the parts are all alike, there's not much you feel you accomplish. The big thing is that steady push of the conveyor—a gigantic machine that I can't control.

You know, it's hard to feel that you are doing a good quality job. There is that constant push at high speed. You may improve after you've done a thing over and over again, but you never reach a point where you can stand back and say, "Boy, I done that one good. That's one car that got built right." If I could do my best I'd get some satisfaction out of working, but I can't do as good work as I know I can do.

My job is all engineered out. The jigs and fixtures are all de-signed and set out according to specifications. There are a lot of little things you could tell them, but they never ask you. You go by the bible. They have a suggestion system, but the fellows don't use it too much because they're scared that a new way to do it may do one of your buddies out of a job.

Interviewer: "Who do you talk to, Joe, when you're working?"

There's only three guys close by—me and my partner and a couple of fellows up the line a bit. I talk to my partner quite a lot. We gripe about the job 90 percent of the time. You don't have time for any real conversation. The guys get along okay—you know the old saying, "misery loves company."

Interviewer: "What sort of a person is your foreman?"

Oh, I think as a man he is an all right guy. I see him once and a while outside, and he's 100 percent. But in the shop he can't be. If I was a foreman, nobody would like me either. As a foreman, he has to push you all the time to get production out so that somebody above won't push him. But the average guy on the line has no one to push—you can't fight the line. The line pushes you. We sometimes kid about it and say we don't need no foreman. That line is the foreman. Some joke.

The worker then discussed the general working conditions in the plant—the lighting, ventilation, safety conditions, housekeeping, cafeteria facilities, and the plant hospital. He thought these conditions were all good, and that in this respect at least the company had done all it could to make work as pleasant as possible for the workers. Then he added:

But you know it's a funny thing. These things are all good, but they don't make the job good. It's what you spend most of the time doing that counts.

His Chances of Promotion

The interview then turned to the subject of promotion opportunities:

My chances for promotion aren't so hot. You see, almost everybody makes the same rate. The jobs have been made so simple that there is not much room to move up from one skill to another. In other places where the jobs aren't broken down this way, the average fellow has something to look forward to. He can go from one step to another right up the ladder. Here, it's possible to make foreman. But none of the guys on the line think there's much chance to go higher than that. To manage a complicated machine like that, you need a college degree. They bring in smart college boys and train them for the better jobs.

Interviewer: "What does your wife think about your job?"
At this point his wife spoke up:

I often wish he'd get another job. He comes home at night, plops down in a chair, and just sits for about 15 minutes. I don't know much about what he does at the plant, but it does something to him. Of course, I shouldn't complain. He gets good pay. We've been able to buy a refrigerator and a TV set—a lot of things we couldn't have had otherwise. But sometimes I wonder whether these are more important to us than having Joe get all nervous and tensed up. He snaps at the kids and snaps at me—but he doesn't mean it.

The worker was then asked if he had considered working elsewhere:

I'll tell you honest. I'm scared to leave. I'm afraid to take the gamble on the outside. I'm not staying because I want to. You see, I'm getting good pay. We live according to the pay I get. It would be tough to change the way we live. With the cost of living what it is, it's too much of a gamble. Then there's another thing. I got good seniority. I take another job and I start from scratch. Comes a depression or something and I'm the first to get knocked off. Also they got a pension plan. I'm thirty-seven and I'd lose that. Course the joker in that pension plan is that most guys out there chasing the line probably won't live 'til they're sixty-five. Sorta trapped—you get what I mean?

His Views on the Union

The subject of the worker's relationship to his union came up in the course of the interview:

The union has helped somewhat. Before they organized, it was pretty brutal. The bosses played favorites—they kept jacking up the speed of the line every time after they had a breakdown. But the union can't do much about the schedule and the way a job is set up. Management is responsible for that.

We had a walkout last year. They called it an unauthorized strike. Somebody got bounced because he wouldn't keep up his job on the line. The union lost the case because it should have gone through the grievance procedure. The company was dead right to insist that the union file a grievance.

But it was one of those things it's hard to explain. When word got around that the guy was bounced—we all sort of looked at each other, dropped our tools and walked. Somehow that guy was every one of us. The tension on the line had been building up for a long time. We had to blow our top—so we did. We were wrong—the union knew it and so did the company. We stayed out a few hours and back we came. We all felt better, like we got something off our chests.

Some of these strikes you read about may be over wages. Or they may just be unions trying to play politics. But I sometimes think that the thing that will drive a man to lose all that pay is deeper than wages. Maybe other guys feel like we did the day we walked out.

Toward the end of the interview, the worker spoke of the company he worked for:

They are doing what they can—like the hospital, the safety, the pay, and all like that. And the people who run the plant I guess are pretty good guys themselves. But sometimes I think that the company doesn't think much of the individual. If they did they wouldn't have a production line like that one. You're just a number to them. They number the stock and they number you. There's a different feeling in this kind of a plant. It's like a kid who goes up to a grown man and starts talking to him. There doesn't seem to be a friendly feeling. Here a man is just so much horsepower. You're just a cog in the wheel.

Let's just take this interview apart for a moment.

Notice, first, that this worker's dissatisfaction was not due primarily to the things that are usually considered important to a job. People often say: "Pay a man enough and he'll be satisfied." But this man's pay was good. His job was secure. He worked for a sound company. He had substantial seniority. He had a pension, hospitalization and disability benefits when he became sick, and a good boss; at least he did not hold the kind of job he had against the boss. Working conditions, heating, lighting, cafeteria facilities, and safety conditions were, I would say, as good as if not better than average.

Yet Joe despised his job.

The simple fact is that the impact of "sound" engineering principles had had a marked effect on his total outlook on the job.

What "Sound" Engineering Has Taken Away

For this man, and for hundreds of others with whom we have had experience, the engineer, in applying the principles of mass production to the extreme, had factored out virtually everything that might be of real, personal value to the worker. The sense of anonymity implicit in much of what this particular worker said can be traced back to some of the basic characteristics of his immediate job.

The conveyor belt determined the *pace* at which he worked. He had no control over his pace.

Because it was broken down into the simplest motions possible, the job was highly *repetitive.*

Simple motions meant that there was little or no need for *skill.*

The tools and the work procedure were predetermined. And when techniques changed, it was the engineer—not the worker—who controlled the change.

He worked on a *fraction of the product* and never got a sense of the whole. (He admitted that in 12 years of work he had almost never seen a finished car roll off the final line.)

Some attention was required—too much to allow him to daydream or carry on any sustained conversation with others, but not enough to allow him to become really absorbed in his work.

The technical setup determined the character of his work relationships. This man identified himself with the partner who worked with him on the opposite side of the line, but beyond that he displayed almost no identification with a work group as such. Men on the line work as an aggregate of individuals with each man performing his operation more or less independently of the others. The lack of an intimate group awareness appeared to reinforce the same sense of anonymity fostered by the conveyor-paced, repetitive character of the job itself.

The worker's comments about promotion and job aspirations are interesting. He saw little hope for advancement because most of the production jobs paid about the same. By applying principles of work rationalization, the industrial engineer, in the best interests of efficiency, had simplified the tasks so that differences in skill from one job to the next were all but eliminated. It was difficult for the average worker to move vertically through a series of distinct steps in promotion. In this connection, it should be added that over the years the union itself, through collective bargaining, had encouraged the trend toward uniform wage standards by raising minimum levels without increasing the relative amounts between job classes.

From a careful examination of the actual work careers of over 200 workers we have found only a few who had experienced any substantial change in job classification during a period of from 12 to 15 years. Collectively, all the workers had improved their overall economic status; individually, few had experienced much change in their relative job status. The net effect of this condition was to increase the depersonalization of the job.

Social and Economic Costs

What did the total job picture add up to? The worker's own words sum it up: "You're just a cog in the wheel."

So what? This company and the thousands of others that had adopted mass production methods were making a profit and giving the public what it wanted. The workers were making good wages. But against these plus factors we found that over and above the social costs to the men involved, there were economic costs to the industry. Turnover was high. Quality performance was not maximized because of the inherent lack of interest in the job. Labor–management relations were in a state of constant tension.

Ways of Bringing About a Better Adjustment

Does this imply that I am advocating that we scrap mass production methods? Certainly not. But it does imply that industry and labor must take steps to bring about a better adjustment of man to machines. Here are some ideas suggested by our studies.

Wherever possible, those responsible for equipment, layout, and job design should try to re-introduce a certain amount of flexibility in the way work is set up and performed by the work group. Job rotation is one answer. We have seen this done successfully and not at the expense of sound engineering practice; but it should be emphasized that such rotation cannot be carried out by arbitrary orders from supervision. It is a *group* function and the members of the group must have a share in determining how the system should operate.

Job enlargement, a term originally coined by my colleague, Charles R. Walker, is another effective technique that reduces boredom and restores greater interest to the job itself. Stated simply, job enlargement means that the individual worker performs more operations over a longer cycle of time. Such a method involves considerable initial training costs, but the evidence now coming in shows clearly that it improves quality and increases job satisfaction.

Many other techniques designed to maximize interest in the immediate job have been tried out with success. In my judgment we have only begun to strike pay dirt. The problem arose in the first place through the failure of those responsible for the purely technical branches of management to understand the basic needs of the men who must operate the machines.

"Will not automation solve the problem in the long run?" a friend recently asked. Possibly so. It looks as if intrinsic skills will be changed and enlarged. The debilitating effects of highly fractionated, repetitive work, with man a mere physical extension of the machine, will be eliminated. Skills of the hand will yield to skills of the mind. But automation will not make job satisfaction automatic, especially if those traditionally concerned with the technical phases of production continue to operate independently of those who manage men.

The challenge is clear. In the jobs of today that are rationalized in the tradition of Taylor and in the jobs that will be rationalized under automation tomorrow, management must look at work as a mutually interdependent function of both engineering and human relations.

8

Job Design
and Productivity:
A New Approach

Louis E. Davis

IT has long been taken for granted that specialization is the organizing principle of modern industry and the mainspring of its phenomenal productivity. However unfortunate some of the by-products of specialization, they have been accepted by and large as necessary evils. Better to put up with them, it seemed, than to attempt remedies that might impair efficiency and thus jeopardize the material gains of industrialization.

But are these actually the alternatives today? In the light of recent research and experiment, it appears to be high time to re-examine the issue. Has specialization perhaps been carried too far—to the point where productivity is *adversely* affected? Are fatigue, tension, low morale, absenteeism, turnover, and other causes of inefficiency actually the result of overspecialization? Can increases in productivity be achieved by *reversing* the principle of specialization?

NOTE: The author wishes to express his appreciation to Dr. Ralph R. Canter, Systems Development Division, the Rand Corporation, for his collaboration in developing the concepts and supervising the experiments reported in this paper.

Specialization and Job Design

The approach to these questions has always been blocked by the assumption—accepted implicitly by management, engineers, and social scientists alike—that *the content of each job in an organization is fixed by the requirements of the production process and the organization structure* and therefore cannot be altered without jeopardizing economic efficiency.

It is this assumption that has persistently biased the judgment of both experts and laymen and ruled out the possibility of an objective approach to the problems created by specialization. Engineers and industrial managers have designed jobs on the basis of this assumption, and their concepts and methods of job design, reinforced by the economists', have set the pattern of industrial organization.

In its classic form, then, job design incorporates the principles of specialization, repetitiveness, reduction of skill content, and minimum impact of the worker on the production process. The basic criteria for job design are minimizing immediate cost and maximizing immediate productivity.

Social philosophers, it is true, have long deplored the dehumanizing effects of this type of job design—monotony, the lack of mental stimulus, rigid adherence to job specifications and standards of output and, not least, a hierarchical social order in which subordinates depend upon their superiors for the satisfaction of basic needs and aspirations. Whether the worker subjected to such a life experience could ever become a responsible citizen in a free democratic society seemed open to question.

Although the social scientists, beginning with Mayo, were the first to put to the test some of the basic assumptions of industrial society, they too took for granted the critical assumption that job content is fixed by technology, and hence focused their investigations for the most part on *other* aspects of the work situation, leaving job content to be prescribed by the engineer.

More to the point, therefore, are the criticisms being made today of the concept of job design itself.[1]

---

[1] See, for example, J. C. Worthy, "Organization, Structure and Employee Morale," *American Sociological Review*, Vol. 15, No. 2 (April 1950), p. 169; C. R. Walker and R. H. Guest, *The Man on the Assembly Line*, Harvard University Press, 1952; F. L. Richardson and C. R. Walker, *Human Relations in an Expanding Company*, Yale University Press, 1948; R. H. Guest, "Men and Machines: An Assembly-Line Worker Looks at His Job," PERSONNEL, Vol. 21, No. 6 (May 1955), p. 496.

Drucker has argued, for example, that the use of the worker as a single-purpose machine tool is poor engineering and a waste of human resources. As he states the case:

> The principle of specialization is productive and efficient. But it is very dubious, indeed, whether we yet know how to apply it except to machinery. There is first the question of whether "specialization" as it is understood and practiced today is a socially and individually satisfying way of using human energy and production—a major question of the social order of industrial society.[2]

Or as Walker, even more boldly, has suggested:

> We are only at the threshold of a scientific understanding of man's relation to work and especially his relation to the new technological environments within which much of the work of the modern world is being performed.[3]

It may well be, then, that society has bowed too soon to the expert in accepting the principle of specialization as inviolate. Once the critical assumption of fixed job elements is put to the test, it may prove to be invalid, and the traditional concepts of job design may have to be reformed.

It is from this point of view that current trends in job design will be analyzed in this article and the outlines of a new approach to the problem presented.

Current Approaches to Job Design

Job design [4] is a phase in production planning that follows the planning and design of product, process, and equipment. It specifies the content of each job and determines the distribution of work within the organization.

This simple definition of job design does not take into consideration the many choices open to the job designer in specifying the content of a particular job. Generally speaking, however, the job design process can be divided into three phases:

---

[2] P. F. Drucker, *The New Society*, Harper & Bros., 1950, p. 171.
[3] C. R. Walker, "Work Methods, Working Conditions and Morale," in *Industrial Conflict*, ed. A. Kornhaumer *et al.*, McGraw-Hill, 1954, p. 358.
[4] This and other technical terms used hereafter are defined in the Appendix.

1. The specification of individual tasks.
2. The specification of the method of performing each task.
3. The combination of individual tasks into specific jobs to be assigned to individuals.

The first and third determine the content of a job, while the second indicates how the job is to be performed. It is possible, therefore, to distinguish between the design of *job content*—content design—and the design of job methods—*methods design*. There is a large body of knowledge about methods design—it is the subject of a specialized branch of industrial engineering, called methods engineering [5]—but there is relatively little information about content design.

According to a recent survey,[6] however, it is the prevailing practice in designing the content of industrial jobs to rely upon the criterion of minimizing immediate costs, as indicated by minimum unit operation time. To satisfy the minimum-cost criterion, the following rules are generally applied: [7]

In specifying the content of individual tasks:

1. Specialize skills.
2. Minimize skill requirements.
3. Minimize learning time.
4. Equalize workloads and make it possible to assign full workloads.
5. Provide for the workers' satisfaction (no specific criteria for job satisfaction are known to be in use, however).
6. Conform to the layout of equipment or facilities or, where they exist, to union restrictions on work assignments.

In combining individual tasks into specific jobs:

1. Limit the number and variety of tasks in a job.
2. Make the job as repetitive as possible.
3. Minimize training time.

In contrast with this *process-centered approach*, another concept of job design has been developed in recent years—the *worker-centered*

[5] L. E. Davis, "Work Methods Design and Work Simplification," *Progress in Food Research*, Academic Press, Vol. 4 (1953), p. 37.

[6] L. E. Davis *et al.*, "Current Job Design Criteria," *Journal of Industrial Engineering*, Vol. 6, No. 2 (1955), p. 5.

[7] See, for example, H. G. Thuesen and M. R. Lohman, "Job Design, Parts I and II," *Oil and Gas Journal*, Vol. 41, No. 35–36; H. B. Maynard *et al.*, *Methods-Time Measurement*, McGraw-Hill, 1948.

approach, which emphasizes the participation of the worker in certain areas of decision making as a way of giving meaning to the work situation.

Representative of this approach are the group planning method and job enlargement. In group planning,[8] a team of workers participates in deciding the content of the various jobs to be performed by members of the team. In job enlargement,[9] the job is specified in such a manner that the worker performs a longer sequence or a greater variety of operations and may be responsible as well for testing the quality of his work, setting up and maintaining his equipment, and controlling his own production rate.

There is a third approach which combines the process-centered and worker-centered approaches. In job rotation, for example, the operator is assigned a series of jobs to be performed in rotated order.[10] This method is often used to counteract the unfavorable effects of process-centered job designs in circumstances where the basic job specifications cannot be altered for one reason or another.

Some Criticisms

These new approaches to job design—the outgrowth of social science research and experiment in industry—may be welcomed on the whole as a step in the right direction.[11] By calling attention to the critical role of the worker himself in the modern industrial system, they have challenged some of the basic premises of traditional job design.

A strong word of caution is in order, however. Most, if not all, social science research in industry, as was pointed out earlier, has been based on the assumption that the contents of a job are technically inviolate. If this assumption is invalid, as it may well be, the research findings cannot be accepted without question.

[8] E. A. Woodhead, "Jobs Break-Down Under Group Study Plan," *Electrical World,* Vol. 120, No. 4 (1943).

[9] C. R. Walker, "The Problem of the Repetitive Job," *Harvard Business Review,* Vol. 28, No. 3 (1950); E. J. Tangerman, "Every Man His Own Inspector, Every Foreman His Own Boss at Graflex," *American Machinist,* Vol. 7, No. 3 (1953), p. 7; J. D. Elliott, "Increasing Office Productivity Through Job Enlargement," AMA *Office Management Series,* No. 134 (1954), p. 3.

[10] A. Wood and M. L. Okum, "Job Rotation Plan That Works," *American Machinist,* Vol. 90, No. 9 (1946).

[11] They have been greeted with enthusiasm in many quarters. See, for example, "Broadening the Job," *Time,* Vol. 63 (April 12, 1954), p. 100; D. R. Wright, "Job Enlargement," *The Wall Street Journal,* March 11, 1954, p. 1; D. Wharton, "Removing Monotony from Factory Jobs," *American Mercury,* October 1954, p. 91; J. K. Lagemann, "Job Enlargement Boosts Production," *Nation's Business,* Vol. 42, No. 12 (1954), p. 34.

Given this basic limitation, it is not surprising that most of the recent experiments in job design have been haphazard—a kind of trial-and-error attempt to remedy the defects of completely "engineered" job specifications. As yet, there has been relatively little systematic analysis, under controlled conditions, of the actual relationship between job content and other variables (long-term cost, productivity, motivation, and so on). Hence, in the absence of adequate theories of job design and experimental evidence to back them up, the doctrine of minimum costs still holds the field.

There are, however, three pioneering studies of job design to which this criticism does not apply. Since these investigations focused on actual job content and were carried out under controlled conditions, they may serve as models for future research in this area.

The first of these is the study made by Walker and Guest of the Institute of Human Relations at Yale University,[12] one of the first systematic investigations into the consequences of job specialization. Using depth interviews to explore workers' experiences on automobile assembly line jobs, the investigators analyzed the effects of mass production technology on job satisfaction and human relation.

Job Design on the Assembly Line

The characteristic principles of mass production technology are defined in the study as follows:

1. Standardization.
2. Interchangeability of parts.
3. Orderly progression of the product through the plant in a series of planned operations at specific work stations.
4. Mechanical delivery of parts to work stations and mechanical removal of assemblies.
5. Breakdown of operations into their simple constituent motions.

The study focuses on the consequences of these principles as translated by the engineer into specific job designs—that is, the resulting gains and costs, both social and economic, for workers and for the company. Looking first at the gains, it is evident that the "engineered" job has yielded high levels of output per man-hour at low cost, provid-

---

[12] C. R. Walker and R. H. Guest, *The Man on the Assembly Line,* Harvard University Press, 1952; Walker and Guest, "The Man on the Assembly Line," *Harvard Business Review,* Vol. 30, No. 3 (1952), p. 71; Guest, "Men and Machines," PERSONNEL, May 1955.

ing profits for the company and a relatively low-priced product for the public.

In examining the social costs, however, we discover some disturbing facts. These can be summed up in the one overwhelming fact that the workers despise their jobs. This dissatisfaction does not seem to arise from the circumstances usually considered important by management such as pay, security, working conditions, pension plan, and supervision—the workers regarded these as satisfactory on the whole—but from certain features of job design:

1. *The anonymity of the individual worker* (what has been referred to previously as the principle of "minimum impact of the worker on the production process"). This is a consequence of designing *out* of the job virtually everything that might be of personal value or meaning to the worker. Specifically:
   a. The worker has no control over his work pace.
   b. His job is highly repetitive, having been broken down into the simplest motions possible.
   c. There is little or no need for skill because of the simple movements required.
   d. Methods and tools are completely specified and the worker has no control over them or any changes made in them.
   e. Because he never works on more than a small fraction of the product, the worker does not see the final results of his work, has no identity with the product, and cannot estimate the quality of his contribution to it.
   f. Since the job requires only surface attention, the worker does not become really absorbed in his work.
   g. The geographic arrangement of the production line severely limits social interactions. Men on the line work as individuals rather than as a work group, and the lack of group awareness seems to reinforce the feeling of anonymity.
2. *The depersonalization of the job,* as evidenced in the lack of job progression vertically. Since tasks have been simplified, skill differences between jobs are practically eliminated. Very few workers in the study had experienced any substantial change in job classification during a period of 12 to 15 years.

The manager and the engineer, of course, may feel that these social costs are more than justified by the gains for the company and the consumer. This, however, is not the point. Granting that low unit cost production—or minimum total economic cost, which amounts to the same thing—is the fundamental requirement for progress and well-being in an industrial society, the main question is this: Is the method of job design chosen by the engineer the *optimum* one for achieving minimum total economic cost, *which includes social costs by definition?*

The question implies, of course, that the engineer's criteria for measuring the effectiveness of job design are inadequate, and this inference is strongly supported by the evidence of this study. As Walker and Guest point out, turnover was high; the quality of performance was far from optimum; and labor–management relations were in a constant state of tension.

An Experiment in Redesigning Jobs

The second study to be examined,[13] one of the first controlled experiments on job design in an industrial plant, was aimed at investigating how productivity could be improved by altering job content. The experiment was designed to test the hypothesis that higher economic productivity could be achieved by:

1. Increasing the number of tasks in a job.
2. Combining tasks that (a) have similar technological content and skill demands; (b) are sequentially related in the technical process; (c) include final activities in the process or subprocess; (d) increase worker responsibility by enlarging the area of decision making concerning the job; and (e) increase the opportunity for the worker to perceive how his contribution is related to the completion of the work process.

Two major criteria were chosen for analyzing the effectiveness of these modifications in job design: quantity of production per manhour, and quality of work. Certain measures of attitude and satisfaction were also used.

The experimental setting was a manufacturing department of a unionized company on the West Coast. The department had been the subject of detailed engineering study for some years and its activities

---

[13] A. R. N. Marks, "An Investigation of Modifications of Job Design in an Industrial Situation and Their Effects on Some Measures of Economic Productivity," Ph.D. dissertation, University of California, 1954. This study was under the direction of Dr. R. R. Canter and the author. A detailed report of the study is to be published.

were organized according to the latest engineering practices. A similar department in the same company was used as a control group to permit monitoring of plantwide changes that might affect employee attitudes and performance.

At the start of the experiment, the product—a hospital appliance—was being made on an assembly line at which 29 of the department's 35 members worked, the rest of the workers being engaged in supplying the line and inspecting the product. The 29 line workers were unskilled women with an average of four-and-a-half years' experience on the line (the range was from one to seven years, approximately).

Each job on the line consisted in performing one of nine operations (these had similar skill requirements and technological content) as well as inspection in the form of rejecting defective parts. The operations were spaced at stations along the conveyor line, and the women rotated between hard and easy stations every two hours. Since the conveyor line set the pace, the workers were not responsible for the rate of output, and job rotation in effect eliminated any individual responsibility for the quality of output.

The experiment was divided into four phases (the details are given in Figure 1):

1. *Line Job Design.* The original assembly line job, used as a reference base.
2. *Group Job Design.* In this modification, the conveyor is eliminated and the workers set their own pace. Otherwise, the operations are the same as above.
3. *Individual Job Design No. 1.* Workers perform all nine operations at their own stations, control the sequence of assembly, procure supplies, and inspect their own product.
4. *Individual Job Design No. 2.* Job content is the same as in (3) but workers are located in the main production area.

The changes in productivity resulting from the modifications in job design may be seen in Figure 2. In Group Job Design, which eliminated conveyor pacing, productivity fell markedly below the Line Job Design average, indicating how conveyor pacing maintained output. The introduction of Individual Job Design, however, raised productivity above the Group Job Design average.

Although productivity under Individual Job Design did not reach the Line Job Design norm of 100, the level actually achieved is nonetheless impressive in view of the fact that the workers had only

Figure 1
Experimental Conditions for the Modification of Job Design

Type of Job Design	Purpose	Criteria	Locations	Number of Workers	Total Number of Days Assigned	Number of Days Each Worker Assigned	Production Method
Line Job Design	Obtain reference base of job design where separate tasks are performed on rotated basis.	Quantity, quality, some measures of attitude and satisfaction.	Main department.	29	26	26	Workers rotate among nine stations on belt conveyor, performing minute specified operations at pace of conveyor.
Group Job Design	Eliminate conveyor pacing. Other conditions same as above.	Quantity, quality.	Adjacent room.	29	14	2	Workers rotate among nine individual stations using batch method.
Individual Job Design No. 1	Give workers experience on experimental job design.	Quantity, quality.	Adjacent room.	29	16	2	Workers perform all nine operations at own stations, plus inspection and getting own supplies.
Individual Job Design No. 2	Obtain measure of experimental job design.	Quantity, quality, some measures of attitude and satisfaction.	Main department.	21	27	6	Same as Individual Job Design No. 1.

six days' experience on Individual Job Design No. 2 (only two days' experience on Individual Job Design No. 1), whereas they had an average of over four years' experience on Line Job Design. Moreover, the daily averages shown in Figure 2 do not reflect the trend resulting from consecutive days of experience with the modified job designs, since workers were assigned to the experimental designs on an overlapping basis. The data given in Figure 3, however, showing the average output of the whole group for *each successive day* of the trial period, indicate that the trend was consistently upward and that, on the sixth day, the group achieved an average productivity *higher* than that reached under Line Job Design.

Figure 2
Average Daily Productivity Indexes

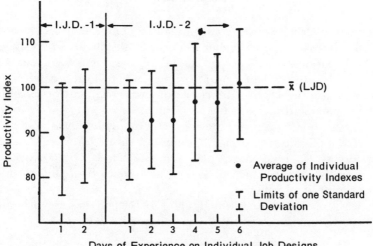

Figure 3
Average Individual Productivity Indexes

An examination of the dispersion of datum points about the averages in Figure 2 reveals an even more significant result. The narrow dispersion about the average for Line Job Design reflects the fixed work pace imposed by the line—workers could not deviate from this pace unless there were absences on the line. On the other hand, when the workers set their own pace, individual differences came into play, as indicated by the wide dispersion about the average for the three

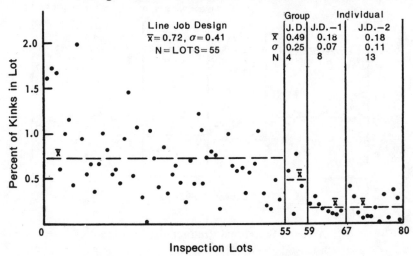

Figure 4
Percentage of Kinked Assemblies in Consecutive Lots

experimental designs, and some individual performances were as much as 30 to 40 percent higher than the Line Job Design average.

The superiority of the experimental job designs is demonstrated further in the quality data shown in Figure 4. (The number of kinked assemblies produced gave a direct measure of workmanship, since the quality of parts and subassemblies was not involved.) Beginning with a high level of quality under Line Job Design, quality levels rose with the removal of conveyor pacing. Under Individual Job Design, when responsibility for quality was placed in the hands of the workers, quality levels rose still higher, kinked assemblies dropping to one-fourth the original value.

It was concluded that Individual Job Design, besides bringing about improvements in productivity and quality, had:

1. Increased the flexibility of the production process.
2. Permitted identification of individual deficiencies in productivity and quality.
3. Reduced the service functions of the department such as materials delivery and inspection.
4. Developed a more favorable attitude toward individual responsibility and effort—after experience with Individual Job Design, workers disliked the lack of personal responsibility characteristic of Line Job Design.

The third piece of research, a study carried out in an Indian textile mill, highlights the importance of the organizational component in job design.[14]

An Indian Textile Mill

The research problem was posed by the fact that the mill's production was unsatisfactory, although new equipment had recently been installed and workloads assigned on the basis of an intensive study by engineers.

In reviewing job designs, it was found that existing worker-machine assignments produced organizational groupings and interaction patterns that mitigated against continuity of production. In one room containing 240 looms, for example, 12 activities were organized as follows:

A weaver tended approximately	30 looms
A battery filler	50 looms
A smash-hand	70 looms
A gater, cloth carrier, jobber, and assistant jobber each	112 looms
A bobbin carrier, feeler-motion fitter, oiler, sweeper, and humidification-fitter each	224 looms

Since these activities were highly interdependent, the utmost coordination was required to keep production going.

Each weaver came into contact with five-eighths of a battery filler, three-eighths of a smash-hand, one-quarter of a gater, and one-eighth of a bobbin carrier.

After a study of travel and communication patterns, the work groups were reorganized so that all of the workers who were interdependent became part of the same work group. Each group was then made responsible for the operation and maintenance of a specific bank of looms—a geographic rather than a functional division of the weaving room, which produced regular interaction among individuals whose jobs were interrelated. As a result of these changes, efficiency rose from an average of 80 percent to an average of 95 percent after 60 working days, and the mean percent of damage dropped from 32 percent to 20 percent. In those parts of the weaving shed where job design remained unchanged, efficiency dropped to 70 percent, finally rising again to 80, and damage continued at 32 percent.

[14] A. K. Rice, "Productivity and Social Organization in an Indian Weaving Shed," *Human Relations,* Vol. 6, No. 4 (1953), p. 297.

Some Basic Questions

The results of these investigations underscore the criticism made earlier of the usual approaches to job design. Relying as it does on extremely narrow criteria, traditional job design has often failed to yield the gains in efficiency that have been anticipated. On the other hand, it has produced a host of *unanticipated* and disturbing secondary effects—monotony, dissatisfaction, resistance, and even obstruction. These failures have often been laid to the "contrariness" of human nature, but this is merely another way of saying that, given the current state of knowledge, the effects of job design are unpredictable.

Yet when jobs have been manipulated or redesigned in order to enlarge job content or personal responsibility, even within a given state of technology, *reduced costs have been reported as well as gains in productivity and morale.* These results could not have been achieved on the basis of the classic theory of job fractionalization.

In short, the traditional concepts and methods of job design have obviously failed to provide satisfactory answers to two fundamental questions:

1. *What criteria should guide the design of jobs?*
2. *What criteria should be used to evaluate the effectiveness of job designs?*

If adequate criteria for job design are to be developed, research and experiment toward this end must be based on the following conditions:

1. A recognition of the limitations of the traditional minimum-cost criterion.

2. A new approach to job design that encompasses not only the technical requirements of production but the organizational requirements, the social elements in the work situation (the individual's relationship with fellow workers and with management), and the interaction between the human and the technological imperatives of the job.

3. The formulation of explicit theories of job design that will permit prediction. This requires systematic analysis of how specific changes in job content affect productivity, morale, and other variables.

4. Validation of these theories by experimental evidence gathered under controlled conditions so that causal factors can be identified and general principles established.

A New Approach

Since many of the flaws in job design can be traced to the inadequacies of the minimum-cost criterion, what is needed is a criterion of *total economic cost* that takes account of the multidimensional character of job design and includes relevant long-term changes for economic, engineering, organizational, social, psychological, and physiological costs.

To determine how such costs are to be measured poses, of course, some formidable research problems. Among the variables that would have to be measured are the following:

◻ Labor turnover and absenteeism.
◻ Learning time.
◻ Flexibility of work skills.
◻ Quality deficiencies and production bottlenecks associated with job performance.
◻ Grievances and interpersonal conflicts arising out of job and process requirements.
◻ Organizational rigidities.
◻ Service requirements such as supervision and inspection, engineering, maintenance, and personnel services.
◻ Other overhead costs.

These considerations dictate a new approach to job design—the *job-centered approach*—which goes beyond the process-centered and worker-centered approaches. The job-centered approach operates on the premise that a job cannot be adequately designed without taking into account all three of the basic variables—process, worker, and organization—as well as the variables arising from their interaction, and that changing any of these in isolation may affect economic productivity—that is, total economic-cost—adversely.[15]

It is hoped that this approach will point the way for future research and lay the basis for a more satisfactory theory of job design.

The Outlook for Research

Research and experiment must reflect the multidimensional character of job design. While job content remains the focus of research, other variables should be included in experimental designs, and certainly the range of data required is such as to call for a problem-centered, research-team approach by engineers, psychologists, sociologists, anthropologists, economists, and others.

[15] L. E. Davis and R. R. Canter, "Job Design," *Journal of Industrial Engineering*, Vol. 6, No. 1 (1955), p. 3. See also, L. R. Sayles, "Human Relations and the Organization of Work," *Michigan Business Review*, November 1954, p. 21; R. H. Guest, "A Neglected Factor in Labor Turnover," *Occupational Psychology*, October 1955.

Job design research can be expected to pay off in a number of areas: For management, in re-examining organizational designs, reward systems, control devices, communications, and the administration of the personnel function; for the engineering sciences, in improving design theories and methods in every area—product, process, equipment, plant layout, control systems, and so on; and for the social sciences, in re-evaluating human relations, programs, leadership methods, personnel techniques, communication networks, and organizational design at all levels.

The need for more effective job design, though urgently felt at present, will become even more acute as our economy moves into the era of automation. The introduction of automatic equipment makes rigorous demands on job design theory and methods in determining what processes should be automated, how automation systems should be designed, and how the human links in the control system should be related.

Even where automation is not applicable—and only a small number of jobs relative to the total will actually be transformed by automation—the design of nonautomated jobs, either in automated plants or elsewhere, will be a critical factor in maintaining operations and meeting competition.

Hence—despite the popular illusion that automation will solve most of our problems by making the machines do the work—job design will remain a central problem for industry not only in the area of production and clerical jobs but, in view of the requirements of functional organization, at supervisory and managerial levels as well.

Appendix
Definitions of Terms

1. *Job:* The structure of tasks assigned to an individual together with the work methods and the setting. The *content* of a job comprises the following:
   a. *Work Content:* The assigned series of tasks that arise from the requirements of the technical process or the equipment used or from traditionally established needs.
   b. *Methods Content:* The specification of the ways in which the work activities are to be performed, including tools, equipment, and location. It is often referred to as methods design.
   c. *Organization Content:* The organizational setting in which the assigned tasks are to be carried out—for example, the location of the job in a work group, hierarchical relations, and so on.
   d. *Personal Content:* The factors in the job that affect personal behavior, growth, motivations, and so on.

2. *Job Design:* the process of specifying the content of a job (work, methods, organizational, and personal content) in terms of a job definition or a job description.

3. *Total Economic Cost:* The total cost of producing a unit of product or service. In addition to the immediate charges for labor, materials, overhead, and so on, it includes the relevant long-term charges for economic, engineering, organizational, social, psychological, and physiological costs.

4. *Economic Productivity:* Productivity measured on the basis of total economic cost—that is, direct productivity modified by the addition of appropriate overhead or hidden charges stemming from absenteeism, labor turnover, quality failures, inflexibility, and so on.

5. *Minimum Cost:* The cost of producing a unit of product or service that includes only the immediate charges for direct labor, materials, and overhead.

9

Human Factors
in Production

Alfred J. Marrow

THE use of psychological techniques during World War I gave great impetus, in the period that followed, to work in the field of applied psychology. Unfortunately, the quantity of this activity frequently exceeded its quality; aptitude testing almost assumed the proportions of a fad. Inevitably the overoptimism and exaggerated claims of such enthusiasm led to disillusionment, and the testing movement soon found itself in a position analogous to that of the public opinion polls after the presidential election of 1948.

As the 1920s progressed, with capable test researchers insisting upon more rigid standards, aptitude testing was restored to a position of scientific acceptability. And, although industrial psychologists interested themselves in a number of other problems, their field continued to be largely a selection psychology.

Within the present decade, however, there has developed a growing interest in the importance of interpersonal relationships in industry. Stemming largely from the field theory concepts of Kurt Lewin, many investigators are now approaching industrial problems from the social psychological viewpoint. The individual is no longer to be studied as an isolated unit, but in relation to his environment, as he interacts with those about him. The industrial organization is considered a social unit, governed by laws of social interaction. And if we would treat properly the personnel ills that beset us, we must first determine the social structure of our industrial organizations. Through this approach lies the possibility of understanding and eliminating many of our personnel problems, and by so doing we create a healthy social unit.

For the past decade, personnel research at the Harwood Manufacturing Corporation has been based on these concepts. Let us consider some of the theoretical considerations underlying our experiments.

Time Perspective [1]

Morale is a much used and much abused term, defying adequate definition. Nevertheless, we all know (too well!) what is meant by low employee morale.

The level of morale is dependent, to a large extent, on one's attitude toward the future. The unemployed man who expects to find employment momentarily will maintain morale. Once he loses hope completely, his morale drops. We are all given, at times, to contemplation of the future. We may be overly optimistic, be unduly pessimistic, or alternate between these states; and rarely does the future unfold as we expect. Nevertheless the psychological future that an individual projects has a strong influence upon his moods and actions of the moment. In like fashion are the psychological past and present of importance; an individual's total time perspective will largely define his actions, emotions, and certainly his morale at any given instant.

"Tenacity in the face of adversity" is a military definition of high morale; you must be able to "take it when the going gets rough." And, while this may not be a generally acceptable definition, it contains an element that is applicable to the industrial situation.

Persistence (a few degrees less determined than tenacity) is obviously a quality of value in an employee and is definitely dependent upon an individual's time perspective. Actually, there are two chief factors that make for persistence: (1) the value of the goal; and (2) the outlook for the future. If the psychological force toward the goal (the strength of the desire) is sufficiently great, and if there is a felt proba-

---

[1] The discussion in this section is derived from Kurt Lewin's chapter on "Time Perspective and Morale," in *Civilian Morale,* edited by Goodwin Watson, Houghton Mifflin, 1942.

bility of reaching the goal, then we may expect persistent behavior.

The felt probability of reaching the goal (time perspective of positive morale value) is a concept of some importance, as we shall see later. To possess motivational value, a goal must be attainable in the eyes of the goal-seeker; otherwise it has no goal value, it is no goal at all. Few of us continue to reach for the stars very long.

Should a goal lack the probability of achievement, in terms of the individual's time perspective, the imposition of such a goal may very well lead to negative attitudes. This is true for organized groups as well, and the negative attitudes developed may assume the form of organized aggression. In this case, the group's time perspective serves to lower morale.

Level of Aspiration and Time Perspective

In setting goals, or fixing upon a given level of aspiration, we are in effect expressing our wishes and hopes for the future. The level of aspiration is therefore intimately associated with time perspective.

A successful person will set his next goal somewhat higher than the last, but not so high that it cannot be attained. In this manner, he is continually raising his level of aspiration. He may have an extremely high ultimate goal, but he is realistic enough to approach it by achievable steps. The unsuccessful person, on the other hand, will do one of two things: (1) He will set a goal that is too low, an admission of defeat; or (2) he will set a goal that is too high, and then either make superficial gestures toward reaching it without really trying, or continue unreasonably to pursue the unattainable goal.

Frequently a goal will not be accepted as realistic if there has been no demonstration that the goal is achievable. We are all familiar with the "It can't be done!" response to a new piece rate. Yet once the goal has been achieved, it acquires a social reality, and is thereafter more readily accepted by others. Their time perspective has been changed by the demonstration of achievement. "If he can do it, so can I."

The foregoing theoretical considerations have been basic to the design of our research. In demonstration, let us turn to the experiments.

Turnover

Excessive turnover of personnel has always been a costly and disturbing problem, and so it became to us during the war. In an attempt to understand the reasons for turnover, group interviews were held with supervisors. The usual reasons were advanced: moved out of town, took another job, no transportation, disliked the work, not enough pay, not enough overtime, and so on. As a follow-up, exit interviews were conducted with all workers who left during a period of two months. The workers mentioned a few additional reasons for quitting (for example, disliking their supervisors), but in general the reasons given were the same. The opinions of supervisors and workers did not seem to give a final answer concerning the causes of turnover, nor were they of much practical help in prescribing remedies except for the elimination of rather specific grievances.

The pressing problem of turnover demanded further psychological research. From the viewpoint of factory management there were two purposes to the research: (1) Why do employees quit their jobs? (2) What can be done to correct this problem?

Kurt Lewin, while visiting the Harwood Plant in 1944, expressed the belief that much of the turnover might be caused by a feeling of failure on the part of the employees who left the organization.

To examine this possibility, the turnover of the previous month was analyzed. The findings supported Lewin's hypothesis: Of the 116 operators who were rating above standard production for the month, not one had left, but of the 211 who were rating below standard, 28 had quit during the month.

The data also revealed the interesting fact that turnover increased as the worker approached the standard of an experienced operator (60 units per hour); that is, there was greater turnover among those who were approaching standard production than there was among those who were considerably below standard. This pointed to the possibility that the high quit rate of "almost skilled" workers was caused by increasing frustration as they approached their goal. It was theorized that this frustration was caused by the conflict of two factors: First, the strength of the worker's desire to reach standard increases as the goal comes within sight. Second, the difficulty of improving production increases as the distance to the goal decreases; that is, the higher the level of production, the greater the difficulty of increasing production. Thus the conflict between (1) increased desire to reach standard and (2) increased difficulty of reaching standard, seemed responsible for the frustration that led to a feeling of failure.

The frustration-failure hypothesis was explored further. The employees who quit during 1944 were divided into seven groups, classified by amount of production at time of quitting. For each classification the percent turnover per month during 1944, based on the total number of employees in that classification, was computed.

These data further substantiated the hypothesis. It was found that the rate of turnover increased as the learner approached the experienced level of 60 units per hour and decreased sharply once the success feeling of exceeding 60 units per hour was attained. The monthly turnover at 30 units per hour (about half the minimum skilled level) was 1 percent; at 45 units per hour it rose to 5 percent; and at 55 units per hour (almost equal to a skilled level) it rose to 8 percent. On an annual basis, the turnover figures were equivalent to 12 percent, 60 percent, and 96 percent, respectively, for the three indicated numbers of units per hour. Once the standard was achieved, the turnover rate dropped to 13 percent.

If the frustration-failure hypothesis of turnover was valid, as the data seemed to indicate, then we had the answer to our first question: Employees quit their jobs (at least many of them) because of a sense of failure. We were then faced with the second problem: What could be done to correct the situation?

To eliminate failure experiences, insofar as possible, the training program was redesigned. The trainers were instructed not to put the slow learner on the defensive, but rather to accept without criticism the explanation that the trainee offered. Trainees were encouraged to accept the factory situation realistically, with all its unavoidable difficulties and minor irritations. In addition, though the trainee was told of the ultimate goal she was expected to reach, she was also encouraged to set weekly goals that seemed reasonable. In this connection, the trainers were carefully instructed to recognize unrealistic goal setting; it was necessary to avoid overoptimistic levels of aspiration that might result in failure. Trainees, in conference with the trainer, often set as many as eight or nine substitute goals during the training period. Probably many more were set unofficially on a daily or two-day basis (perhaps hourly) once the habit was formed.

The results seemed to substantiate the hypothesis. As a result of the trainer's encouraging, sympathetic attitude, as well as the establishment of realistic substitute goals (as contrasted with the less realistic goal of standard production) the turnover rate dropped about 50 percent for the entire plant. More significant was the drop in turnover at the "almost skilled" level, the high frustration period; turnover at this level dropped to 75 percent in 1947. In 1944 it had been 300 percent.

Effect of Transfers

American industry has characteristically changed models and products as frequently as competitive conditions and engineering progress dictated. When this happens, it is necessary to transfer workers to different jobs. In addition, the high rate of turnover and absenteeism in recent years resulted in unbalanced production lines, which also necessitated shifting of workers.

The resistance of workers to such transfers was one of the major problems of the production staff. When transfers occurred, the resistance would become evident in grievances concerning piece rates on the new jobs, high turnover, low efficiency, restricted output, and overt aggression toward management. But there was no way of avoiding the transfers; plant operation required the changes in methods and jobs.

Here again we seemed faced with a failure situation. As the first step in the investigation, an analysis of turnover was made, comparing transferred operators with those who had not been transferred recently. Data were gathered for the period from September 1946, to September 1947. Each group was divided into seven classifications according to production rating at time of quitting. For each classification, the percent turnover per month, based on total number of employees in that classification, was obtained.

When the curves were plotted, it was discovered that both the level of turnover and the form of the curves were quite different for the two groups. The nontransfers showed an average monthly turnover of about 4½ percent; among the transfers, the average monthly turnover was approximately 12 percent. In comparing the curves, both groups showed a sharp drop in turnover for those beyond the 60-unit standard; this was consistent with the findings of previous studies that turnover was low among those who had experienced success. However, whereas both groups had high turnover at the "almost skilled" level, again consistent with previous studies, the transfers also had a peak turnover at the lowest production rating, evidence that many of the transfers quit just after their production fell upon being transferred.

How were these findings to be interpreted? The high turnover at the "almost skilled" level already had an explanation in the frustration-failure hypothesis previously described. But whereas the learners experienced greatest frustration at the level just below standard, the transfers experienced even greater frustration immediately after transfer. It seems likely that the frustration resulted from "loss of face," the contrast between the previous high status and present reduced status.

Still another revealing finding was made in the investigation of resistance to transfer. For the simplest type job in the plant, the average learning time for beginners was five weeks. Yet experienced operators, when transferred to this same job, required an average of eight weeks to reach standard. Nor could it be argued that the skill habits on the old job were interfering with relearning on the new job. Transferred operators rarely complained that they wanted to do it the old way, and time and motion studies showed very few false moves after the first week of change. Thus the slow relearning of transfers seemed primarily a motivational problem. In support of this was evidence obtained from interviews with transferred workers. The group was characterized by a general pattern of low morale. There were expressions of resentment and aggression against management, but largely, the picture was one of resignation, with evidences of frustration, loss of hope of ever regaining the former level of production and status, feelings of failure, and a very low level of aspiration.

All the standard approaches were used in attempting to solve the problem of resistance to change. Special monetary allowances were made, the cooperation of the union was enlisted, layoffs were attempted on the basis of inefficiency; very little was accomplished.

Here again, special research procedures were required. Starting with a series of observations about the behavior of transferred groups, a general overall program was devised. The first step consisted of developing a theory to account for the resistance to change. Next, a real-life action experiment was designed to be carried out as an integral part of plant operation. Finally, the results of the experiment were interpreted in light of the theory, accounting for the experimental differences and providing effective means for overcoming resistance to change.

The experiment consisted of selecting four groups of operators, three experimental and one control; selection was based upon similarity in efficiency and other important variables. A change, comparable in degree, was then made in the operation of each group. Thus the four groups became experimental transfers.

The manner in which the operations of the groups were changed varied; this was the experimental variable. For the control group, the usual factory routine was followed. A meeting was called at which it was explained that the change was necessary because of competitive conditions, that a new piece rate had been set; the rate was explained, questions were answered, and the meeting was dismissed.

The operations of the experimental groups were changed differently. Included in the method of change was a forceful technique for making the group aware of the need for change, and an opportunity to participate in planning the details of the change. Group 1 was represented in the planning by selected members; Groups 2 and 3 all participated in the planning.

The results of the experiment were fairly clear. The control group dropped in production immediately upon change, and by the end of the experiment showed no appreciable amount of recovery. Resistance developed almost immediately. There were marked instances of aggression against management, deliberate restriction of production, lack of cooperation with the supervisor. Nine percent quit during the first 15 days after the change. Grievances were filed about the piece rate which, upon checking, was found to be even a little "loose."

The recoveries for Groups 2 and 3 were dramatic. Both groups recovered to their pre-change level of production the second day after change, and by the end of the experiment they had actually surpassed their pre-change level by about 14 percent. They worked cooperatively with their supervisors, there was no indication of aggression, and there were no quits during the 15-day period.

Group 1 required more time to recover (possibly because of an unavoidable operational problem), but reached the pre-change level by the 14th day after change, and by the end of the experiment had exceeded its pre-change level. Here, too, no quits were recorded. One particular act of aggression was observed that was neither prolonged nor serious.

In analyzing the negative attitudes that make for resistance to change, there seem to be four component forces in operation. These correspond to the goals of pay, security, status, and success. When an operator is at a production level above standard, the situation represents high pay, security, status, and success—all of a positive nature; when at a level below standard, we have low pay, insecurity, lack of status, failure. Because management's standard of production is well accepted, any action that tends to place the operator at a level below standard is strongly resisted.

The success of the experiment seemed to be attributable largely to the fact that experimental transfers were given the opportunity to participate in planning the change, in planning their own work future. Thus, where such external motivating forces as monetary rewards, management pressure, and other means had failed, group involvement and decision developed internalized motivation for the accomplishment of a goal mutually desirable to management and worker.

Group Standards as a Restraining Force

It has been demonstrated that a group member will tend to set his goals in accordance with the standards of the group. An interesting illustration of the restraining forces that group standards bring to bear upon goal-setting is found in the following report:

In 1937, management was confronted with the problem of training hundreds of workers for a newly erected plant in the South. It was assumed at that time that skill was the major, and motivation the minor, determinant of the rate of learning. During the first year of the plant's operation, a traditional training program was introduced. The average output after a week's training ranged from 10 to 20 percent of the standard production for skilled workers. The trainees were informed at that time that their first week's rate of production, frequently attained at great physical and emotional effort, was only a fraction of what they would be expected to produce at the end of 12 weeks. The disparity between their accomplishment and the stated future goal, an imposed goal, was so great that many workers expressed scepticism of ever being able to attain that goal. Since the plant was newly organized, there were no skilled workers who were actually doing the job at standard speed; the goal therefore seemed impossible to attain. The wages these learners received were already more than they had been accustomed to as domestics, farm hands, or waitresses. There was nothing either inside or outside the plant to give the higher standards social reality for the group. As a result, despite the dissatisfaction of management, the learners were well satisfied with their progress. Consequently the learning rate was slow, plateaus were common, and at the end of the 12-week training period the majority of the trainees were only producing about 50 percent of the minimum standard for experienced workers. Pressure methods were introduced to increase production. Rewards and punishments of many kinds were tried. The result was a frightening increase in voluntary quits. Finally, after some 40 weeks, the first few workers reached the minimum level for rating as skilled.

It had become clear by this time that an individual will slacken his efforts and set his goals far below those he could reach if group standards are low. Conversely, he will raise his goal if the group standards are raised. In other words, both the ideals and the action of an individual depend upon the group to which he belongs and upon the goals and expectations of that group.

A comparison of the training period of the first year of plant operation with that of the second year illustrates the effect of group goals on the individual. At the beginning of the second year, a number of the older workers had already exceeded the skilled level of production. Moreover, there had been a migration to the plant of a group of experienced workers from a nearby community. Thus the group standards had been appreciably raised. In addition, the changed reality of the goal had an effect upon learning and the level of aspiration. As a result, the average training time of 34 weeks in 1937 was reduced to 14 weeks in 1938.

So much for the vivid testimony to the great restraining force of a seemingly unattainable goal, as exemplified by the experience in 1937 and its sequel in 1938. Let us turn our attention now to the present.

During the war a popular model was discontinued. After a lapse of four years, this item was reintroduced. At the time of the reintroduction, there were no longer any workers in the plant who had formerly made the product. Consequently, it represented a new item for which there were no accepted group standards, just as it had in 1937. Since there were actually no workers doing the job at a standard speed, the goal once again, in 1948 as in 1937, seemed too difficult and unattainable. As a result, the learning curve flattened out to the level that had prevailed some 10 years earlier when the plant was first established.

Note that the average training time, which had been 34 weeks in 1937 and had been reduced to 14 weeks in 1938, has been still further reduced in 1948 to seven weeks. Yet on this one item, for which there are no group standards, there is every evidence at the moment of writing that approximately the same 34 weeks will be required to reach standard. And so we have completed a full circle.

There are several elements in common between the 1937 and 1948 situations. In both cases, the job was new to the plant personnel. In both cases, the goal seemed unattainable. And in both cases, the group established standards that restricted production, though for different reasons. In 1937 the group standard remained low because additional pay did not constitute a motivating factor. The 1948 low group standard is an intentional restriction of production, an aggression against management.

There have been many instances in the past when a new job required extended learning time because the goal seemed unattainable to the original group of learners. And after the first group had attained the goal and given it social reality, succeeding groups were able to reach standard production within a shorter learning period. And so we predict that, once the present slow learners reach standard, succeeding learners on the same job will reach standard in much less time.

Conclusion

These experiences emphasize that in investigating the general problem of job satisfaction and morale, we must explore beyond the limits of the worker in his job. We must do as the medical scientist did in his search for a cure for malaria. So long as the therapy was focused on the patient's temperature, little progress was made. But when such undreamed of measures as draining swamps and stocking ponds with fish were tried, they turned out to be the preventatives that had really been needed all the time. Similarly, our investigations of the problems of human adjustment must be broader than the symptom and the patient. We need to seek out the environmental causes of conflict and dissatisfaction, its media of communication, the unhealthy social conditions that make for low resistance to its transmission or persistence, and in general, its social pathology and therapy.

10

Consultative Supervision and Management

H. H. Carey

"WHAT is 'consultative supervision'?" That question was asked by a new foreman attending a foremen's discussion group.

"It's the opposite of 'insultative supervision,' " came quickly from one of the other foremen present. This is, in fact, a rough and ready way of distinguishing between two methods of supervision—one which, among other things, tends to maintain an employee's self-respect and one which tends to destroy it.

This aspect of the supervisory problem was stressed by the General Foods Corporation under the heading of "Consultative Supervision" in its booklet, "Employee Relations in General Foods," issued in May 1941:

> Because it places emphasis upon respect for the personality and human dignity of each individual employee and allows maximum development of his natural capacity the management believes that the most enduring—and in the long run most satisfactory—personnel relations will be attained by means of consultation and explanation—up and down the organization—through the channels of communication shown on organization charts.

This means:

1. That employees should be encouraged to express their views on matters affecting their jobs and interests.
2. That consideration should be given to their views before reaching decisions materially affecting their jobs and interests.
3. That all those who direct the work of others should see to it in the daily operation of our business that no one is ignored on those things about which he thinks he has a right to be consulted.
4. That all matters affecting employee relations should be fully and freely explained.

Employees are assured there will be no discrimination as a result of their exercising their rights under this method of administration.

This constitutes the first formal declaration of policy by any company under the heading of *consultative supervision.* The term "consultative supervision and management," originally suggested in a magazine article in 1937,[1] did not refer to a new idea or method; it was only a new name for the method of leadership in which supervisors or executives discuss *in advance* with employees or the representatives of employees plans or policies that will materially affect employee interests. This is a supervisory procedure that is applicable at each organization level to the working relationships of the supervisor with his subordinates—that is, between top executives and supervisors and lower-ranking executives or supervisors, and between the lowest-ranking supervisors and nonsupervisory employees. It is also a management procedure in that it is applicable to the group relationships between different management levels and those between management representatives and representatives of employees.

What Is Consultative Supervision?

Certain questions have arisen about this method of dealing with individuals and groups which indicate that a more explicit statement concerning it is needed, particularly with respect to the underlying principles and their application. Some persons concerned in industrial relations matters have construed the consultative method as something that strikes at the root of management prerogatives.

[1] H. H. Carey, "Consultative Supervision," *Nation's Business,* April 1937.

Others have thought it a means of letting everybody run the business.

Consultative supervision and management does not imply a spineless supervisory and managerial body "turning over the business to the boys," nor does it mean endless individual and group wrangles. Obviously, responsible individual supervisors and executives must make decisions and initiate action. The point is that decisions and actions that affect employees must be understood by the employees in question and accepted by them as fair; otherwise there will be passive or overt resistance, and management objectives will not be achieved to the extent that they might be.

One supervisor, referred to by his subordinates as a man they would "go through hell and high water for," frequently calls in small groups of men one and two levels below him and asks them to pitch in with their ideas on the problem at hand. Because of his obvious sincerity in opening the door for the presentation of different points of view, the group members "shoot the works."

After an adequate discussion this supervisor usually ends up, "Well, there seems to be quite a difference of opinion on what we ought to do about this. But somebody has to make a decision. In the light of all the discussion here it seems to me that we ought to . . . and we'll proceed on that basis. Maybe those of us who hold this view are wrong, but let's give it a try and see where we come out. If we're wrong, we'll even let you other fellows say 'I told you so'!"

And when the group members go out they're saying to each other, "He's a swell guy" . . . "Well, anyway, I had my say" . . . "I'm willing to give it a whirl."

Contrast that scene with the one where the "boss" always calls the boys in and "tells 'em." When they leave his office, they are thinking, although perhaps not saying: "What a guy." . . . "He just don't know what it's all about." . . . "What does he think we are—dumbbells?" . . . "I could tell him a few things he didn't even consider." . . . "Well, I guess that makes us just a bunch of office boys."

The principle of consultation has been used by many supervisors and executives from the beginning of human organization. It is seen in its simplest form when a supervisor says to one of his subordinates, "What do you think about this, Joe?" or "How do you think we ought to tackle this?" In vocational adjustment matters, it is exemplified when the supervisor says at the appropriate time and place, "What kind of work would you like to get into?" or "There's a job opening up in the new mill; would you like to have a crack at it?" In wage matters it appears if the supervisor says at appropriate intervals, "I'm due to make a recommendation to the boss about your rate of pay. Before I do it I want to hear what you have to say and what you think I should do about it. I won't make you any promises. I won't argue. I just want to listen and make sure that your ideas and point of view are considered before we make a decision."

Action initiated by the responsible head to bring his subordinates into the picture on matters of mutual concern *is not a sharing of prerogatives or authority. Rather, it is an extension of the opportunity of participation in the development of points of view and the assembly of facts upon which decisions are made.*

Such a supervisory procedure implies recognition that the individual is worthy and competent to contribute to the formation of plans or methods that are vital to the job and offers positive evidence that his ideas are given consideration by those more directly responsible for decisions. It provides a chance to give the employee background information that will enable him to understand the situation better. And after having experienced this procedure, the employee will be much more willing to accept the decision when it is made, even though it is directly contrary to what he considers his own interest.

Extending the Area of Consultation

In the relationships between higher and lower levels of management, the adoption of a consultative procedure means that upper levels extend the normal area of consultation to include those who are one, or perhaps two, levels of organization below that on which the particular decision is ordinarily made. For example, some matters ordinarily decided by a company president and his vice-presidents might be referred for advance recommendation and comment to those reporting to the vice-presidents; similarly matters usually decided at the plant manager's level might be referred one or two levels down—and so on down the line, each managerial or supervisory group being given the opportunity to contribute to a greater extent in the formulation of plans affecting its own immediate responsibilities and operations. In some matters, such as the formulation of basic employee relations policies, the consultative procedure might be extended to the lowest level of supervision, giving all those responsible for administering the policies on the daily job an opportunity to make suggestions. The principle back of this is that "men carry into action best that which they have had a part in forming."

Such a procedure within the managerial or supervisory group tends to develop each individual and to knit together the various organization levels. It is a practical demonstration, particularly to those in the intermediate and lower supervisory levels, that they are actually considered part of the management group. In addition, they get a larger view of company problems and operations together with a better understanding of the plans or policies which they have to carry out.

In Labor Relations

In the field of labor relations the consultative method is illustrated in the following statement from a management representative to a labor representative: "It is management's job to manage the business, and we intend to do it. However, we recognize that employees' interests and welfare are involved in many of our problems, and we want to make sure that the employees' point of view is adequately considered before we make a final decision. It will, therefore, be our policy to consult employees or their representatives on all matters materially affecting their status or welfare before formulating any final policy or taking action. Through such consultation we shall give employees the opportunity to present their point of view, and we shall take only such action as we consider justified after a thorough consideration of all interests involved—those of stockholders, customers, and employees."

In any discussion of the process of management through advance consultation, it should be understood that there are many management problems in which employees have no proper interest and many cases in which consultation may be neither desirable nor necessary— such matters as refinancing, plant expansion or contraction, introduction or discontinuance of products, allocation of manufacture among different plant locations, allocation of funds to surplus or dividends, prices of product, and so on.

Management by Defense

During the past few years we have had management by defense. It has been the tendency of most employers to make decisions without giving employees or their representatives a chance to discuss matters affecting them. Management has said in effect: "This is our decision; if you don't like it, complain, and we'll talk it over with you." Consequently, management prerogatives and actions have been challenged, and management has found itself in the position of having to justify its action after the fact. This is an untenable position from the standpoint of good employee relations. No management action, however fair and just to all interests involved, can be acceptable to employees or provide the basis for real cooperation if the door to advance consultation is closed and provision is made only for complaints and grievances.

Consultative supervision is not a method of supervision to be used in every supervisor-employee contact. In the normal course of day-by-day operations, direct orders are necessary, but if a high degree of cooperation is to be obtained by an individual supervisor or by the management group as a whole, the procedure can and should be used often enough to make employees or their representatives feel that they are an important factor in the business and not just cogs in the wheel. Where it is used occasionally, in a manner that indicates an honest willingness to give the individual employee an opportunity to participate to a reasonable degree in matters on which he feels he has a right to be consulted, it should establish the employee's confidence in the supervisory and management group, and this confidence will carry over to all its decisions and actions.

What the Employees Want

Stated another way, consultative supervision and management is a way of enlisting a higher degree of cooperation and work effort from employees than they normally give in the work situation.

An individual's job is one of the most important things in his life; to a large extent it determines his whole life. Because it is so vital, the employee is naturally interested in everything that happens to him on the job and in any changes that will affect him or his interests. Management people in general have looked at the management job from the management point of view; in most instances they have not given an equivalent amount of consideration to the employee's viewpoint. If a high degree of employee effort and cooperation is desired, it would be advantageous to give further consideration to the attitudes of employees that determine *willingness* and *desire* to apply themselves to their assigned jobs, and to what might be done to induce more favorable attitudes that would be reflected in greater cooperation, higher productivity, and more confidence in the company management.

On the basis of practical common sense, we know already some of the essential facts about what employees like in the way of treatment on the job and what they respond to favorably. Among the things employees like is to be "in on the know" concerning their job and factors related to it; also, they want some kind of voice in job matters and in changes that may affect them; in other words, they want consideration for their point of view that they may not feel like pawns, messenger boys, or just "order takers."

Consultative supervision gets right to the heart of these desires. Supervisors using it are more likely to explain the background of particular problems. And the essence of the consultative procedure is that *the supervisor opens the door for employee participation.* While an individual may have a constructive viewpoint about his job and other matters affecting his interests, he may be unwilling to bring his ideas into the open for fear of offending his superior in some way. When the supervisor opens the door, however, the situation is just right from the psychological standpoint.

One well-informed national labor representative has observed that a large measure of the success his union attained seemed due to a widespread feeling among employees of personal frustration in the work situation—a resentment against what they considered arbitrary treatment on the part of the employer and insufficient respect shown them as individual human beings.

"He Done It All"

The desire of employees to participate to some extent in matters affecting their interests is well illustrated by a situation that developed some years ago in a Pennsylvania plant where company policies and working environment were considered ideal by most outsiders.

When a strike occurred in the plant, it attracted widespread attention. A reporter talked with one of the strikers in an effort to find out what was really at the bottom of the whole thing, explaining that in the face of all the company benefits, it was hard for him to understand why the employees should go out on strike.

The striker said: "But *he* done it all. We didn't have anything to do with it. I don't want anybody to be good to me. I want to be good to myself."

While management people recognize that it is in the interest of management to enlist the fullest possible cooperation of all employees, further consideration needs to be directed toward methods by which this objective may be attained.

It is beginning to be generally recognized that employees are not motivated solely by economic incentives and that companies cannot purchase their complete loyalty through high wages. Any executive who had an eight-cylinder car that was functioning on only six cylinders would be totally dissatisfied until all the cylinders were taking their full load and performing satisfactorily. My guess is that it is highly probable that the average employee is giving not more than two-thirds, and perhaps not more than one-half, his full measure of cooperation and ability to his employer.

Basic Considerations in Developing Cooperation

The causes for this lack of cooperation, loyalty, and effort are numerous, and they do not need to be enumerated here. It would be worth while, however, to give attention to some fundamental considerations underlying the problem of developing a well-integrated, effective, highly cooperative employee group. Some of these considerations may be listed as follows:

1. Cooperation of a high order cannot be enforced. It can be achieved only through establishing conditions from which it naturally springs.

2. Cooperative responses are natural to the individual who, through his experience on his daily job, is convinced that he is a significant part of the business.

3. One of the essentials in developing effective cooperation is that employees, supervisors, and managerial officials at all levels identify their own interests with those of the company.

4. Statements of policy or company intent, while desirable, are not convincing in themselves or wholly effective in building up proper employee attitudes. The individual will be convinced that he is a significant part of the business only if his experiences on the daily job itself give him a feeling of worth, dignity, and general satisfaction.

5. Since the development of a well-integrated, cooperative working force must be brought about largely by the middle and lower supervisors, it is essential that these middle and lower supervisors be accorded treatment on the daily job that will induce in them appropriate attitudes, methods, and action in dealing with their own subordinates.

6. Executives and supervisors must have the genuine respect of subordinates by virtue of their individual characters, abilities, and personal qualities—not merely the kind of respect that is accorded position and rank, or arises from fear.

The consultative method of leadership should go a long way toward establishing the kind of job conditions that promote responsibility, self-respect, a "sense of belonging," and a recognition of common interests—things that tend to unleash the full energy and abilities of employees. Giving an individual the opportunity to participate in such job matters as planning, improvement of methods, wage adjustments; affording him the chance to state his job preference—perhaps giving him some share in decisions concerning his vocational adjustment— may reach the core of the problem of enlisting the maximum interest, cooperation, and work effort of employees.

New Methods of Leadership

To those who may still feel that the process is inconsistent with management prerogatives, it may be said that possibly the management prerogatives that have been undermined during the past few years might have been sustained if the average employee had felt that he could make his weight count as an individual in his immediate work situation, and if there had been sufficient management and supervisory attention to his individual problems, viewpoints, and ideas. No one brought up in the traditions and customs of our country wants to be pushed around or to be considered a pawn or a peg to be moved here and there. If he cannot get this feeling or sense of participation through company channels, he will endeavor to get it through some other means.

Times are changing and the kinds of leadership methods and abilities required are changing. Leaders who grew up and learned leadership tactics in the era of "respect your elders" are likely to find it increasingly difficult to use the same methods in the current "oh yeah" times.

As the Supervisors See It

In discussing consultative supervision, a group of supervisors listed the advantages of this procedure as follows:

- Employees feel that they are working *with* and not *for* the supervisor.
- The supervisor gets the benefit of the individual's experience and training.
- It gives employees a chance to "sound off."
- It develops the individual's initiative and self-reliance.
- It increases the individual's confidence in management.
- It builds up the individual's self-respect.
- It builds up the individual's confidence in the supervisor and increases his willingness to cooperate.

□ The supervisor can get to know the employee better and to understand his attitude and feelings.

□ It makes the individual feel more responsible for his job and not merely a cog in a machine.

□ It keeps the individual on his toes.

□ It improves employee–company relations as the employee feels that the supervisor and the company are interested in him as an individual.

□ In making work assignments the supervisor can more easily make sure that the individual understands the job.

□ It broadens the employee.

□ It tends to improve job performance.

□ It develops straight thinking.

They considered the possible disadvantages to be:

□ The supervisor may lose "face" with a certain type of employee.

□ Such a system may overdevelop the self-esteem of some employees.

□ It takes too much time (the supervisor's and the individual's).

□ It may give the employee the idea you don't know your job— can't make up your mind.

□ The employee may think the supervisor is trying to shift responsibility.

□ It will destroy morale if the employee's ideas or point of view are asked for and then ignored, or if insufficient credit is given to them.

Consultative Supervision and Organized Labor

Consultative supervision and management does not exclude collective bargaining. In fact, it can be applied in the handling of management–labor relations and may minimize the area of conflict and build up a greater degree of collaboration. Some companies have actually used this method in solving such basic problems as the evaluation of jobs, the establishment of output standards, and setting rates of pay by making these matters projects for joint study. Such action does not mean that the management abandons its prerogative of making decisions in these vital areas, but it does mean that after the use of this process, such decisions are more likely to be understood and accepted by the labor organizations and the rank-and-file employees.

Such a consultative procedure used both with individuals and with

labor groups gives management and supervisory people better information upon which to make decisions. It opens the door for employee
ideas and viewpoints that can be profitably utilized. It gives an opportunity for management representatives to present management difficulties, problems, and viewpoint in such a way, as to increase the
individual employee's willingness to accept company decisions. It
gives supervisors and management an opportunity to catch grievances
and complaints in their very early stages and to iron out such difficulties before the misunderstanding or resentment spreads and becomes
a serious matter. It will tend to support rather than to impair the right
of management to manage the business and, in the larger sense, the
consultative method could be considered as one way of managing a
business so as to develop and utilize to the fullest extent the entire
human resources of the organization.

The Democratic Method

More than 25 years ago Congress appointed the United States
Commission on Industrial Relations to study the "underlying causes
of dissatisfaction in the industrial situation." After two years of study
and investigation one of the commission's conclusions was as follows:

> The question of industrial relations assigned by Congress to the
> Commission for investigation is more fundamental and of greater
> importance to the welfare of the nation than any other question
> except the form of government. The only hope for the solution of
> the tremendous problems created by industrial relations lies in the
> effective use of our democratic institutions and in the rapid exten-
> sion of the principles of democracy to industry.

It can be said with some degree of assurance that the policies and
methods in business and industry should conform to a great extent
with the political ideals and practices of the democracy within which it
operates. Consultative supervision and management is a democratic
procedure that will help to develop among employees the conviction
that they have a stake in the free enterprise system. In some respects
the opportunity to participate in matters closely related to their daily
jobs is more vital to them than participation in political matters.

In conclusion, it should be stressed that the consultative process is
not a "slick" way to get by with employees. It cannot be merely a
"technique"—as such it would surely be detected by employees as a
sham. It must spring from a genuine respect for the personal integrity
of employees, for their experience and point of view.

11

Building a Democratic Work Group

Leland P. Bradford and Ronald Lippitt

PRACTICALLY everyone in America would readily agree that he believes in democracy, though in almost the same breath many would say, ". . . but this is a factory [or office] and we have to get the work out."

This tragically curious contrast of beliefs symbolizes the confusions, inabilities, and lack of knowledge that prevent most supervisors from developing efficient work groups. Dominating, autocratic control is the technique of ignorance and inability to lead in industry and business—and disastrous in the end. Just as democracy is a more civilized method of leadership in government, so it is, equally, with other groups. But democratic leadership demands skill and knowledge.

Efficient group leadership must be based on understanding of the dynamics of group growth and action. Successful groups seldom grow haphazardly. It is only as supervisory training develops efficient group leaders that high production, employee development, and good morale will be the rule instead of the exception.

Any efficient work group, whether in an industrial establishment or an office, is more than a collection of individuals. It has a personality and a unity that grows and changes according to the pressure upon it. Whatever the supervisor does has an effect not only on the individual but also on the group as a whole. To an extent greater than usually realized, the personality and efficiency of a work group depend upon the supervisor. It is important to note that frequently supervisors' actions, correct for the individual, prevent rather than develop work efficiency of the group.

It is unfortunate that the majority of books and articles on supervision and group leadership have laid almost their entire stress upon the techniques of group leadership and put little emphasis upon understanding the causes of varying degrees of group productivity and morale resulting from different patterns of leadership. By so doing they have failed to underscore for the potential leader or supervisor the cardinal principle that group efficiency must always be a joint responsibility of leader and group and that only through the interactive participation of both in leadership does such efficient production result. They have turned the attention of the supervisor only toward what he does and not toward the effects of his actions on what the group does. This has resulted in an overemphasis upon dominance and submission, whereas the basis of any truly efficient group is joint responsibility, participation, and recognition.

Increasingly will supervision be the responsibility of the entire group. The day of sharp distinction between the leader and the led must gradually disappear if high production and harmonious working relations are to be attained. This means that the responsibility of supervision is to lead and develop the members of the work group so that they may share in the supervision of the group. This does not mean the disappearance of the supervisor; rather it increases his importance as the central figure in group productivity.

To appreciate the importance for productivity of the group spirit of employees, it is desirable to examine certain types of supervision and the resultant group personalities. Four of such types follow.

1. The Hardboiled Autocrat

Characteristics. This is the supervisor who believes that he must constantly check up on everyone to keep up production. He gives the orders and employees carry them out. He believes that the only way to get conscientious performance is to expect and secure discipline and immediate acceptance of all orders. He is careful not to spoil the employee with too much praise, believing that because the employee is paid to work he needs nothing else. It is the employee's place to carry out directives, not to question or always understand them. This supervisor is usually very conscious of his position and authority and believes that employees cannot be trusted very long on their own initiative.

Group reactions. The results in this group are as follows: There is some submission to the supervisor's authority, but resentment and incipient revolt underneath (of which the supervisor probably is not aware); no one assumes more responsibility than he is forced to take, and buck-passing is a common pattern of behavior. Employees display irritability and unwillingness to cooperate with each o'her, and there is considerable backbiting and disparagement of the work of others. Only a fair level of production is maintained, and the work slips markedly whenever the supervisor is not present.

2. Benevolent Autocrat

Characteristics. The benevolent autocrat would be startled to realize that his method of supervision is autocratic. In contrast to the hardboiled autocrat, he is interested in his employees, wants to see them happy, praises them as much as he criticizes them, is seldom harsh or severe, and likes to think that he is developing a happy family group. He urges employees to bring their problems to him and is interested in all the details of their work. Actually, he trades benevolence for loyalty. The crux of his autocracy lies in the technique by which he secures dependence upon himself. He says, with a pat on the back, "That's the way I like it. . . . I am glad you did it that way . . . that's the way I want it done," or "That isn't the way I told you to do it . . . you are not doing it the way I want it." In this way he dominates employees by making himself the source of all standards of production. Any failure to live up to these standards he receives with hurt surprise and intense anger as personal disloyalty to him.

Group reactions. This group has a very different personality from that under the hardboiled supervisor. The employees are fairly happy in their work, and most of them like the supervisor. Those who see through him, however, dislike him intensely. Careful examination shows a great amount of dependence on the supervisor for direction in all work situations. No one shows initiative without first ascertaining the reactions of the supervisor, and there is a definite reluctance to accept further responsibility. No one develops ideas for improving work techniques or procedures. The group is characterized by submissiveness and lack of individual development. Lethargy and some incipient revolt exist, which may flare up if employees are called upon for heavy emergency work. Because of their desire to meet the supervisor's expectations, productivity is fairly high as long as he is on hand to give directions.

3. Laissez-Faire

Characteristics. The laissez-faire supervisor may be the supervisor who has no confidence in his ability to supervise and consequently buries himself in paperwork or stays away from employees. He may also be the one who believes that to be a "good fellow" means license. He leaves too much responsibility with the employees; sets no clear goals toward which they may work; is incapable of making decisions or helping the group arrive at decisions; and tends to let things drift.

Group reactions. This group has by far the lowest morale and productivity. The work is sloppy, output is low, and the employee has little interest in his job or its improvement. There is much buck-passing and scapegoating, and considerable irritability and unrest among the employees. There is practically no teamwork or group cohesion, and no one knows what to do or what to expect.

4. Democratic

Characteristics. The democratic supervisor endeavors wherever possible to share with his group the decision making about work planning, assignments, and scheduling. Where a decision must be made by him, he helps the group to understand clearly the basis for his decision. He is careful to develop as much participation, opinion giving, and decision making as possible, and a feeling of responsibility for the success of the work on the part of everyone. He is concerned that each employee clearly understand his work and have opportunities for success in it. His praise and criticisms are always delivered objectively in terms of work results and never personally in terms of what he may or may not like. He encourages worthwhile suggestions and the development of new procedures.

Group reactions. This group displays a high degree of enthusiasm for the work. The quality and quantity of production are the highest of all groups, and the degree of teamwork within the group is noticeably greater. Employees grow and move on to greater responsibilities. They more frequently feel that their work is successful because the members of this group willingly praise each other's efforts. Because

there are far fewer problems of employee performance and motivation, the supervisor is more relaxed and can devote more time to
planning and to constructive leadership.

Differences in Group Personalities

The personality of each of the above groups [1] resulted from
specific actions on the part of the supervisor concerned. The pattern
of each group was inevitable. An examination of the causes of differences in group patterns will indicate certain basic principles of leadership and group action that must be followed if successful group production is to result.

1. *Hardboiled autocrat.* The lack of teamwork, intense competition
among employees, buck-passing, knifing of others, lack of acceptance
of responsibility, letdown of production when the supervisor was absent, resulted from the employee's being frustrated in achieving basic
personal needs from his work efforts. First, every employee needs to
belong to and participate in a work group. When this need for "belongingness" is blocked, the individual stands alone and this increases
his insecurity. Under the hardboiled autocrat there was no group to
which to belong, but merely a collection of individuals dominated by
one person. Second, every person needs a feeling of individual importance and satisfaction from personal effort. The position of merely
carrying out orders prevented any sense of personal accomplishment.
The only status possible to the employee was to be recognized and
possibly favored by the supervisor. The supervisor, by assuming the
central role of total responsibility and credit, frustrated any efforts of
the employees to gain a sense of personal achievement and worth.

---

[1] Although these observations of the four types of supervisor are drawn from
examples in business and industry, basic experimental research confirming these patterns of leadership and the effects of them has been carried on in university
laboratories. For reports of some of these studies see:

Alex Bavelas, "Morale and the Training of Leaders," Chapter 8 in *Civilian Morale*
(edited by Goodwin Watson), Reynal and Hitchcock, New York, 1942.

"An Analysis of a Work Situation Preliminary to Leadership Training," *Journal of
Educational Sociology*, March 1944 p. 17.

K. Lewin, R. Lippitt, and R. K. White, "Patterns of Aggressive Behavior in Experimentally Created Social Climates," *Journal of Social Psychology*, Vol. 10, No. 2, 1939.

Ronald Lippitt, "An Experimental Study of Authoritarian and Democratic Group At-
mospheres," *University of Iowa Studies in Child Welfare*, Vol. 16, No. 3, 1940.

R. Lippitt and R. K. White, "An Experimental Study of the Social Climate of Children's
Groups," in *Child Behavior and Development* (edited by Barker, Kounin, and Wright),
McGraw-Hill, New York, 1943.

Frustration leads to aggression, either toward the frustrating cause (the supervisor) or, if that is impossible, toward other employees or work. Such aggression was seen in backbiting, jealousies, irritability, inability to work with others. Frustration also breeds disinterest and indifference, feelings of "what's the use?" absenteeism, and employee turnover.

Finally, under autocratic supervision the employee is made less secure. Security is determined by the extent to which the individual feels confidence in his ability to cope with new situations and the extent to which he can predict favorable conditions in the future. Neither of these conditions was present under autocratic supervision. Because no responsibility was released by the supervisor, employees had little opportunity to take initiative and grow in ability. The future, so far as employees could tell, was up to the whims and decisions of the supervisor. The result was insecurity, and insecurity usually produces nervous tension, egocentricity, aggressiveness toward others, and inability to work with others.

2. *Benevolent autocrat.* The pattern of causes for the actions of the group under the benevolent autocrat is similar to that of the hardboiled autocrat. The difference lies in the degree of frustration present. The needs for belongingness and personal achievement were secured in part through employees attaching themselves to the supervisor. As dependents, they shared in credit coming to the supervisor and they gained some sense of belongingness because of the paternalistic interest of the supervisor. Insecurity was less dominant in this group. So long as employees submitted to the subtly dominant leadership of the supervisor, they had security in his protection.

Perhaps the most dominant cause of the actions of this group lay in the slowly regressive reaction to frustration. The frustration was never sufficiently dominant to produce active aggression. Rather, it produced a gradually developing regression to more childlike levels of dependency. Instead of advancing to greater responsibility and initiative, employees retrogressed toward submission, dependency, and inability to accept further responsibility. They approached a state where they could exist only under strong autocratic supervision.

3. *Laissez-faire supervision.* The picture of frustration, failure, and insecurity was greater for this group than for any other. Because there was no leadership, there was no group to which to belong. Without leadership there was no work goal and thus low production and no sense of personal achievement.

Adequate prediction of future conditions was impossible when there was no direction in the present. The only prediction posssible was that the future would be as directionless and chaotic as the present, and this prediction could hardly produce security.

Frustration produced not only aggression in this group but also indifference and disinterest to the point of little work accomplishment. Thus laissez-faire leadership did not even result in a fair level of productivity.

4. *Democratic supervision.* Only in this group did employees satisfy their basic personal needs. Because of the participation in decision making, the understanding of the "whys" of directions, the sharing in group credit for achievement, here was a group to which the employee could belong. Because of these factors, each employee felt that his planning and efforts contributed importantly to group achievement. Security was relatively high under this type of supervision, for two reasons: Sharing in planning and decision making gave employees a clearer picture of the importance and continuity of the work. Prediction was more realistic, less likely to be based on rumor and guess. Again, participation in planning increased the ability of the individuals concerned and enhanced their confidence that they could handle new or emergency situations.

The above analyses of various group patterns of action open up fairly clearly certain fundamental principles of efficient group productivity. These principles must be met if high production, high morale, ability to meet emergency situations without conflict and strain, and ability to adjust to new situations are to be secured. They are:

1. *Adequate space of free movement.* Every employee needs to feel free to move and initiate action comfortably, within certain limits. If he is too greatly restricted, as is the case under autocratic supervision, when opportunity for initiative and responsibility are denied, he is frustrated and reacts with aggression or indifference and submissiveness. If the space in which he can move is too wide and uncircumscribed, he has no direction for his movement and is equally frustrated. Under laissez-faire leadership, with no direction or control of the employee, he is essentially less free than the employee under rigid autocratic control because he has no clear direction or goal toward which to move and consequently cannot move at all. Complete license is the most restrictive of all controls and the most frustrating. Thus it was that the laissez-faire group showed greatest aggressiveness and lethargy, and yielded lowest production.

Democratic leadership entails encouraging the employee to assume that responsibility of which he is capable, but no more. It entails making certain that the employee understands clearly the direction and goal of his efforts, and that he be given help *where needed* in resighting his goals in evaluating his progress toward those goals. Then, and only then, will the employee have adequate space of free movement. Then, and only then, will he be free from frustration producing indifference or irritability toward others.

2. *Basic human needs.* Every employee needs to feel that he belongs to a cohesive work group. Equally or more important, he needs to feel that, no matter what his contribution, it is important, and, consequently, he, as an individual, has meaning and importance to others. Opportunities for participation in planning and decision making help to meet both these basic needs. Under autocratic control both these needs are blocked because the supervisor assumes all responsibility, initiative, and credit. This is true no matter how benevolent or honey-coated the autocratic control may be. Under laissez-faire leadership there is no group to which to belong and no production achievement with which to be satisfied. Again, only democratic control meets these basic needs adequately.

3. *Security.* Employee insecurity is one of the greatest factors in low productivity, tension, aggression, and work problems. Individual security is essentially a feeling of confidence in personal ability to meet new situations and to predict favorable conditions in the future. Where supervisory control is autocratic, the only security possible to the employee is dependence upon the supervisor. Such dependence too frequently takes on an emotional tone and becomes more and more based on the likes and dislikes of the supervisor, a weak reed upon which to lean. Laissez-faire leadership provides no prediction and no employee growth. Democratic leadership provides security in that the employees not only participate in responsibilities and planning, thus increasing the degree of prediction of future events, but also develop through the process of participation, thus increasing their confidence in ability to cope with future problems.

4. *Success.* Essentially, an individual feels successful only when he has attained a goal important to him after considerable effort. If the goal is arrived at too easily, no sense of success is experienced. Under autocratic leadership only the supervisor had success experiences, because he was the only one to assume responsibility. The employee merely carried out orders, and the result was not his success. Success is the best possible motive for more efficient production. Democratic leadership that enables the individual employee to participate makes it possible for the employee to feel success after accomplishment.

Developing the Democratic Work Group

It is clear from this summary of the results of different types of leadership in employee groups that management has a vital stake in the question, "How does the supervisor go about developing the most productive work group?"

Proper selection of supervisors and training in democratic group leadership is, of course, the obvious answer. Consideration of these skills is usually neglected in selection procedures, and omitted from the content of training conferences and coaching on the job. In fact, the unfortunate idea seems to have cropped up that this "democracy business" just means "holding more meetings—just more talking and less work." This is a sad misunderstanding that blocks the way to greatly improved morale and productivity in many factories and offices.

Rather than talk about training, however, let us take a look at the performance of the adequately trained supervisor who has just been assigned to his job:

Having problems is permitted. First of all, the democratic supervisor takes steps to demonstrate that he does not view as a reflection upon himself the group sharing and discussion of problems that employees feel exist in their work situation. Only the supervisor who is convinced of the basic superiority of group airing and group solution of most group frustrations will have the personal security to heed the public expression of problems in his work unit, and to stimulate thinking about them, without becoming defensive and even blaming in his reactions. The real solution of work tensions before they arise to a dangerous pressure can be achieved only if the supervisor is felt to be "one of us" toward whom there can be continual freedom in communication of feelings.

Regular time for group thinking and action. Our supervisor discovers that under the previous supervisor "calling the group together" was an irregular occurrence that usually was the occasion for exhortation to special effort or the issuance of new orders making some change in the work routine. These meetings had been rather tense affairs, with no one except the supervisor saying much. Often employees remained standing and became painfully conscious of how hard the floor was. This is now changed. The new trained supervisor has meetings held regularly, which everyone can plan for well ahead of time. These are occasions for sitting down and thinking, as a group, about work problems and the interpretation of new management plans and policies. The supervisor does all he can to stimulate reactions to the ideas and suggestions that he or group members present. They are not long meetings, but they are regular and they "belong to everybody who comes to them."

Democratic group meetings more than "talk." These meetings begin to have a very definite and important meaning in the lives of the work group. They are not college "bull sessions," which ramble on and on; they are not uncomfortable gatherings where one listens to the boss "sound off"; nor are they "gripe sessions," which never arrive at anything constructive. The supervisor, with his agenda committee of three representative employees, has a definite plan for each meeting. It is the responsibility of the agenda committee to see that the concerns of their fellow workers are taken into account in the agenda planning. In the discussions at the meetings, the group members do not just talk about the problem or topic under consideration and then hope that the supervisor will make a decision that takes their talking into account. Most of the discussions actually move on from group thinking to group decision and shared responsibility for "doing something about it." The supervisor shares frankly with the group his own limitations of power to do anything about certain conditions. This helps the work group to be realistic about the necessary limitations to their own thinking and decisions, but at the same time gives them the experience of partnership in doing the best they can within the work environment in which they operate.

Definite group goals. If the work group is to develop a sense of unity and of responsibility, it must have a sense of direction and must see that it is making progress in that direction. The good supervisor helps his work unit see its place in the overall job of the organization. Together he and his group discuss and set immediate production goals for their work unit. The supervisor realizes that feelings of success are basic to high morale and sustained productivity. He further realizes that success involves a sense of progress—of moving forward as the result of one's own effort. This feeling of moving forward occurs only if there is a definite destination or goal, and some signposts that tell you you are moving toward the goal. So the supervisor, as a group leader, stimulates the work group to set distant and immediate work objectives. Only if these objectives are their own, set by themselves, will they serve fully as motive power for increased quantity and quality in production.

Performance standards mutually accepted or determined. Most supervisors have some responsibility for rating the employees working under them. Our democratic supervisor discovers that under the previous supervisor these ratings were never clearly understood by the employees. Several times the opinion had been voiced by disgruntled employees that the supervisor played favorites and was biased in his ratings. The new supervisor takes quite a different tack in developing this aspect of a democratic work atmosphere. First, he has a full discussion with the group about the desirability of work performance standards as the basis for a fair system of recognition. The group then has a discussion of the meaning of the performance standards that are in use. The definitions are fully explored. Or, if he is free to, the supervisor invites the group to participate with him in creating adequate definitions of good performance in the particular work unit. When ratings are made, he uses them as a basis for a personal conference with each worker. In these conferences and at all other times, his praise or criticism are accepted by employees as fair because it is based on mutually understood standards rather than on standards known only to the supervisor.

Understanding the reason for decisions outside the work unit powerfield. Often the supervisor must see that plans and decisions from higher up the line are passed down and followed through in his work group. Our democratic supervisor has helped his group think through and accept the fact that many decisions are outside his or its field of power but are usually made in the best interests of the total work organization. Then, when such decisions and plans do come down the line, the supervisor gets all the information he can as to the reasons for them so that he can inform his group. He realizes clearly that a main factor in the work morale of those under his leadership is that the work assignments and activities must "make sense."

Supervision of the individual as a group member. All these observations stress the importance of group communication of feelings and group thinking in a democratic work group. Actually the democratic supervisor still spends most of his time in personal contacts with individual workers. But he realizes keenly that every decision he makes with regard to an individual worker's request, every grievance he handles, and every word of praise or criticism he voices have group repercussions—either constructive or destructive. He sees that newcomer Sam is pretty much an outsider yet so far as feeling at home in the work group is concerned, so he enlists the aid of Jim, the natural leader of the group, to take a friendly interest in seeing that Sam gets pulled into things more at lunch hour. He recognizes that Nate feels quite insecure about his work and needs more recognition than the others, but he realizes he will only make it worse for Nate if the special attention should look like favoritism. He notices the little clique in the corner whose members are becoming rather lax in some of their work habits. The supervisor knows Max is the person who is "listened to" in that subgroup, so he has a friendly personal chat with Max and the problem disappears. To sum it up: (1) This supervisor knows that in a democratic work group social control of the individual can usually come best from within the group itself; (2) he knows that every personal contact with a worker must be thought of in terms of its possible group implications.

Progressive growth in independence and responsibility. The most important point about the performance of this democratic supervisor as we watch him on the job month after month is the flexibility, the progressive changes, in his supervisory behavior. He does not have one set of leadership habits or tricks for keeping people at work under him. Week by week his work group grows in its ability to assume responsibility and in its desire to take initiative. Week by week he becomes progressively unnecessary as a motivator, director, and pusher of workers. The group personality has matured to the extent of taking on many of the functions of maturity—self-starting ability, internal sources of motivation, ability to get satisfaction from work progress rather than external praise and rewards, a clear sense of direction, and creative capacity for seeking new, more efficient directions. And so week by week the supervisor is able to spend less time on problems of employee morale and satisfaction and more on thinking about and trying out new work methods and ideas for improving the quality of production.

Concluding Remarks

Democratic leadership is not easy of accomplishment. It demands continuous effort and growth on the part of the supervisor. It demands psychologically secure supervisors not circumscribed in their effectiveness by their personal needs for power and status. But once this style of leadership is established in a work unit, there is stability. Many of the tensions and problems occupying most supervisors' time in the autocratic work atmosphere are eliminated. Production is not only more efficient but shows progressive improvement with time.

Certain cautions need to be noted. Every supervisor must realize that he starts from where the group is. If the group has been accustomed to rigid supervisory control, with no opportunity for initiative or responsibility, to give complete responsibility in the beginning would only result in a laissez-faire situation. In such cases responsibility must be gradually extended, with more careful encouragement and leadership given to the employees.

It is usually the wisest policy to share with the group the knowledge that efforts to develop a more democratic working relationship are being planned. Get across the idea that success will depend on the group as well as the supervisor. Discuss and plan with the work group ways in which the group members can assume more participation and responsibility.

Be prepared for suspicion, indifference to responsibility, efforts to get away with less achievement. These are natural employee reactions to previous autocratic control. They have been observed again and again as transitions take place in the type of leadership. The supervisor should be prepared for discouragement. Participation in democratic work groups is not an experience for which many of us are well prepared as yet. Democratic leadership is a long-time process, though certain gains in morale and productivity are often almost immediate results.

12

Organizational Research and Organizational Change: GM's Approach

Howard C. Carlson

PRACTICAL problem-solving and action strategies probably have never been more welcome in industry than they are today. Increasingly serious problems pose complex requirements, a seemingly endless array of new demands, and the need to deal rapidly and effectively with change in almost every industrial organization. In this action-oriented context, traditional modes of personnel research inevitably seem to fall short of producing the fundamental changes necessary for enhancing the profitability, growth, or survival of an organization or for enhancing the quality of worklife of its members.

Thus many behavioral scientists in industry have attempted to reorient their research to important issues in the context of change. Dr. Michael Beer, for example, found it useful to distinguish research action (traditional) from action research (change-oriented) in his work at Corning Glass. The model to be described here—which evolved out of an experimental change program initiated in 1969 at four General Motors plant sites—attempts to provide an organizing framework for doing research in the context of change.

From the outset, research was closely tied into the experimental change program at General Motors. For example, a careful research design guided the selection of the four plant sites that participated in the first effort. This design called for plants that had similar geographical location, labor-market and workforce composition, products, and production technology but markedly different operating performance.

Two assembly plants in Atlanta and two foundry plants in Saginaw, Michigan met these requirements. Each city provided what later became casually identified as a "good" plant and a "poor" plant in terms of operating performance, making possible the program's research objective of learning what elements of leader behavior, organizational climate, and structure accounted for the difference.

Unfortunately, however, the research design also had an unanticipated impact on the program: It actually got in the way of using the research findings effectively in bringing about change. Upon being informed of the design, one of the "good" plants found it difficult to see why it should change at all: A "poor" plant, on the other hand, found it easy to reject the very basis for its inclusion and participation in the change program. These difficulties were never completely overcome.

Other growing pains also became apparent in early attempts to couple research and the change process at General Motors. But perhaps the program's most serious mistake was neglecting to consider research as an *intervention* in itself. Since then, however, recognition of this mistake has helped to recast the traditional employee research perspective at General Motors. For example, the company no longer uses any systematic procedure for gathering research information without giving considerable thought to its impact on either the present functioning or potential modifiability of the organizational unit involved. Beyond this, research at General Motors has been given a more direct action orientation to the business of change.

Nevertheless, persisting stereotypes about research can easily operate to cloud such an orientation. They can make it difficult to find full acceptance among managers, OD consultants, trainers, and even researchers of the potential value of research as an intervention. Most of these stereotypes are already familiar: Research is academic, impractical, neverending, not tied to profits, a quest for knowledge, an elegant design, an anal-compulsive interest in precise measurement, or the technical ability perhaps to record change but certainly not to help bring it about. It might even be expected, so the stereotype goes, that some researchers have never really accepted World War II because there was no control group!

The research model that grew out of the GM experimental change program was designed to help eliminate some of these stereotypes. It attempted:

- To begin to pull together the concepts and strategies of research as an intervention, providing an organizing framework for a total research program likely to reduce internal barriers to change.
- To assist in "reaching" managers and OD specialists with a way of looking at and thinking about research as a dynamic, action-oriented process.
- More generally, to provide a guide for people who want to use research, watch research, or evaluate research in the context of change.

In each of these ways, the GM research model has proved useful. Its main drawback as a framework for research is that it is abstract; the model is concerned only with broad kinds of research strategies and their assumed relationship to change. It is free of specific "how-to" content. A research manager or specialist must specify the projects ann project mechanisms required in any real application of the model to change in an organization.

Model Design

In general appearance, the GM research model has led some people to call it a "Paper Airplane (Delta Wing, no less) Model of research strategies that will hopefully fly." However, some of its lines have been neatly drawn for effect and should not be interpreted too literally (see Figure 1). The real importance of the design is its attempt to portray research as a multifaceted process or framework of different strategies—and not as just one stereotypic approach.

At the top of the model is a problem-techniques-program dimension to the framework of research strategies. At the base is an organizational dimension. Along either dimension, strategies to the right are regarded as short range and operating closer to the cutting edge of change. Strategies to the left are regarded as long range in nature (typically six months or longer in the auto industry).

Figure 1
Breaking the Internal Change Barrier: Some Research Strategies

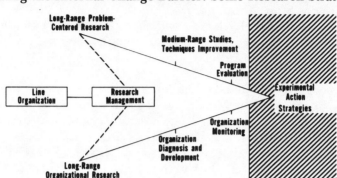

Although each strategy and its relationship to change will be described separately, the total framework must be considered in thinking about research as an intervention. Consequently, a continuous single example or case experience will be presented to illustrate each strategy that is embodied in the model. Briefly, the case involves one of GM's car divisions that had experienced a consistently increasing rate of employee absenteeism and turnover over a period of five years. In late 1969, this division decided to take some research action even though its current absolute levels of absenteeism and turnover were neither the worst nor the best being demonstrated at that time in General Motors.

Involvement of the Line Organization

An important feature of this research model is the involvement of key representatives of the line organization from the beginning and throughout all stages of the research process. This involvement should not be merely token in nature but rather should provide line representatives the chance to *influence* project design and implementation, analysis or interpretation of results, and development of recommended action steps. It also should enable line people to *get up front* in the process when it comes to related internal presentations and communication steps, implementation planning and action, and follow-up assurance of effective action.

Put simply, the basic assumption underlying this model is that only people, and not research *per se,* can bring about any needed changes in an organization. This is evident whenever reports of research findings and recommendations simply gather dust in someone's desk drawer. Researchers in the context of change can thus ill afford to sit in their offices or next to their computers designing and carrying out projects without real involvement of the line organization.

At the GM car division that will serve as an example, an absenteeism and turnover task force was formed at the start. It comprised representatives of line management, production, industrial engineering, and personnel from within the division along with representatives of GM's supporting staffs from employee research, education and training, and manufacturing development. An industrial engineer from the manufacturing development staff chaired meetings of this task force while also performing a liaison and integrative role between meetings. The task force designed a multifaceted research program, deciding to focus the total effort solely upon the engine and assembly plants to permit later comparisons of any progress with the experience of other plant operations in the car division.

Long-Range Problem-Centered Research

When a specific and narrowly defined problem or felt need is apparent to the line organization and when it also seems likely that any real solution will be complex or long range in nature, long-range problem-centered research may be applied. Some specific problems to which this kind of research can be addressed include excessive grievances, low or declining productivity, poor quality, rising absenteeism, and declining employee morale.

In adopting this research strategy, whether the problem appears symptomatic or seems more fundamental in nature is of little immediate consequence. The idea is to begin research where the organization is or where it is "hurting" and aware of this in some way. As an intervention, research should clearly *not* begin with a problem defined primarily by the researcher, with a new concept in the theoretical literature, or with an armamentarium of techniques seeking to fit and thus define their own problem.

At GM, preliminary analysis by the car division's task force suggested that the great bulk of turnover occurred during the first four weeks of employment. It also suggested that early job experiences might predispose employees who were retained longer to exhibit either high or low rates of absenteeism. The problem for research, then, was to identify critical factors in the early job experiences of new hires that contributed to turnover and led to different levels of absenteeism among employees who were retained.

An in-depth tracking study of 200 randomly selected new hires was conducted over a six-month period. Results showed, for example, that persons oriented to their new jobs as individuals (rather than as members of a group) and assigned to an above-average operator for training (rather than to one rated by the foreman as average in performance) were less likely to be absent. In addition, the results showed that foremen could predict very accurately—on the first day of a new hire's employment—whether a person would or would not be frequently absent in the future. Perhaps as a kind of self-fulfilling prophecy, foremen behaved differently (in their orientation and training assignments, for example) toward persons identified as a future problem. These and other results of the long-range research endeavor led to a number of specific changes in how new hires were treated early in their work experience with the car division.

Medium-Range Studies: Techniques Improvement

Research interventions can also begin where the line organization is impeding techniques already operating, believed to be operating, or existing largely on paper and in the minds of their authors for solving people problems. Techniques of human resource planning, recruitment, selection, orientation, training, career planning and counseling, management development, communication, and motivation are but a few of these. In other words, research can be aimed not only at changes in personnel management techniques but also at identifying factors that constrain a given technique from achieving its intended result, confronting the organization with data on such constraints to bring about needed change and integrating the technique into other organizational processes more effectively.

For example, research in the GM car division had sought improvement in the orientation and training foremen were expected to give new employees. The results pointed to many constraints upon the foreman, including one introduced by his own reward system. Any time spent by a new employee in orientation would weigh against the efficiency of a foreman's area. Upon recognizing this constraint, management was easily moved to apply no charge against an area for the first day a new hire was on the job. Foremen were thus given greater latitude to orient an employee without jeopardizing their efficiency. Additionally, special training aids were provided the foremen to ensure more consistent attention to the adjustment of all new employees to their jobs.

Program Evaluation

Any new program or technique introduced into the line organization should be systematically evaluated. Unfortunately, this step is often regarded as "something we really should do as professionals" and also a kind of academic concern or check on "something we already know intuitively or from our experience." Since neither of these points of view is very compelling, evaluation is usually neglected as an intervention in itself.

The basic intent of this strategy, however, is to provide the initiators or authors of a new program with some kind of objective feedback mechanism that will lead to real change and needed revision in the program. Furthermore, whether or not a program is evaluated is likely to have an important impact on the climate for change in an organization. The model shown in Figure 2, for example, points out some expected consequences of evaluating versus not evaluating training programs.

Figure 2
Evaluating vs. Not Evaluating Training Programs: A Model of Some Expected Effects

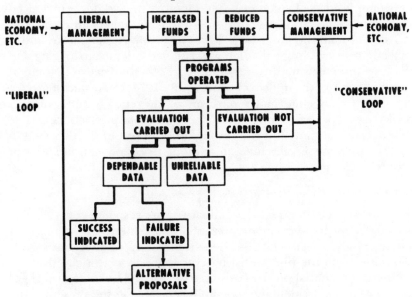

As this model shows, two things can obviously happen to training: Management can either increase funds or reduce funds during the life of a given program. These two possibilities, in turn, are related to a "liberal" loop and a "conservative" loop of management attitudes toward the use of expenditures of time or money for training. Under the same general conditions and economic climate, one or the other loop will be dominant in the thinking of managers making decisions about training.

The model shows that whenever evaluation is *not* carried out, the conservative loop is strengthened 100 percent of the time. And when evaluation is carried out but unreliable data (data not permitting us to know whether or not the training worked as intended) are used, the effect is still one of feeding into the conservative loop. On the other hand, using reasonably dependable data in carrying out an evaluation will always contribute to increasingly progressive management attitudes. When success is indicated, of course, this will happen almost by definition. But even when a failure becomes evident, alternative proposals for a revision in the training program can be expected to feed into the progressive loop. The major point of the model, then, is that evaluation affords at least some possibility of a progressive change in management climate while the lack of evaluation will always contribute to increasingly conservative attitudes among managers.

In the car division's absenteeism and turnover research program, for example, an evaluation plan developed by the task force produced at the start some knowledge of results and later an expanding interest in going beyond the program as it was originally designed. An industrial engineer within the division was assigned full time to logging and tracking absenteeism, turnover, and many other indicators that might potentially affect the indices of concern. By 1971, the results showed a demonstrable decline in absenteeism in the engine and assembly plants (8 to 9 percent drop in absenteeism without prior notice), while absenteeism continued to rise throughout the rest of the division (25 percent increase in absenteeism without prior notice) and also in another plant in the same city.

Experimental Action Strategies

This strategy emphasizes initiative or response to the line organization—helping the organization *now* rather than proposing a lengthy study or very elaborate research design. In effect, it involves "shooting from the hip" with whatever immediate action appears to have some potential on the basis of past research, experience, sheer intuition, or an accidental opportunity available in the present situation. Ideally, a member of the line organization itself will suggest trying something and perhaps put into operation a practical application of some principle of the behavioral sciences—one that might have entered the picture along with the researcher.

Any such experimental actions should probably be introduced in a limited and reasonably controlled way and not applied across the board in an organization. Efforts should then be directed toward measuring how well the strategy works and, if it does, toward diffusing it into other parts of the organization. Thus the emphasis in taking the action initially should not be entirely on getting results but also on getting experience and educating members of the line organization who can assist effectively in diffusion later.

For example, while not part of the original GM car division program design, four experimental employee task forces were established in the engine plant to put some group involvement and dynamics immediately to work on the problem of absenteeism. Each task force included a foreman and six to eight hourly employees, including a union committeeman. After two days of preparatory training for the foreman, a series of five meetings—each lasting two hours or longer and held about a week apart—was structured for each task force.

At the first meeting, the approach was introduced and task forces formed. (Although an effort was made to control the mix of groups in terms of seniority, sex, race, and individual absenteeism rates, final participation was voluntary—which, of course, limited conclusions that would later be drawn from this research.) At the second meeting, the task forces discussed how absenteeism was not only a problem to management but also a problem to the employees who did come to work. Subsequent meetings were structured around identifying causes, brainstorming possible solutions or corrective actions, and evaluating these possible solutions to arrive at specific recommendations for management.

Absenteeism at meetings of the four groups of employees was virtually nonexistent. While comparison groups of employees displayed typical rates of absenteeism, some (but not all) of the experimental groups showed reduced rates of absenteeism during a scheduled work period of five months after their task-force participation. None of the recommendations made by the task forces were rejected by management, and meetings with all employees in the departments involved were used to provide feedback on the work of the task forces and on what short- and long-range actions would be taken. Subsequently, with both management and employees enthusiastic about this approach, employee task forces were set up to deal with a wide range of other operating and employee relations problems in the car division.

Organizational Monitoring

The next strategy, organizational monitoring, really parallels and ties in with the evaluation of programs. The difference, obviously, is its focus on monitoring or tracking the status of organizational units instead of programs. Doing this effectively requires adequate measures not only at the level of results or relevant end-state variables (such as profits, cost savings, product quality, or employee morale) but also at the level of organizational processes essential to these results (such as leader behavior, decision-making and information systems, or the operational readiness of a work team).

Virtually all of the measures now widely used in industrial organizations are historic in nature. That is, they evaluate yesterday's, last month's, or last year's performance, making it difficult to see a problem until it already exists. But once the results begin to dip substantially, organizations monitoring them begin to experience internal pressures or forces for change. By developing measures of the processes behind such a dip, it should be possible to predict or project future levels of results and thus mobilize internal forces for change earlier—hopefully to get ahead of the problem.

Beginning steps have been taken to develop lead-time indicators in the case of the GM car division under discussion as well as in other GM units. It is already clear that absenteeism, turnover, and grievances can be predicted reasonably accurately on a monthly, quarterly, or even yearly basis. In addition, a well-controlled study showed that absenteeism is functionally related to in-process quality. Once defect detection and repair systems have operated, however, the relationship of absenteeism to final quality measures prior to shipment drops to zero (debunking, incidentally, the popular speculation in some quarters that cars built on a Monday or Friday are of lower quality because of higher absenteeism on those days).

Organizational Diagnosis and Development

A broad organizational diagnosis and development strategy is probably the most essential element in a viable and on-going research program. Its users in the line organization seem to become more receptive to behavioral science research in general and to the utilization of specific research findings when such an overall strategy exists.

This strategy enters the model parallel to techniques improvement. Yet while it may seem that OD is technique-oriented in its present state, any techniques being applied are usually hooked together in some sort of process that makes sense to the OD consultant and, it is hoped, to people in the line organization. To summarize the literature on the subject: We know a great deal about many different intervention techniques, something about their effects, and very little yet about the change process that we seek to tap into or accelerate through organization development.

By 1972, and even earlier than that, the GM car division was institutionalizing many of the principles and techniques developed in the course of its research. In addition, different programs seeking to re-emphasize the individual's sense of doing an important job; to provide for a regular interchange of ideas, information, and problems between hourly employees and their supervisor; and to adopt interdepartmental problem-analysis task forces utilizing hourly employees and technical resources were all beginning to take form outside the research program. At this point, the industrial engineer who chaired the absenteeism and turnover task force accepted and received intensive training for a broader role in the division as coordinator of organizational development. By now, he has a very small staff, and the car division has an expanding program of organizational development that extends to plants beyond the original engine and assembly plants.

Long-Range Organizational Research

Long-range organizational research is a far more encompassing strategy than its parallel on the problem-techniques-program dimension. Generally, this strategy attempts to focus research on problem combinations or complexes, underlying causal variables, and broad issues of sociotechnical and structural relevance to the organization. Some of the targets for this strategy might include the design of new plants, new organizational structures or forms, and organic problem-solving systems.

A Model of the Change Process

The model and outline shown in Figure 3 describe the change process as it was hypothesized by Dr. D. L. Landen, GM's director of organizational research and development. It is conceived as a naturally inherent, though in some ways, perhaps, often a slowed or blocked, process in every organization. A shorthand description of the overlapping stages (as opposed to the steps) of the model might include:

—Unfreezing (awareness, acceptance, readiness).
—Planned intervention (diagnosis and search, application).
—Refreezing (measurement, institutionalization, renewal mechanism).

Research might seek to *describe* in terms of the model techniques such as job enrichment, human resource planning, training, or team

Figure 3
Process of Organizational Development

Awareness of a disturbance, of organizational problems of growth, identity, destiny and revitalization; of human satisfaction and utilization of human resources; and of problems of organizational effectiveness.

Acceptance of the nature of organizations, of the existence of alternative modes of organizational management and of the range and depth of human and organizational potentialities.

Readiness and commitment to act, to undertake change process and provide required resources and actions beyond mere verbal support.

Diagnose problems, search solutions, to gain understanding of where the organization is, what produces disturbances, where the organization should be, and which improvement strategies are appropriate to its needs and goals.

Application of new behavior, to experimentally test new methods of operating, to modify organizational processes, and to seek congruency between organizational goals and individual needs.

Measurement of the degree of improvement, of the means by which effective change occurs and of the standards and methods by which organizations should be evaluated.

Institutionalize as an integral part of the enterprise, to incorporate into the management system the principles of human resources management and the mechanism and strategies of organizational development.

Renewal mechanism, to introduce a means of activating steps to renew awareness of problems, of recycling the entire organizational development process as the principal means by which organizations carry out day-to-day operations, and of incorporating relevant values and practices into the management system to ensure the continuity of the enterprise.

building to determine which elements of the hypothesized change process are well covered and which elements are not. Given knowledge of a technique's descriptive status in terms of the model, relating this status to results obtained with the technique might—over many such comparisons—establish the utility of the model. Improvement in the techniques themselves could also result from this process.

Implications of the Model

While other models are imbedded within the overall model that has been proposed here as a framework of research strategies, it is the overall model that carries implications for a total research program. This model should lead us to organize research and select projects in terms of all of the elements described. In these times, long-range research will simply not survive without action strategies operating in the short range and up front on current issues relevant to the organization. On the other hand, "shooting from the hip" is not likely to survive very long either without some more fundamental and long-range research coming along behind it.

From the model, it is also clear that research may fall into disuse and perhaps atrophy without real involvement of the line organization. And finally, it seems clear that coupling organizational development into the program will help research acquire a more dynamic and integrated posture with respect to both the theoretical and real world.

PART III

Defining
the Function

MANY ideas offered each day as new, problem-solving insights are really old wine in new bottles. A review of past issues of *Personnel* tends to confirm this because it reveals that in decades past many able human resources specialists foresaw the positioning and functioning of human resources management that modern-day proponents are recommending. In this context, then, as in most others, a study of history provides perspective—and informs judgment.

If we go back to 1933, for example, we find an article authored by W. J. Donald, at the time a partner of James O. McKinsey and Company, that identifies organization planning, clarification of the staff role of executive personnel management, the use standards of performance as the basis for appraisals of executive performance, and the development and use of incentive compensation programs tied to organizational objectives as the major tasks of personnel management. Interestingly, his article, "Effective Executive Personnel Organization," posits that *executive* personnel organization and management is the area in which this new specialty can make its major contribution to organizational performance—a modern concept indeed.

Paul Pigors changed the focus of the function somewhat in his 1947 article, "The Challenge for Personnel Administration." Written when he was an associate professor of industrial relations at Massachusetts Institute of Technology, this article forcefully represents that human resources management is what line supervisors do, not what is done in the personnel office. Pigors's rationale is clear: The effectiveness of a human resources activity is measured by its effects on the efficiency and effectiveness of the organization's employees and no staff activity can possibly have the same cumulative effects on these measures as the day-to-day behavior of the organization's supervisors. Who is right, Donald, with his emphasis on executive-level personnel, or Pigors, who focuses on first-level supervisors? The obvious answer: both, then and now.

Why single out executives and supervisors, though? Isn't sound human resources management the responsibility of all managers. James C. Worthy said yes in 1948 in "Changing Concepts of the Personnel Function," but he said yes in a special way. Undoubtedly influenced by his work in the personnel department of Sears, Roebuck and Company, Worthy advised that in carrying out its staff role, the human resources function should avoid developing elaborate systems for conducting the human resources business of the organization because operating managers, the *real* human resources managers of the enterprise would flee in horror from involvement with such complex processes. His message was twofold: All managers manage human resources, and to help them do it well, keep your systems simple. Who can disagree?

It is now 1953 and Ewing W. Reilley, a partner in McKinsey & Company, has taken the human resources function back into the executive suite, this time at the right hand of the president. In "Bringing Personnel Administration Closer to the President" Reilley listed three major questions a human resources department should ask:

1. What can we do to improve the ability of our present executives?

2. How can we motivate and reward our management people to give them the greatest incentive for promoting the long-range profitability of the company?

3. How can we do a better job of selecting individuals with high potential and developing them for greater responsibility?

These are still good questions for a human resources executive to ask.

As human resources management has grown in stature, it has attracted stronger and stronger executives. Given their ability, it is often difficult for these executives to accept their staff role. But staff role they have, as Louis A. Allen pointed out in his 1956 article, "Personnel Staff and the Line Organization." Written when he was manager of organization planning for Booz, Allen & Hamilton, Allen's article emphasizes that the role and responsibility of the personnel department is to provide advice and service to the line organization, not to do the line organization's human resources management job. Amen.

At one time Charles A. Myers was considered the dean of human resources management specialists. In 1964, when he was a professor of industrial relations and director of the Industrial Relations Section at Massachusetts Institute of Technology, he wrote "New Frontiers for Personnel Management." His message in this article was clear, and is still relevant: In the context of a changed labor force, the new information technology, a better educated workforce, the need to move faster to integrate minority-group members into the workforce, and increases in government regulation, human resources managers must now and will increasingly in the future need to concern themselves with the external environment. The forecast of 1964 has become the fact of 1979. Here again—the past is prologue.

13

November 1933

Effective Executive Personnel Organization

W. J. Donald

NEARLY every management problem resolves itself finally into a question of securing or developing and of properly organizing the executive personnel of a corporation—in other words into a balanced executive personnel program.

It is not enough that a corporation shall have good executive personnel—it is also essential that the executive personnel shall be well organized and that they shall, at least subconsciously, understand the principles of organization that are in effect.

The importance of effective personnel organization lies in two major elements:

1. The external pressure to which every business corporation is now subjected.

2. The importance of the conservation of executive energy and the requirement that the energy of every executive in a company shall be fully released to accomplish the utmost.

External Pressure

Probably never before has management been subjected to such overwhelming and uncontrollable external factors. Even before the end of the first year of the depression, Europe, which had envied our much heralded modern management, began to take the position that American management had not succeeded in saving the day. As an appraisal of American management as a whole, the attitude of European business was correct. Even the best of our executives, while capable of swimming against the tide, could not maintain the profit position held in the boom period.

It would be useless to claim that management can ignore external economic and industrial trends. On the contrary, the best of management will anticipate those trends and muster every ounce of energy, every element of sound organization, every sound policy for the business, and every economical procedure in order to establish and maintain a high position in its field of endeavor and to seize upon adversity as an opportunity to advance its relative position.

Those from abroad who undertake to appraise American management would do well to draw a clear line of differentiation between the effect of economic conditions external to an individual corporation, and the quality of executive personnel and executive organization that affects directly the position of an individual corporation in its chosen field.

The major elements in external pressure on a business are general economic conditions and competitive conditions in an industry.

Gradually we are coming to realize that American management has been faced with general economic conditions that none of the present generation of corporation executives have ever faced before. Among these conditions is the fact that for three years we were in the midst of a long downward trend in the general price level. This we accept very reluctantly. Manufacturers individually, trade association groups, individuals as home owners and as security owners, sales executives, production managers, financiers, all alike, very slowly, if at all, accept the idea that property values are going through a process of decline, at first precipitous and later gradual. The home owner hangs on to his property, in which three years ago he had only a small equity, in the belief that values of 1926 to 1929 will return and that his investment in an equity will be recovered. Security holders fondly hope that losses will be recovered, and to do so cover their declining values by purchasing issues at fractional prices, anticipating that a relatively small gross advance per unit on many units will wipe out previous large losses on a small number of units. Manufacturing executives maintain manufacturing capacity and postpone contracting the organization, all largely on the assumption that old prices *must* return, and usually they assume that these price levels must return *soon*.

It is quite usual to forget that for 25 to 30 years the consumer declared that prices could not move higher; that there must be a change downward in the cost of living.

Over and over again one listens to discussions of management policies, especially pricing policies, in which the basic assumption is that the price levels of 1926 to 1929 surely will return in the course of the next few months or a year or two at the most, in terms of our former standard of value. What we seem to forget is that the general price level is determined not by costs but by what the public can pay in terms of the unit of value. We seem to forget entirely that there are forces external to management that have a significance as inevitable as death and taxes; that the general price level is beyond the control of management and that the general price level has its ultimate bearing on the price level of particular commodity groups.

What has been going on during the first three years of the depression has been not merely a decline, which was at first rapid and then gradual, in the general price level, but also, and far more important, a rapid and growing deviation of the prive levels of different commodity groups from the general price level. If all prices had come down together, and equally, it would have been possible to have a declining price level without a contraction in either physical volume of production of goods and services or a decline in employment, but a precipitous decline in the general price level as affected by gold and the credit structure built on gold has always resulted in wide deviation of the prices of some commodity groups from the general price level. The price paid for previously borrowed capital remained static. The price of governmental services rose. The obligations involved in rentals and other contractual agreements were only slowly revised. In other words, some prices actually advanced, others remained static, some declined very little. In contrast, the prices of some commodity groups or of some services declined much more rapidly than the general price level. In fact to the extent that some prices were not reduced along with the general price level, the price reduction of other commodity groups became exaggerated.

In such a situation exchange relationships between different commodity groups previously fairly well established and accepted are thrown completely out of balance. The inevitable result is a contraction of physical volume of production of goods and services and a contraction in employment, and consequently a contraction in consumer purchasing power. It is true that the process of the exchange of goods has broken down very largely during the last three years.

Under such conditions, the management of an entire industry or of all the units in that industry is faced with external pressure over which it has little or no control. If there ever was a time when corporations required the most in adaptable, courageous, and realistic management organization it is in such a period as that through which we have been going—the end of which has not yet been reached.

The contraction in physical volume of production, goods, and services that follows the unbalancing of price ratios inevitably leads to excessive productive capacity compared with consumer purchasing power. As a consequence, competitive conditions within an industry become an abnormal challenge to the executives of an individual corporation. It has become customary to assume that all industry is grossly overbuilt, that the major problem is one of controlling production, of keeping it within the bounds of demand. Undoubtedly, many industries are overbuilt. This is true of certain types of recessive industries, the products of which are no longer in such demand as formerly, even in terms of the number of physical units.

In some industries the rapid development of capacity abroad and of textile manufacturing in India and China, has brought domestic capacity in America or in Great Britain into a state of relative chaos. The establishment of tariff barriers, rapid expansion of domestic industry within new European national boundaries has adversely affected more than one American industry that ten years ago counted on a certain proportion of exports.

Certainly there is excess capacity in particular American industries. In such situations competitive conditions in an industry are quite beyond the control of the individual management and call for all the ingenuity and cohesiveness of the management organization of an individual corporation.

Conservation and Release of Energy

Under the most favorable conditions, profitable business requires the utmost of business executives, and the utmost requires not only the full release of the best capacities of every executive but also the conservation of those energies in order to best accomplish objectives.

To date we have regarded executive organization as something God-given, beyond the possibility of learning or acquiring. We formerly thought this way about salesmanship, an attitude acquired and strengthened during a 25 year period of rising prices and a seller's market. During the last decade we have accepted the idea that selling ability is a matter not only of native ability but also of training; but the very executives who insisted on the importance of training for salesmen or of training for rank and file employees, generally took it for granted that the ability to select and organize executives belonged in the realm of genius. They also assumed quite naturally that to have arrived at some point of executive responsibility was evidence of destiny and beyond the influence of intelligent analysis.

The cumulative results of three years' depression have gradually brought us face to face with the fact that there is nothing permanent or predestined about executive organization or executive ability. Too many reputations have been strewn to the side of the road to warrant any such attitude. Too much adaptability to new conditions, ingenuity to contrive new policies and new procedures, is required in these times to warrant a sense of security in any executive or in any executive organization. The more violent the character of an industry, the more apparent this becomes. In fact, where extraordinary profits seemed evidence of genius a few years ago, violent reduction in gross and net earnings, receivership, and bankruptcy today demonstrate that genius is close kin to insanity.

If there ever was a time for the release of every potential of imagination, vigorous effort, or intelligent analysis, or for the conservation of the use of every executive talent, this is the time when we discover the possibilities. The shrinking in the numbers of executive personnel in individual corporations, while executive problems multiply, demand not only the release of all capacities but their conservation and direction into channels of major use.

The day of complacency of executive organizations is or ought to be over. No longer is anything certain about the economic or business outlook or about the future of an individual corporation or the future of an individual executive. Only ability and merit ensure an executive future for anyone or for any executive organization. There are still some serious dangers characteristic of many organizations and present to a lesser degree in some large organizations.

Inbreeding

The first of these probably is the amount of inbreeding among the executive forces of organizations. Sometimes even among our most reputable and apparently best managed companies one finds a degree of group and individual self-satisfaction that was all very well during a period of rising or stable prices, but all wrong for the decade that lies ahead. Bigness alone is taken by many as evidence of competence when often it is nothing more than protection from easy and quick discovery of incompetence. Promotion by seniority, in fact if not in theory, shields upper and senior executives from effective challenge. In many organizations only a business earthquake will modify policies or procedures in less than 20 years. Pride in policies a decade or 20 years old can be discovered in any city. Such pride ought to be *prima facie* evidence that policies need revision.

Glibly, we comment on patriarchal and hereditary characteristics of executive organizations abroad, particularly in Great Britain. To be sure it is harder to detect in America, but look over corporations of all sizes and one will find appointments of relatives, of persons with "right social connections," of former bank executives who for some reason had to be dislodged and were easily dumped on an industrial creditor.

In companies large and small one will find individuals clinging to executive positions because others in the next rung of executive responsibility find it difficult to dislodge what was at first a business associate but has now become part of the business "family." How often, too, one finds subordinate executives who know and confidentially admit the truth, but have not the courage or the ability to make a superior face the truth. It may be high time to go on a man hunt for nepotism and to throw promotion by seniority overboard.

Security

A second prevalent danger is the sense of security that prevails in many organizations. This is especially true of large corporations. Almost every businessman can think of those who must keep their mental dynamos working at full force to prevent themselves from sinking back into a sense of security that is not good for them, their jobs, or for their companies. Often there is a hesitancy to do things that are new or challenging—almost everywhere one finds men who, knowing the evil that lies in the existing policies and procedures of an organization, hesitate before undertaking the uncertainty that may lie in a change of policies or procedures.

I have in mind, for instance, a man of great capacity who has deliberately followed the policy of not making himself too conspicuous at this time in an organization that has long been wed to tradition.

A man of corresponding capacity in the same organization made himself too much of a thorn in the side of those who were responsible for the "damning total." The more aggressive and correspondingly intelligent of the two is no longer part of the organization. The equally able but deliberately less conspicuous executive is still there quietly modifying the organization but carefully protecting his security. It remains to be seen which of the two will accomplish the most in the long run.

There is another type of security that is likely to come on many of us in the course of the next five years, namely, security that will be induced by a sense of gradually improving conditions. It is almost inevitable that when an up-turn comes there will be a great temptation after this period of strenuous exacting effort to lean back on our oars with the feeling that security has once more returned. The most we should hope for is an opportunity to view business problems under more favorable conditions with more perspective and more temperately. But not within a decade except possibly for short periods shall we be relieved of strenuous competition and never again probably shall we find conditions changing as slowly as in the past. The only safe position for the executive organization of a company or for the individual to take is that the *tempo* of business in the future will exact more from us than ever before.

Reliance on Cooperation

A third danger lies in a very prevalent attitude that a spirit of cooperation within an organization is more important than, or a substitute for, scientific executive organization. This is often a protective coloring for failure to define executive responsibilities and to hold executives definitely responsible. It provides a cloak for considerable alibiing for inadequate results or for lack of courage to deal with executive appointments and assignments of responsibility and for failure to make them understood. It is a counterpart of the idea that capacity for organization finds its origin in executive genius. It is a natural corollary of our general failures to think rightly and act in terms of organization principles or to admit that organization theory is or can be a body of scientific knowledge. It recognizes by implication that something is wrong or lacking in executive organization, but contributes nothing to its advancement. In fact, the less we talk about cooperation in business management and executive organization, the more likely we are to attack the problem of organization at its roots.

Reliance on Good Personnel

A fourth danger is an often expressed assumption that given good executives, good results will be obtained. Usually it is assumed that the selection and training of a good personnel are the elements that constitute a valuable organization.

It is weak thinking that assumes that good personnel are more important than good organization. Such thinking dodges the major issue. Good executive personnel *properly organized* ought to be the objective of every major executive. The results obtainable from the selection and training of good personnel are only one-half the results that should be obtained. Nothing short of a sound organization of well-selected and well-trained personnel should be the objective of any company.

Policies—The Prerequisite of Effective Organization

The building of an executive organization properly presumes a prior determination of objectives in terms of business policies. There has been some discussion of executive organizations in terms of theoretical standards, but it makes considerable difference what the objectives of an organization are. After all, an organization is constructed to accomplish some definite purpose and the policies adopted to accomplish that purpose have an important bearing on what organization is required to reach the objective.

For instance, a marketing policy of being a style leader, of seeking customers who will purchase well-styled products at a price for style goods sold direct to the dealer, will have an important bearing on the organization relationships of production and marketing executives and on the type of marketing organization required.

Production policies of manufacturing all parts, of owning sources of raw materials and preparing raw materials for manufacture or the production policy of manufacturing to demand, rather than manufacturing in advance and storing, will all have an important bearing on the necessary executive personnel organization for production.

Obviously, a policy of purchasing raw materials and parts or a policy of speculating in raw materials will influence in an important manner the executive organization for purchasing functions and the relation of the purchasing personnel to marketing, production, and financial executives.

Whether a corporation sells direct to dealers or through wholesalers, whether it finances its operations entirely by issue of securities or partly through commerical loans, whether it has a far-flung sales organization with branch office personnel and local bank accounts, whether it has branch factories, or one large manufacturing unit, will have an important bearing on the extent and quality of its financial executive personnel. Whether a corporation follows the policy of promotion from within or whether it welcomes new blood from without, whether it believes in retiring executives in the middle sixties, or in retaining them indefinitely, whether it believes in retaining men to the pension age, irrespective of merit, or in dismissing them with or without a dismissal allowance, will have an important bearing not only on the executive personnel department organization, but also on the whole organization structure and the spirit of the executive personnel.

Analysis of Jobs

Assuming that we recognize the importance of effective executive organization, the dangers that lurk in this relatively undeveloped field of management theory and the significance of the objectives of organization as expressed in management policies, we come necessarily face to face with the problem of analysis of executive jobs. The term "job analysis" used freely and loosely throughout the last 15 years has to do essentially with a process rather than with a result. The essential elements of executive job analysis are:

1. Job description
2. Definition of job requirements
3. Job classification
4. Job evaluation

Job Description—What Is To Be Done

In the realm of executive jobs what one most commonly discovers is an illogical, almost inexplainable assortment of activities collected by or assigned to different executives. The first reason for this state of affairs is that it is usually the nature of an executive to have an acquisitive attitude toward responsibilities and authority. Executives often are where they are because they like power. The higher up one goes in a corporation the more this is true. The second reason is that, by and large, major executives have not been offered theories by management or have not thought out for themselves any basis for determining to whom in the corporation particular activities ought to be assigned. A third reason is that it is a common attitude for executives to feel that one ought to be ready to do whatever falls at hand to be done. This is an attitude in which the spirit is good but the intelligence weak.

What most corporations need in effective personnel organization is a complete description of *all* of the activities of each executive—the particular things that are done week by week and day by day, and for that matter hour by hour. The importance of this description of jobs lies partly in the discovery of all of the responsibilities and activities, all the duties that have to be performed within the organization, and partly in the inevitable discovery of the illogical assignment or acquisition of activities of many varieties by different executives—often overlapping, often conflicting.

Job Requirements and Job Classification

The next step in the process of analyzing jobs is the determination of requirements for different types of activity. At this point we refrain from undertaking to define the requirements for positions. Considering the variety of activities of different types of executives, one must admit that it would be almost impossible to find in any one man all of the capacities usually required for performing all of the functions that have become attached to him.

Definition of the requirements for particular activities, however, is comparatively simple. These requirements include types of knowledge, analytical ability, the extent to which counselling with others, and so on are required. On the basis of the requirements of individual activities, it becomes relatively simple to determine what kinds of activities naturally group together.

Considerable thinking is yet to be done in the definition of job requirements and the classification of activities under different major executives. Gradually we are beginning to recognize that analytical ability is to some extent required of all executives. It is not the prerogative of the comptroller, of the personnel man, of the statistician, or the economist alone. The ability to make decisions is, of course, essential in all major operating executives and to some extent among staff men. There is, however a great difference between a major executive making an operating decision on his own responsibility with the advice and counsel of the comptroller or other staff executive, and the making of decisions for operating executives by staff men who are not responsible for results. Gradually we are coming to recognize that the important ability in many positions in carrying out many duties is the ability to help determine policies *along with others,* to share knowledge, opinions and facts with them, and even at times to refuse to assume a share of responsibility for operating decisions for which others must be responsible.

The ability to put decisions into effect is clearly different from the ability to make decisions or to determine policies. Frequently we find men capable of determining what ought to be done but utterly incapable of carrying it through to completion.

The ability to "command" needs some differentiation from a common interpretation of the word "authority," which too often conveys the concept of abuse. The ability to persuade, to give counsel, is a requirement that large-scale organization, in particular, demands increasingly from all executives. The production or financial executive must counsel with marketing executives, but subject to proper coordination from above, and appeal to the general management. Counsel does not mean usurping the responsibility for decision in the province of another individual executive.

Job Evaluation

The next major step in the process of analyzing jobs is to determine what a position representing a classification of jobs is worth. In the executive field this is an almost completely neglected aspect of job analysis. Standards for appraisal by comparison with similar positions in other companies are scarce. Every effort I know to determine the value of an executive position has stumbled over the impracticability of comparing jobs and positions in different companies even in the same industry. To be sure, they do afford some broad comparisons, but none of very practical use, fortunately or unfortunately, depending on the point of use. A much more profitable approach lies in the candid appraisal of the relative importance of different positions in different levels of executive responsibility. To be sure, such an attack on the problem is almost certain to disclose some wide variations from what ought to be, and occasion some embarrassing moments, but does result in profitable, because fair, adjustments. For the individual business some standard of judging the worth of individual positions can be found, and must be found if the release of executive effort is to be achieved.

Definition of Responsibilities

In the process of organizing executive personnel usually too much is taken for granted. Definitions of responsibility and lines of authority are under the most favorable circumstances subject to some degree of interpretation. Written statements of responsibility and lines of authority at best leave room for misunderstanding and for varieties of meaning. The lack of written statements almost inevitably results in confusion, overlapping, and a degree of pulling and hauling that creates disorganization and doubt in the minds of subordinate executives as to the location of superior responsibility.

There are a number of prevalent reasons as to why a statement of responsibility need not be prepared. It is assumed by many that they are established, that they are understood, and that there is no overlapping. By others, a certain degree of overlapping and duplication is defended on the ground that the executives ought to be able to "double" for each other. In actual practice they often do double, but usually in a conflicting manner—the job is done twice, but differently. Misunderstandings arise regarding the border line of responsibilities. The lack of written statements leaves room for the assumption of authority and responsibilities of others, or for dodging responsibilities that ought to be assumed on the supposition that someone else has assumed them.

Evidence of the value of written statements of responsibility and lines of authority can be gained in the attempt of any company to set down in written form the responsibilities of various executives. How heavy the lines of demarcation are, how much misunderstanding there is, and how much overlapping will almost inevitably appear. In addition, some functions will seem to have ño particular home within the organization and, consequently, will be largely neglected. This is particularly true of some of the activities that have been added to the management process in recent years.

But it is not enough to have a written statement of responsibilities. It is equally important that they should be understood, that they should be explained and that they should be practiced. Any written statement of responsibility and lines of authority will need interpretation, especially in the period immediately after their preparation. The English language leaves a good deal to be desired. The understanding of the English language leaves even more to be desired. Different individuals are inclined to read into what is written what they wish to understand, and in that respect the definition of responsibilities, like the law, needs adjudication. With explanations, adjustments, and interpretations will ultimately come a degree of understanding that naturally makes for smooth functioning.

Ultimately the full benefits of a clear-cut definition of responsibilities will come only through practice. There is no training except through the establishment of new habits of action and it is only through practice that new habits of action are formed.

The full benefits of the proper analysis of jobs and classification of activities into a written statement of executives' responsibilities come not only through written statements properly explained and interpreted but also in their practice.

Understandable Relationships

It should be apparent that an executive organization cannot consist of a number of major sections living unto themselves and communicating with each other only through the general manager. The production program is vitally affected by the marketing program and to be successful must be supported by the economical and well-organized production of products that meet a standard at a price.

Financial management can be wrecked on the altar of rapid expansion of sales, or on the failure to control manufacturing inventory, or again inadequate financial management can cripple the sales program, and so handicap production and increase costs of manufacture.

This interrelationship between the major operating functions of a business is quite different from the relationships between an executive and his subordinates. In a properly organized company the head of a major department, like manufacturing, is responsible for decisions affecting his own operations, but in making his decisions he must take into consideration the point of view, the needs of, and the limitations imposed upon him by finance and marketing. This fact, too frequently ignored, brings into being a relationship between these major executives that is somewhat similar to the relationship between a facilitating department such as the budget bureau, comptroller's office, or personnel department and any operating organization. The production department has something of an advisory, consulting relationship to the marketing department and the financial department. No one of the major operating divisions of a company controls the other but each inevitably serves the other. Only through the general management does one division exercise control over another and the exercise of that control in the sense of command is a responsibility of the general manager rather than of coordinate department heads.

Thus it is that current business requires of its major operating executives not only that they shall be able to make decisions and exercise the function of command within their own departments— that is, that they should be operating executives within their respective fields—but also that they should have the capacity for assuming an advisory and something of a consulting relationship to their confreres in other major operating departments. It is at this point that the greatest weakness in business executives often appears; namely, an inclination to make decisions for others in fields to which their operating responsibility does not extend.

The most complicated and misunderstood relationships in business arᵥ the relationships between operating executives and those specialists ın business who have been added in the last few decades, in the course of the expansion of the analysis of business activities. I refer especially to those executives who have come into being by reason of the introduction of budgeting, modern personnel administration, and merchandizing in its newer and more accurate sense. These functions have frequently been referred to in terms of functional control.

The term *function* is generic. In the whole of management terminology there is probably no other term so badly abused, misused, and misunderstood. It applies to the activities and the responsibilities of every type of executive—to the general manager, the works manager, the treasurer, and the sales manager quite as much as to the comptroller or manager of the personnel department. All perform functions in the generic sense of that term.

Likewise the term control is a generic term but its use has been even more abused than the use of the term function. To some it means command or the right to exercise command; to some it means the right to disapprove the decisions or actions of a coordinate executive; to others it means the influence brought to bear on decisions of operating executives by the staff men through the analysis and interpretation of the results of decisions. Even within the same company these several various interpretations of the relationship between staff executives and operating executives exist. Some operating executives have one interpretation of the function of staff executives, others have a different interpretation. The understanding of the functions of the budget department or of the comptroller's office may, in turn, be quite different from the understanding of the relationship between the personnel department and the operating department. Much depends upon the attitude that the staff executive takes toward operating departments and on his interpretation of his relationship to operating departments.

What is needed in most organizations is the acceptance of two main principles:

1. That an operating executive should make his decisions and

assume full responsibility for them and for their execution, subject only to his superior, but with the advice and counsel of staff executives.

2. That the staff executives such as the budget director, the comptroller, the manager of the personnel department, and so on, do not have any responsibility for command in operating departments, and that there is a facilitating relationship between staff and operating departments in the sense that staff men help establish standards of operation by which operating executives may more easily arrive at decisions and by which they may be judged more fairly by the general management. It is not the function of staff executives to control in the sense that they may make operating decisions for the operating executives. If the operating executives make decisions that are contrary to the evidence presented by the staff executive, or if they fail to execute decisions made in such a way as to maintain standards that are adopted, the responsibility for control in the sense of command belongs to the general manager and not the staff executives.

Of all the violations of sound organization principles, the failure to observe this latter principle has been the most frequent in management organization. Personnel management went through its violent stages of bad handling in this respect with subsequent deflation of "authority" and ultimate rise in effectiveness. Budget directors and comptrollers went through a similar period a few years later. Some of them have not yet emerged from the stage of thinking in which they accept the functions of command of the general manager. Until they do they will not serve the operating executives as effectively as they should.

Decentralization of Responsibilities

With the growth in size of corporate operations, especially in those organizations brought about through mergers, which have several plants and branch offices, it has become impracticable for operating executives, including the general manager, to form adequate judgment regarding the efficiency of the conduct of the business through personal contacts alone. Many organizations suffer from the habit of extreme centralization of the control of operations. There is an endless debate regarding the respective merits of large-scale organization, medium-size organization, and the small type of organization; this debate revolves around the question as to whether or not it is possible to maintain the advantages of small-scale operations while gaining the advantages of large-scale operations. The problem exists even in relatively small organizations although, of course, on a smaller scale.

The most successful efforts to reconcile these advantages and disadvantages lie in the direction of the breaking down of operating units through decentralization in such a way as to make individual executives down the line in the organization responsible for an operating unit of a size similar to that in which the chief advantages of small-scale operation appear, providing these decentralized units are given facilities that afford knowledge commensurate with that of the personal knowledge of the manager in the small company.

In the sales organization this means the establishment of branch offices covering territories of appropriate size, embracing a sales force that is within the capacity of a manager to supervise. It also means that the branch office manager should have authority and responsibility that make his job insofar as possible correspond to the operation of an independent business. His compensation should correspond to the compensation he would receive for success in operating an independent business.

In a manufacturing organization this means breaking down into branch plants and operating units within the plants, each supervisor in the organization being responsible for a unit within the capacity of supervision of one man.

With decentralization into what, so far as possible, amounts to subordinate business units there should come a considerable degree of latitude for experimentation and encouragement of consultation upward from the bottom and inward from the territories. It means that a program of standardizing operations of branch offices or factories, which puts a blanket on all independence of thought in the units, is almost certain to be the death of progress and destruction of that development of executive material without which men will not be adequately available for promotion.

From decentralization of responsibilities should come constantly improving standards of operation that may be seized upon here or there for adoption or modification for the whole organization. Experience and responsibility are great teachers. Taking orders does not of itself produce executive material except by using the proper kind of advice and help without abdicating responsibility. Decentralization produces executive ability and produces it more effectively in most cases than if top management superimposed standard practice in all details.

Any small-scale business management is usually accountable only to itself or, at most, only to one's superior level, but it usually requires of one man more ability than it is fair to expect of any man. In a small manufacturing organization, the president, usually owner, is in effect not only president and general manager but also treasurer, works manager, sales manager, and accountant. In a medium-sized business he acquires a general sales manager, production executive, treasurer and accountant. Often, however, the standards of effectiveness are a matter of guesswork and of opinion, and in consequence injustice of appraisal and uncertainty result, but lack of established standards for appraisal of results is particularly compensated for by personal contacts.

The more an organization grows in size and the more the principle of decentralized responsibilities is established the more difficult it becomes for a major executive to appraise the quality of the management of decentralized units. The solution of this problem lies in setting up standards of operating efficiency and modifying them as external business conditions, technological factors, and the efficiency of the organization change.

There are, of course, a great variety of operating standards that may be used as a basis for judgment of the quality of operating units in different corners of the business. Some of these are: sales quotas for territories by lines of product, personnel standards for jobs to be filled, minimum credit ratings, standard manufacturing costs, and so on. All of these standards assembled lead naturally to budgets, which when properly prepared and adopted provide the most satisfactory means of appraisal of the execution of policies by those responsible for operating various units of activity.

Staff or Facilitating Departments

It is in the preparation and adoption of standards that the use of staff executives has increased. Left to themselves with the constant pressure of operating responsibilities, operating executives would find altogether too little time for establishing standards of efficiency. Indeed they might be tempted to feel that the possibility of higher standards could not be detected. While no staff organization should be established as a system of espionage, on the contrary staff organizations should be established with the point of view that the operating organization will gladly use it to devise new methods, to establish better standards, to analyze and interpret results, and to help make comparisons and, consequently, improvements.

In this sense all staff departments perform a facilitating function rather than a control function, at least in the sense of command. The process of setting up standards and of getting operating executives to use these standards effectively are both essentially an educational and training process. If the standards of efficiency and standard methods are developed in an atmosphere of cooperative effort, the constant setting-up and revision of standards is of itself an educational process.

The trouble with staff departments in the last two decades in too many cases has been that they perform a command function rather than an executive educational and training function. As such they have received far less cooperation from the operating organization than they might, and the operating organization made less use of their services than they would otherwise have done. This is probably the most difficult relationship in modern business organization—the one least thought out and the one in which greatest mistakes have been made by corporations as a whole and by staff executives individually.

No permanent progress will be made without full recognition that operating executives are fully responsible for their decisions and that staff executives are responsible only for analysis, interpretation, service, comparison, and training, and that they will produce new standards and new levels of results only through the medium of the operating organization.

In the last 20 years the management movement has placed considerable emphasis on methods and procedures. To some these have become almost an end in themselves. In many a corporation some methods have scarcely been reviewed in a decade. Frequently one gains the impression that there is no adequate conception of their purpose, that in the minds of the management they have a meaning more important than the results.

Standard practices ought to be viewed essentially as a means of relieving executives from infinite attention to detail so that they can concentrate attention on variables that constantly appear in business experience that call for modifications to be made in policy, standards, and methods.

Lack of methods and procedures in many companies accounts in large degree for the fact that there are no consciously recognized policies. The executives never get beyond consideration of individual cases. It is only when variations are viewed in relation to standards that new policies, new standards, and new methods are developed as promptly as they are required.

When we put methods and procedures in their proper place as tools to relieve staff management of consideration of all details and permit them to consider variations, there is possible a full release of executive capacity for concentration on problems that changing conditions always create. When we view methods and procedures in these terms as tools for conservation and release of managerial effort, then methods and procedures serve their true function.

Executive Compensation

The advantages of sound executive organization combined with decentralization of responsibilities and with facilitating service that help to establish standards to which are added methods and procedures that permit executives to devote themselves to major problems rather than details, however, will fall far short of the best results unless executives are compensated in such fashion as to place a premium not only on individual effort but also on coordination between departments and cooperation between operating executives, department heads, and staff or facilitating departments. The unfairness of the compensation of executives, even though unintentional, can destroy a large part of all the values that may be created through adopting other sound organization principles.

There are two principal methods of providing fair executive compensation. The first is salary revisions based on a determination of the value of the position, combined with a comparison with problems against a standard. The second is the provision of extra incentives that are dependent upon variations from standards.

It ought not to be assumed that straight salaries cannot involve the principle of incentive. They do, provided salaries are intelligently and fairly revised, taking into consideration standards adopted and results obtained and provided lines of responsibility are so drawn as to permit location of responsibility, and therefore determination of the contribution of the individual or the group. Too frequently salaries are raised or lowered automatically and many salary plans of compensation for executives exist in lieu of extra incentive plans because the management has never adequately tackled the problem of establishing standards with the help of which fair adjustments could be made.

In many cases we have developed standards for judging the effectiveness of minor executives but top management dodges the responsibility of establishing standards against which they may themselves be judged.

The turn is very definitely towards extra incentives for managerial employees. Compared with less than 100 applications a few years ago, there are several hundred in existence today. Some of them have been temporarily nullified by conditions over which business has little or no control. In a period of recovery it may be expected that the principle of extra incentive will expand by leaps and bounds. Many plans will be unscientific, unfair to the executives, and unfair to the company. Many of them will be vastly worse than a straight salary plan. Without clear-cut lines of responsibility properly established, they may be more damaging than helpful. Frankly it is not easy to establish an extra incentive plan without the most careful planning, the most careful establishment of standards of operating efficiency, and consideration of the factors over which the individual executive has control.

It is essential, however, that in a period of recovery, we shall not forget the problem of overhead in the form of executive compensation, and that we shall do our best to solve the problem by making the compensation of executives variable. The danger lies in magnifying what appears to be the best financial interests of the company and fair compensation to the individual or the group and thus losing for the company some of the greatest values that may lie in executive intelligence and growth, as well as the release and conservation of executive ability.

Summary and Conclusion

Sound organization principles and their application to the individual company are the essence of a balanced executive personnel program. No amount of detailed personnel procedures, however scientific, can make up for the defects of organization structure or poor organization relationships. The losses that accrue from improper executive organization probably exceed by far the losses and wastes that are easily visible. Lack of organization destroys the results of the most perfect selection of executive material and makes formal executive training a waste of effort.

The essentials of effective executive organization include the following:

1. Determination of the objectives of a business in terms of policies.
2. Description of the activities required to accomplish objectives.
3. Determination of the main requirements to perform these activities.
4. Logical classification of activities into executive positions.
5. Clear-cut definition of responsibilities and authorities attached to positions.
6. Establishment of understandable relationships understood and practiced.
7. Decentralization of responsibilities.

8. Establishment of standards for appraising executive effectiveness.
9. Provision of staff or facilitating services to help establish standards and make comparisons and, in the process, to develop executive material.
10. Establishment of procedures that relieve executives of detail and permit adequate attention to variables by reason of which new policies and new standards are established and executive changes made.
11. Compensation of executives on the basis of results either through equitable and prompt salary adjustments or through extra incentives.

Symptoms of poor organization are:

1. Lack of recognized policies, particularly written.
2. Lack of written statements of executive responsibilities accompanied by talk about "cooperation" and about executives being able to "double" for each other.
3. Cross currents of authority over the same activity.
4. Extreme centralization of initiative.
5. Lack of standards—costs, budgets, size of customer's account, and so on.
6. Misunderstanding regarding the relationship of staff to operating executives.
7. Immersion of major executives in detail by reason of lack of established procedures.
8. Salary revisions on approximately a flat percentage basis without discrimination or reference to results compared with standards.

It is apparent to any thoughtful observer that executive personnel organization problems have received relatively scanty attention. This is due partly to the prevalent attitude that major executives are born organizers, and the assumption that they would not have reached the position they have were they not able to choose, develop, and organize executive personnel. It is also due in part to the fact that the personnel movement began with attention devoted almost entirely to the rank and file and that many personnel men have found it difficult to graduate upward into either junior or senior executive personnel problems. Moreover, the personnel movement has thus far concentrated too much on personnel procedures and techniques and not enough on management organization principles. Despite the fact that many personnel problems affecting the rank and file depend for their solution on the adequacy of an executive personnel program during this Depression, it is becoming increasingly evident that effective personnel administration embraces the whole range of general management.

Without a sound organization and sound organization relationships adequately understood, even the most successful efforts at scientific selection of executive material or efforts at either formal or informal executive training can accomplish relatively little. The next decade will no doubt witness a rapid development of organization theory and organization principles without which mere technique of production, marketing, finance, or personnel administration promises unnecessarily slim results. It is high time that organization principles should no longer be taken for granted.

14

The Challenge for Personnel Administration

Paul Pigors

ENDURING organizational success can never be achieved merely by technical efficiency and order giving. Authoritarianism can success-fully pose only minimum requirements. Thus the challenge for all representatives of management is to win from workers their voluntary cooperation not only in meeting production demands, but in all other phases of their functioning. This leadership aspect of management, which seeks the plus values of cooperation, is the essence of personnel work.

To those of us who make personnel administration our profession, the challenge of securing cooperation is a double one. First we must win for our point of view the support of operating officials up and down the line, because it is upon them that the organization must ultimately rely for good personnel relations. If we are to succeed in the first objective, our recommendations must be sound in theory. They must also be so persuasively presented that line officials will want to exercise their authority through methods in accord with the personnel point of view. Second, when our ideas are applied by line management, they must prove effective in winning the cooperation of workers. This means that our recommendations should be not only idealistic, but also realistic because they are well adapted to the specific situations in which they are to be used.

Winning Top Management Support

The task of enlisting for personnel work the respect and support of operating management is not always easy. It is especially difficult if the chief executive is not genuinely enthusiastic about the principles that underlie personnel administration. And it is no easier if he thinks that he can reap the benefits of good personnel work without paying for them in advance in time and effort. Until he comes to believe so strongly in the value of personnel work that he is willing to make part payment for it with his own time and thought, the efficacy of any personnel administrator who works for him is necessarily limited. But this limitation need not be accepted as final. It merely means that the personnel administrator's first job is to convince his chief that personnel work is an integral function of line management. As such the responsibility for it cannot be entirely delegated by the chief executive to anyone. The president remains responsible, for and through his personnel administrator, to all his other employees. And the personnel point of view must be his, as well as ours, if it is to win the respect it needs in order to be fully serviceable.

Line and Staff Relationships

When the chief executive has come to realize that personnel administration is a job as important as any in the organization, the personnel man's task in winning cooperation from line management is usually more than half accomplished. With the full support of top management, it should not be difficult for an able personnel administrator to convince line officials that his ideas can be useful to them. In trying to do this, each of us must be prepared to take his chance when it comes. We must be interested in the problems that are recognized by operating officials, and not merely try to impose upon them solutions for problems of whose existence they are still unaware. And above all, we must be able to think along policy lines about major issues, and not allow ourselves to become entirely submerged in details, however urgent.

But we must never forget the limitation of our role as staff officials. We cannot give orders to the line. We should rely, instead, on the power of ideas. We can make sure, however, that our ideas are known and are such as to carry weight. Since our principal aim is to build cooperation, we must see to it that we practice what we preach. In some organizations, tension and frustration, instead of a high degree of cooperation, exist between line and staff. It is an important part of our job to eliminate such barriers to efficiency. The acid test of our success in personnel work is the extent to which our point of view is actualized in the behavior of line officials. If we do our job well, every representative of operating management will be doing it with and for us. This, of course, will make our own contribution less conspicuous. But we need not worry unduly about that. It has been said that one cannot both do things and get the credit for them. It is up to us to do things. We can well afford to let others get the credit. This will make them all the more enthusiastic about our ideas.

Our Part in Labor Relations

If these ideas are of practical value, we can be a constructive influence in labor relations. For one thing, we should be able to set the tone of management–union negotiations. We must try to convince top management that unions are useful when regarded as a check on management's thinking about personnel. Employers who are reasonable and fair need not fear the challenge of any agency that is also reasonable and fair. And management should be ready to take the initiative in developing good relations with the union.

We should help management to be realistic about unions. They are here to stay and they should be accepted, not only in the kitchen as workers, but also in the parlor as equals. Management fights a losing battle when it concentrates on safeguarding its prerogatives. These can never be guaranteed by a clause in the union contract. They can be kept only when they are earned. Progress in personnel relations lies in developing mutual interest between management and workers, and in working toward a common cause. Let's help top management to take and hold this line in union negotiations, remembering that contracts are worse than useless unless they are supported by daily action at the work level.

Long-term results in labor relations depend on a soil-building program. This work has to be done by the first-line supervisors. We can help them to build sound management–union relations from the ground up, by their daily conduct toward workers and union officials. The supervisor's basic rule should be to respect the workers' rights under the law (the shop law of the union agreement) and to see that the workers respect management's rights under the same law.

Understanding in Human Relations

It is part of our job to help the first-line supervisor learn how to get and weigh the relevant facts, both technical and human, upon which judgments must be based. We can help him to see that human facts are subtle, elusive, and variable. In human relations we rarely meet the so-called "plain" fact. Certain events are bound to affect people in different ways, and will often seem quite different even to the same person at different times. Thus every point of view—even ours—is only a *point* of view on the whole arc of human understanding. We need to get other angles and more evidence, to be flexible, and to look for meanings beneath "unreasonable" words. We should try to understand feelings by getting each participant's angle on the situation, then get outside and look at the whole thing objectively.

Policy Thinking

In building understanding for ourselves and others, we have several different kinds of responsibility. Top management may need reminding that policies are for people, and that people respond better when treated not as we think they *ought* to feel and act, but rather as they *do* feel and act. Policies are dynamite unless realistically formulated, and unless they allow room for discretion in border-line cases.

Policies also need to be clearly explained, wisely interpreted, and consistently applied. Supervisors need help in showing workers why policy requirements are more important than purely personal pleas for cooperation. There are exceptions to all rules. But policies should be broader than rules. If many special cases cannot be handled within policy patterns, there is something wrong with the policies. We must find out what it is and try to correct it.

We should be concerned with long-term principles more than with short-term results. Principles are related to people in terms of personnel policies. We should each make sure that all concerned understand the principles that apply to the specific company situation at the time, that we all know what a genuine policy is, and how existing policies are actually working out. Although he has no final word on policy making, the personnel administrator should be top management's key advisor on all policies for personnel. Therefore, we must be sure that our policy thinking measures up to the need.

Getting Down to Cases

When we hear reports of "hopeless" misunderstandings or "incompatible" opinions, we should be willing to get down to cases and see whether we can reconcile the differences. We must try to get inside the situation and piece together the whole story. We must check and weigh the facts, determine the issue, and seek a solution that integrates basic needs. But in planning for the future we should avoid like the plague the temptation to go it alone. We must never emerge on the scene with the results of solo thinking, crying: "Boys, here it is!" The boys will be more likely to agree with our answer if they have helped to work it out.

Interviewing

When trying to create understanding, we need not suppose that we must either always think alone or do all the talking. To create understanding by and between people, interviewing is required. While doing this, we should remind ourselves that for each person what counts most is not what *we* say, but what *he* thinks and feels. We should learn to prepare for an interview so that both participants can make the most of it. We must learn how to listen and help the other person to speak his mind. When he is talking, we may both see new light on what he is asking of the situation, and on what the situation is asking of him. We should use imagination to draw out meaning and use a pencil to pin it down. When the talk is over, we can amplify our notes and evaluate the interview both as an experiment in human relations and as an opportunity to improve our understanding. What happened? Was new insight achieved? How can we do better next time?

The Level of Teamwork and Morale

Our ability to understand should be matched by our readiness to examine the fats. We must never indulge in wishful thinking. How stable are the individuals and groups in the organization? We are certainly not just "one big happy family." What are we? Are we merely an aggregation of people held loosely and temporarily together by economic interest? Or do we possess any sense of united purpose and common membership? Is there more of this feeling in some sections than in others? Have we any real work teams? If so, where? How were they built? How are they maintained? We should think about this, giving credit where credit is due, and help where help is needed.

Learning from Complaints

Often we can gain insight by studying employee dissatisfactions and the methods by which they are being handled. What types of complaints are we getting? Where are they coming from? How does the complaint procedure work? Is it aimed to suppress squawks, to appease troublemakers, or to disclose dissatisfactions? Part of our job is to see that there is a definite and simple procedure, known to all, and that it can function fast. We should try to convince line management that a complaint made officially represents an opportunity and not just another headache.

We can help line management to learn the trick of listening to what speaks *in* workers (for instance, resentment, jealousy, hurt pride, insecurity, or fear) when they present complaints, as well as to what they speak *about*. And we should study complaints ourselves. Sometimes they are eye-openers. In that case, let's open our eyes and look hard, even if this means seeing our department in an unattractive light.

Building and Maintaining Work Teams

The whole employment process is of major concern to us. Is it such that we can be satisfied with every phase of it? Are we, in this process, doing everything that can be done to build and maintain stable work teams?

Recruitment should be both dignified and effective in attracting a suitable number of qualified employees. Placement should be a preliminary decision for routine workers, and part of a continuing experiment for promotional candidates. Our department should set an example for other staff experts by the way in which it works with supervisors to make a success of these initial hiring procedures. Does it?

A key man in the formation of effective work teams is the first-line supervisor. We must try to make this no empty statement in our organization but a fact that can be thought about with pride. We should not be afraid to prove that what the first-line supervisor does, day in and day out, counts for more in personnel relations than what the president says at the annual picnic.

We can help top management select foremen for their skill in human relations as well as for their technical efficiency. We can train them in the personnel point of view, and learn about their problems on the job. If we and they pursue our education together, personnel relations are bound to improve.

Helping Workers Make Good

There is no more vital person in the employment relationship, of course, than the worker himself. We should help him to recognize that his ability to do the job will largely determine his status. Seniority need not be accepted by management as the only standard for decisions on promotion, transfer, downgrading, and layoff. But management need not worry about giving seniority due weight when the earlier steps of recruitment, selection, induction, and training have been followed with care.

Sound procedures of induction and training are essential in helping workers to feel, think, and do as they should. As part of the job of carrying out production goals, these activities are the responsibility of line management. But a personnel administrator can help in developing induction and training programs that fit the company situation. He may also assist in training the instructors who actually do the teaching. Unless this teaching is effective, both technical efficiency and success in personnel relations are inevitably limited.

Employee rating, of which each worker is informed in regular followup interviews, is an essential mechanism for mutual understanding and for the maximum development of employees. When the worker knows where he stands with management, he can adjust his expectations and behavior accordingly. Employee rating also helps management to make sound decisions on promotion. When careful ratings replace snap judgments on employee performance, management, workers, and union leaders will find solid ground for agreement.

A personnel administrator should also be allowed to help top management with its policies and procedures for transfer, downgrading, and layoff. Established avenues of transfer should be soundly built into the organizational structure and generally known. Lack of clarity in this area tempts workers to suppose that management's professed aims to make the most of ability and to stabilize employment are "just a lot of hooey."

Decisions on downgrading and layoff are difficult, both for management to make wisely and for unions to accept. Only on the basis of clearcut policies, consistently and constructively administered, can both sides be assured that all are treated fairly.

Procedures of discipline and discharge also test management's success in applying the personnel point of view. The personnel administrator has not succeeded in his job if line management fails to understand that daily discipline should be maintained within each work team, and chiefly by self-discipline on the part of every employee. Such inner discipline should be encouraged by a constructive discipline policy and supplemented by a few simple rules that are promptly and consistently enforced.

When a worker has to be discharged, every management representative who has regularly dealt with him should look at the record and examine his own memory in search of clues about what went wrong. Was he ever the right man in the right job? Was his follow-up adequate? A skillfully conducted exit interview may throw light on these points. Or management may never learn why it failed in getting this man to cooperate. Was it perhaps that he did not know what was expected of him in time to adjust to the requirements? If so, we must try to use this failure to some purpose by showing management that workers need to have notice and explanation of changes in work routines, in personnel, and in rates of pay.

Other procedures, closely-related to the employment process, are of equal interest to us as personnel administrators.

Earning a Living and Making a Life

For instance, it is up to us to give top management the personnel point of view about earning a living. Wages and salaries are not all that employees work for, though money does matter. They are working for both prestige as well as groceries. Levels of wage rates should be related to those paid by comparable firms in the community or in the industry. The cost of living, the company's financial status, and government wage orders must also be considered. It may be difficult to make the necessary job evaluations and to set up a salary and wage structure that meets all requirements and clearly represents existing job relationships. But the principles are easy to explain. We must see that every interested worker understands them, as well as the facts of his own case. If union officials want to participate in the early stages of job evaluation, so much the better. If not, they should at least be given an opportunity to understand the aims and methods.

When talking money to the chief executive, can we show him that we are cost-minded? As skillful exponents of human values, we may even be able to persuade him, if necessary, that penny pinching is an extravagance in personnel relations.

If the organization has an incentive system, how well does it work? Do employees understand the why and how of output standards? Does the system step up production or keep it down? If it results in gains to the company, are these gains fairly shared with the workers? Does the incentive system divide or unite work groups? Does it convince workers that management values effort, or do they think it is just a device to cut rates? Are time study men regarded by the rank and file as villains, as necessary evils, or as technicians with an understanding of human problems? The personnel administrator should know the answers to these questions and should bend his efforts to see that the answers are right.

In our organization is there a serious conflict for most of the personnel between making a living and making a life? If so, we must do what we can to resolve it. For example, we should try to evaluate for operating management the human aspects of hours and shifts, but without ourselves underestimating technical requirements. It is not hard to plan schedules solely with a view to meeting production demands. Nor is it difficult to adjust one worker's schedule to fit his personal situation. But such adjustments, if made for many people, produce chaotic group schedules. And if made for some people and not others, they may appear to be a form of discrimination. Can we help top management better to integrate all relevant needs?

Mutual Responsibility

It is sometimes difficult for operating management to remember that any serious problem in any area of the worker's life inevitably reduces his total efficiency. It is our job to remind the chief executive that workers' problems are, in part, his problems. And it follows that management should offer appropriate assistance when employees have difficulties that they cannot meet alone. This does not mean doing things *for* people, so much as thinking and acting *with* them. It means helping them to help themselves, and to make intelligent use of plant and community facilities. It also means being realistic and not romantic—not going in for spasmodic do-goodism or utopian experiments, but rather for long-run mutual responsibility in a working relationship.

By an employee service program, management can show that its professed belief in responsibility is neither hot air nor just a one-sided demand on workers. Services depend for success on mutual responsibility. Management should participate with employees in planning an all-around program to meet human needs. Workers should participate with management in administering and paying for the program.

Health and Safety

Mutual responsibility between line management and workers is nowhere more essential than in regard to health and safety. As personnel administrators we, too, have a great responsibility here, and in studying the frequency rate of accidents in the company and the current health data, we should be willing to shoulder our share of the burden. What more could we have done to help prevent accidents and sickness?

For instance, what do the safety records and the results of the accident prevention and health programs show about the success of our department? If top management is not sufficiently personnel-minded to have developed the necessary policies, we may be partly to blame. If operating executives are not so interested in their subordinates as to be constantly mindful of their health and safety, we have not been successful exponents of the personnel point of view. If the safety director and the company doctor do not come to us for advice, we are missing a valuable opportunity for cooperation. If union officials are not invited to take part in safety discussions and in planning for health, our ideas have not proved fully effective in labor relations. And if workers must often be punished for wilful infractions of rules relating to safety and sanitation, our department has fallen down on the job of selecting the right kind of person to join the company community.

Employee Participation in Production Problems

But perhaps our employees participate in these services and not in solving production problems. If so, why? Is it primarily because line management does not want their participation in this area? In that case, what are we doing to correct such a short-sighted and unconstructive attitude? Workers always have ideas about their jobs. The question is whether these ideas are being used to "beat the system," or to step up production. People normally like to make suggestions in order to improve conditions and to gain prestige. If ideas are not coming in through the official suggestion system, it is probably the fault either of this system or of the personnel program as a whole. If workers and union officials do not take an interest in company problems, it is perhaps because they have been given the notion that these difficulties are no concern of theirs. This attitude does not spring from nowhere. But such a sign of cleavage between workers and management is not hopeless. It is a challenge. What can we do to meet it?

The Will to Understand and Believe

We are not, of course, responsible for building a Utopia. But all personnel men are obligated to go on trying, and to interest others in this absorbing occupation. Thoreau said: "Gnaw at your own bone: bury it, unearth it, and gnaw it still." Our "bone" should be the conviction that people can understand each other if they will, and can work together more effectively when they do. We shall never get all the marrow out of this bone, because we shall never reach the point where we know all the answers.

But let us not be discouraged. We have to keep at it, and let neither our own failures nor the mistakes of anyone else convince us that the personnel administrator's job is not worth doing. It is all the more worth doing because it can never entirely succeed. We must keep on learning, and believing that there is a fair solution to every human difference. We can always hope to find it, but in any event we should keep on believing. We must believe in people, in principles, and in our profession. We must also believe in ourselves. Unless we do, how can we ask others to rely on us?

15

Changing Concepts
of the Personnel Function

James C. Worthy

PERSONNEL administration is a relatively new specialized function of management. Because it is new there are wide areas of disagreement as to its proper role. Actually, there is no common understanding as to the responsibilities of the personnel administrator and no generally accepted system of techniques and methods for carrying out his responsibilities. In this respect, personnel administration is far behind such other specialized management functions as accounting, finance, engineering, and the like. In a real sense, personnel may be said to be in its adolescent stage—well past its infancy but not yet grown to man's estate. As is characteristic of adolescents, it is not too sure of itself and not yet quite certain what it wants to be when it grows up.

At the present time, the role of the personnel administrator varies widely from company to company and can be understood only in terms of a particular management's reasons for establishing a personnel department and in terms of the type of individual management selects for personnel work. It is possible, however, to distinguish a number of rather well-defined roles that are fairly characteristic of the personnel function in industry today.

Some Concepts of the Personnel Function

At one end of the scale is the concept of personnel as primarily a record-keeping function, necessary because of the requirements imposed by legislation and the need for centralizing certain fairly routine activities. While many personnel offices continue to function today at this rudimentary level, it is probable that most of us in management have begun to think of personnel in higher terms.

Then there is the personnel department that was established because it was "the thing to do"—because of a feeling on management's part that "no well-run business should be without one." Where personnel departments and personnel activities are established as a means of "keeping up with the Joneses," the resulting program can be little more than a facade to the organization. Its orientation is not primarily toward the organization it is set up to serve, but toward what others are doing, and it is therefore likely to employ techniques and methods poorly adapted to the real problems of the firm.

Another important reason for the increased use of personnel departments is the growth of unionism and management's need for adequate facilities to administer collective agreements. One difficulty with personnel departments that originated primarily to serve this need is that they are likely to become so occupied with the intricacies of collective bargaining that they lose sight of the real problems of human relations in the organization. Thus they may also lose sight of the constructive, rather than the merely defensive, contribution they can make to their managements.

A closely related type of origin is where management becomes concerned at evidences of increasing friction with its employees and recognizes the need for improving employee morale. While this is a constructive attitude as far as it goes, management may be too anxious for quick results from the new department. In such cases, the personnel administrator is in an exposed position. If management does not soon see evidence of improved morale, the administrator is likely to be replaced by someone who will attack the problem more vigorously. He is in a position where he must try to find a panacea that will solve all his problems in one swoop. He has little opportunity to develop the activities and the day-by-day contacts with the organization that are the slow but only sure way of building high employee morale and sound employee relations.

The Scientific Approach

A much more realistic and promising approach to the problems of personnel administration is represented by developments of the past ten years or so, which may be loosely described as "scientific personnel administration." Considerable strides have been made toward the introduction of rational methods and techniques in personnel, and, as a result, personnel work is gradually taking on some of the characteristics of a profession. There can be no question that many products of this approach—merit rating, job evaluation, psychologic il testing, and the like—represent great improvements over former methods.

Valuable as this progress has been, however, the so-called "scientific" approach has shown some serious shortcomings that have undermined the contribution it could be making—and in many cases has made—to management success. Too often the goal of the "scientific" personnel administrator is to install a variety of highly systematic procedures. From textbooks or elsewhere he may have picked up the idea that a well-run personnel program should consist of certain standard parts, each represented by some type of system, and he may not feel that he has his job under control until he has established corresponding systems in his own organization, whether it really needs them or not.

What Is "Good Personnel Practice"?

Many people who have reputations as top-notch personnel administrators today think of their jobs primarily in terms of "good personnel practice," which is often only a euphonious way of saying "bigger and better systems." There is, of course, a rationale for this attitude because in any organization large enough to require a specialized personnel department it is necessary to establish systematic procedures.

The assumption is that if employees are properly selected, well trained, adequately paid, and fairly supervised, job satisfaction will automatically result, production and efficiency will be high, and all will be right with the world. The personnel administrator guided by this philosophy therefore has a relatively simple task in planning his program. All he has to do is catalog the necessary elements of "sound employee relations"—which he can find spelled out in detail in any good book on personnel—and then set up the necessary systems, the "good personnel practices," to see that each element is properly provided for.

Undue Emphasis on Systems

There can be no quarrel with systems as such. In a company of any size there must be an organized means for reaching certain basic objectives, and activities related to personnel—no less than those related to sales, production, or finance—must be systematically ordered if results are to be achieved. But the strong tendency to over elaborate the systems used and to place undue reliance on such systems for building and maintaining sound employee relations is certainly open to question. Let us take an example—job evaluation. The primary objective of a job evaluation program is to provide an orderly set of wage differentials between various jobs in the organization that will be recognized as just and fair by the employees and that will serve as guides in wage administration. So far, so good. Too often, however, a highly complex system results, and the essential objective becomes clouded in a maze of abstruse statistical and rating procedures.

Personnel literature is cluttered with endless arguments on behalf of different sets of such procedures and considerable ingenuity has been exercised in the development of more and more complex job evaluation systems. This welter of activity often results in a system too complex for employees to understand. Far from being convinced of management's fairness in handling the highly important matter of wage differentials, the employees become deeply suspicious of the whole thing.

The same tendency toward over elaboration is apparent in many other personnel activities—training, periodic interviewing, testing, employee benefits, house organs, morale-building programs, and so on. Personnel administrators as a group, in fact, display a remarkable bent toward systemization, a bent so strong that speculation as to its origin and significance may be profitable.

The Struggle for Status

One reason for this tendency, I think, lies in the fact that personnel administration is among the newer specialized functions of management. Personnel administrators as a group are engaged in a struggle for status and recognition in the management hierarchy. Much of the energy of personnel executives goes toward trying to establish personnel as a legitimate function of management, to "sell" themselves to management and the line organization. In this struggle for status, they are under a heavy handicap in the fact that management often has only a nebulous idea of what it expects from personnel, and the further fact that there are no commonly accepted standards by which the personnel job may be judged.

Production, sales, finance, and other specialized management functions have the great advantage of being able to offer relatively objective measures of their effectiveness. Personnel, on the contrary, has nothing to compare with balance sheets or sales and production statistics. After all, what basis does management have for evaluating the importance of its personnel department or the worth of its personnel administrator? As a personnel man myself, I would hate to be judged largely in terms of whether or not I was successful in avoiding labor trouble or in reducing personnel turnover. Such matters are only partially within our control, and in any event represent only limited aspects of the personnel job.

To win the confidence and recognition of management, the personnel administrator must find some means of convincing management that he is operating vigorously and effectively within the areas of his responsibility. In this situation, a "good system" is often highly effective. Management may be concerned with what it feels is a jumbled wage situation. If the personnel administrator can come up with a precise plan backed up by attractive charts and an impressive set of statistical tabulations, management is likely to react favorably because it has the comforting feeling that a thorough and logical job has been done and that this problem, at least, is settled for the time being.

The point is not that thorough, logical work is not important. In too many cases the real purpose of the charts, statistics, and the show of reasoned logic is not so much to accomplish a job as to convince management that it has a very bright and capable personnel administrator. Because management is accustomed to a high degree of systemization in the more technical phases of its work, it may be unduly impressed with evidences of similar methods in the field of personnel. And personnel administrators, being human, are likely to be led to over elaboration of their systems and to the introduction of highly mechanical procedures in areas of their work where more informal methods would produce more effective results for the organization.

Competition for Line Authority

Another aspect of the struggle for status is the attempt, implicit in many personnel systems, to gain a degree of control over the line organization. Staff departments—personnel included—are often painfully conscious of the more solid position of the line, a position whose strength lies largely in its direct responsibility for producing the goods and services that are the lifeblood of the organization. It is a fairly common tendency of staff departments to attempt to inject themselves into the line by establishing control over certain line activities, such as hiring, placement, training, promotion, wage administration, and so on.

These attempts are easily understandable, of course, because in any line organization there are bound to be problems that require correction. However, instead of trying to strengthen the line organization so that it is better able to deal effectively with its own problems, the temptation is to set up some sort of system of control that may have the incidental effect of strengthening the staff department at the expense of the line. It often has the further effect of requiring some sort of policing action that, while it may remedy the immediate problem, very often creates other problems that are as bad or worse. The result is more bureaucracy, more pieces of paper, more "controls to make the controls work." There is a gradual aggrandizement of power and authority by the staff and a weakening of the line.

As a personnel man, I will not deprecate the importance of the personnel job or attempt to relegate it to a lower status in the organization than it should enjoy. But I am very much concerned at misguided and misdirected efforts to achieve the status that I firmly believe a well-conceived and well-executed personnel program would merit. I submit that any effort to secure undue control over line activities, whatever its initial advantages, is a blind alley, essentially unsound, and inevitably self-defeating.

Don't Invite Resistance

One evidence of this fact is the sense of frustration exhibited by many personnel executives. The line will tolerate a great deal, but it can be pushed just so far. Beyond that point, the personnel staff meets increasing resistance, which it is likely to interpret as bull-headed stubbornness. A common topic of conversation when personnel men meet is the obstructive attitudes of the line organization, the need for more power and authority to compel the line to follow "good personnel practices," and the lack of enlightenment on the part of management in not providing personnel with the necessary authority to get things done.

While management is inclined to be system-minded, and is likely to be impressed with charts, statistics, and precise, well-ordered procedures, it is also likely to have a fairly sure instinct about what is really workable in terms of the organization as a whole. And management most probably would back up the line organization in any direct contest for authority and control.

Too often, I fear, the status angle may play a larger part in the personnel administrator's thinking than he may care to admit. In such cases the real needs of the organization might be sacrificed to the ambitions of an individual or group. Such a situation is not only bad in itself, but in the long run can only result in undermining the status and prestige the administrator is working so hard to achieve.

The Human Function of Personnel Management

What, then, should the aims of the personnel administrator be and how should he go about accomplishing them? To answer these questions we must look at the goals of management and explore the possible contributions personnel administration can make to achieving those goals.

In broad terms we may define management's task as that of putting together and maintaining an effective organization that can accomplish the economic aims of the enterprise. This task has both a technical side and a human side. On the technical side, management must provide an efficient plant with the necessary machines and processes, in the provision of which it is aided by its engineering and related staffs who constantly feed in ideas for technical improvements and who assume responsibility for working out various technical problems that require solution. On the human side, management's task is that of building a cooperative organization, an organization of people with drive and enthusiasm, who work together, and who are responsive to management's leadership in the common effort to achieve the economic aims of the enterprise.

The function of the engineering staff is to aid management in the performance of its technical tasks. The function of the personnel staff should be to aid management in the performance of its human tasks—to assist in the development and maintenance of an effective human organization.

Mechanistic Approach to Human Problems

To perform his function adequately, the personnel administrator must develop a considerably broader point of view and an entirely different set of skills than those ordinarily represented by so-called "scientific" management. There has been too great a tendency for personnel people to adopt, more or less uncritically, the methods and points of view of the engineer and to attempt to apply these to the solution of the human problems in organizations.

One of the serious stumbling blocks to effective human organization is a deep-seated attitude characteristic of our times. The physical scientist and the engineer have exercised a profound influence not only on the outward aspects of modern life but on our inner thought processes as well. Among other things, they have strongly influenced our thinking about problems of organization and human relations. The transference of their mode of thought to a field for which it was never designed has distorted our apprehension of our human problems and has seriously misdirected our efforts to deal with them.

If we consider closely our generally accepted theories of organization, we cannot help but note a curious parallel to the machine. Actually, our ideal of an effective organization is a "smoothly running machine," an organization in which all parts function smoothly, with a minimum of friction and maximum economy of effort. Each component is carefully designed for its particular task, and the whole responds automatically to the touch of the operator's hand.

Our very phraseology employs mechanical images. Organization charts are frequently referred to as blueprints. A common argument for the use of psychological tests cites the care with which machines are selected to ensure their suitability for the task at hand and urges that people be selected and placed with at least equal attention to their abilities and capacities. "Management engineering" and "human engineering" have become important and respected professions. Our thinking about organization displays a strongly mechanical turn of mind.

Human Aspects of Organization

The nature of human organization cannot be properly understood in terms of mechanistic concepts. The machine and its component parts have only one purpose—that for which the engineer designed them. The purpose of a human organization, whether business or otherwise, can be defined only in terms of the purposes of the people in it. Unlike the component parts of a machine, the people who comprise a human organization are something more than just parts of that organization. They are flesh-and-blood men and women, with sentiments, ambitions, and needs of their own ranging far beyond the confines of the organization. The extent to which these people serve the needs of the organization willingly and enthusiastically depends upon the extent to which the organization serves their needs as sentient, aspiring human beings.

In these circumstances, the effort to apply primarily technical rather than social skills to the solution of social problems is likely to have grave consequences, since the two kinds of skills are not synonymous and not mutually interchangeable. Elton Mayo, in his book *The Social Problems of an Industrial Civilization* draws the following distinctions between the two skills:

> Technical skill manifests itself as a capacity to manipulate things in the service of human purposes. Social skill shows itself as a capacity to receive communications from others, and to respond to the attitudes and ideas of others in such fashion as to promote congenial participation in a common task.

The attempt to apply to human problems methods and concepts originally developed for the manipulation of things almost inevitably inhibits effective communication and undermines that "congenial participation in a common task" referred to by Mr. Mayo.

Need for Improved Social Skills

Unfortunately, the social skills required for effective cooperation have not been developed to anything like the degree that technical skills have been developed. The task of the personnel administrator comes down to this: If he is to function as effectively in aiding management on its human problems as the engineer aids on technical problems, he must develop as high an order of conscious skill in his field as the engineer has already developed in his.

This is a sizable task, one which cannot be accomplished overnight. For one thing, social skills are poorly understood and many personnel administrators and men in management who have developed intuitive social skills have great difficulty in talking about them or defining them. Until these skills are more precisely identified and until they can be more adequately classified and described, they are communicable only to a limited degree and cannot gain the wide application required.

A great deal of creative work along these lines is being done in some of our universities, which are working closely with business and industry in their areas. Personnel administrators and management cannot wait, however, for the work of the social scientists to come to full fruition. Faced with problems here and now, we must deal with them to the best of our ability. But we can at least make a start, and I think it is important that it be a conscious start—a purposive effort to develop a higher order of skill, which we can place at the service of management.

Pattern for Industrial Democracy

Actually, we have ready at hand, as a deeply ingrained part of our thinking, the ideas that can serve as the basis for our badly needed social skills. This basis is simply the ideals of the democratic society, ideals that are fundamental elements of our culture universally accepted by management and workers alike. These ideals are usually expressed in terms of "rights"—the very word "rights" implying their essentially moral and ethical nature. For our present purposes, we may summarize some of the more significant of these rights as follows:

1. The right of every man to be treated as an individual and respected as a person.
2. The right of every man to a voice in his own affairs, which includes his right to contribute to the best of his ability in the solution of common problems.
3. The right of every man to recognition for his contribution to the common good.
4. The right of every man to develop and make use of his highest capacities.
5. The right of every man to fairness and justice in all his relationships with superiors.

These democratic ideals are not platitudes but actual working principles of effective human organization. Their validity has been proved over and over again, both by our historical experience and by modern research in the social sciences. In my own company, we have cooperated with the University of Chicago on extensive research into the nature of effective organization and the factors that make for cooperation in human relations. Throughout this research we have been impressed with the extent to which the fundamental notions of our democratic society have been validated.

For example, we have been impressed with the number of times the fundamental notions of participation, human dignity, freedom to speak one's piece, and the right to advance on one's own merits have proved crucial factors in the maintenance of a high level of cooperation and teamwork. These are not merely ideals; they are practical principles on how to live and work in a free society.

Control or Cooperation?

Another thing we have learned is that an organization with an extensively developed supervisory hierarchy is more rigid, less adaptive, and less satisfying to employees than a "flat" organization, which places considerable responsibility on the individual and keeps supervision and formal controls at a minimum. In an organization where there are many layers of supervision, employees feel restricted, controlled, and policed. There is little opportunity for creative effort and the development of ideas. In organizations with fewer layers of supervision and fewer controls, there tends to be higher morale, better feeling, more creative effort, infinitely greater adaptability and flexibility, and a higher development of cooperation between employees and management. I hardly need point out that this latter type of organization more closely approximates the democratic ideal than the former.

What are the implications of these democratic ideals in terms of the practical problems of business and industrial organization? In politics we are all familiar with the ideas represented by the democratic and the authoritarian states. Despite our unshakable faith in the superiority of democracy as a form of civil government, a great many managements apply strict authoritarian principles in the administration of their business affairs in the belief, apparently, that business and politics are two different orders of things.

Actually, the two institutions—business and government—are closely similar in their most essential aspect: Both are organizations of human beings, and both depend in the long run on the creative intelligence and effort, on the voluntary support and acceptance, of the people who comprise them. One of the great paradoxes of our society is that we have failed to apply to the internal affairs of our businesses the principles we all recognize when applied to political organization as largely responsible for the tremendous growth in national wealth and the superb social progress we have enjoyed.

Authoritarianism in Industry

Many business organizations closely resemble the authoritarian state in the sense that all direction, all thinking, all authority tends to flow from the top down. While the top administrator may delegate certain parts of his responsibility and authority, the delegation is largely in terms of implementing and effectuating at lower levels of the organization the policies and directives that have already been set up at the top. While a directive may be broken down into a series of parts and parceled out to different people, and while these people may be expected to show initiative and drive in executing their work, their activity is essentially that of carrying out an order.

To make such an organization work, management is forced to set up a rigorous system of controls to see that things get done and that people do not make too many mistakes in carrying out orders. In other words, a minimum of reliance is placed on the people in the organization, and the system depends primarily on the initiative and judgment of those at the top.

A corollary of this tendency is the elaboration of staff organizations, because where the exercise of judgment and skill is largely reserved to top administrators, they must be assisted by specialized advisory staffs. The result is a further extension of the system of controls through the initiative of the staff departments, as well as a considerable complication of the organizational structure, leading in turn to the necessity for other controls to hold the organization together and make it work. At the same time, because of the necessity for operating these controls and because employees at each successive level must be closely directed in their work, the supervisory hierarchy becomes more and more extended.

Effects on Supervision

Let us consider the manner in which the personnel administrator frequently acts in this type of organization. For one thing, he is likely to develop a feeling that supervisors can't be trusted to use good judgment (*good judgment* usually means what *he* would do in a particular situation). He feels impelled, therefore, to establish precise rules to govern every contingency. Or he must appropriate broad areas of responsibility from line supervision and vest them in the personnel department—all for the purpose, naturally, of guarding against the possibility that line supervisors or executives will make mistakes.

Certainly some broad framework of policy is necessary within which the supervisor should be required to work, but this should not lead to the substitution of an elaborate system of bureaucratic controls for the good judgment that should arise from the supervisor's own intimate knowledge of the immediate situation. The effect of such minute controls is to undermine the initiative and judgment of supervisors, so that ultimately their judgment really cannot be trusted because they have never had an opportunity to use it.

What Happens to the Rank and File?

What is the effect of this elaborate system of supervision and control on the rank and file? I refer you to the bitter complaints of management itself over the apathy of employees, their lack of initiative, their lack of interest in the affairs and problems of the enterprise, their antagonism to management, and so on. Instead of blaming this state of affairs on agitators, on faults in the educational system, or on errors in family methods of raising children, many managements need only look within their own organizations.

In effect, all that some organizations demand of lower-level employees is their animal energies, their muscle power. Some managements have done everything possible to take all judgment away from the operator, to relieve him of all initiative, to reduce his work to the lowest possible repetitive, mechanical level. This is usually justified in terms of supposedly greater efficiency, shorter training time, ability to use less skilled workers, and the greater proficiency of the operator that can come from repetition of simple movements.

Granted all this, but how much does industry lose in depriving the worker of all creative relation to his job? I hazard the opinion that industry has lost far more than it has gained. A very serious consequence of this process has been to destroy all meaning of the job for the worker—all meaning, that is, except in terms of the pay envelope. It has had the equally important effect of seriously undermining the confidence of workers in management. Furthermore, because they are restless and discontented, employees are easily influenced by strong leadership, which may arise in opposition to management. Their jobs have made so few demands on their higher faculties, they have had so little opportunity to think, to take initiative, or to make their own contribution to the improvement of their jobs, that when aggressive antimanagement leadership arises, promising workers an opportunity for self-expression that management has not provided, they readily respond. Without question, one of the great appeals of unions is their promise of giving the workers a more effective voice in matters that affect their jobs—their assurance that employees no longer have to do just what they are told but can stand up and be men.

Toward Increased Participation

If management is to restore more cooperative working relations and more efficient production, it must give serious thought to ways and means by which it may restore the highest possible level of individual and group participation in solving problems. This does not imply the necessity for management-worker councils, shop committees, or any other formal devices, although under given circumstances these may have a certain utility. When problems arise at the workplace, however, rather than have someone in supervision or management do all the thinking and tell the workers what he has decided, it is only necessary to call the workers together and say: "Here is the problem, let's figure out the answer." Give them a chance to express their own ideas, and let them know that their thinking is needed and valued.

This is a simple device, but it can be tremendously effective, whether a personnel man is trying to get the cooperation of the line, an engineer is trying to introduce a technical change, or a foreman is trying to increase output. Employees, instead of waiting around to be told, will have the opportunity to express their own ideas with all the satisfaction such expression offers. If people are simply told what to do, they have no responsibility for what happens. But if they have a voice in working out a problem, part of the responsibility is theirs and they'll do everything they can to make it work.

Similar devices can be improvised to deal with a wide variety of situations. They can be of great value not only in dealing more effectively with the practical problems involved but, more important, in building better teamwork and cooperation. Moreover, these devices can be readily applied. They need not wait on changes in the character of the organization structure or in the system of administration.

The fundamental issue, however, must be dealt with in terms of organization structure and managerial attitudes and skill. So long as a company's management is authoritarian, its organization unduly complex, its staff and supervisory heirarchy unduly extended—and so long as controls are over precise and over elaborate—the people in the organization will be stifled, their capacities and creative energies smothered by the sheer weight of the bureaucracy bearing down upon them.

In our efforts to extend the democratic process in industrial organizations I am not suggesting that we take over intact the apparatus of the democratic state. Business cannot be run by the ballot box, or by a Parliament or Congress. These were devised to solve the problem of effective participation by the citizenry in the affairs of its government. We must develop other inventions, adapted to the special circumstances of business, which will give employees at all levels of our organizations a greater sense of personal participation and "belonging," a greater sense of dignity and recognition of their worth both as individuals and as respected members of the industrial community.

Bringing
Personnel Administration
Closer to the President

Ewing W. Reilley

PERSONNEL administration presents one of the greatest uptapped opportunities of any function in management—an opportunity that, properly developed, can give this function an almost explosive increase in importance. And the men who develop this opportunity will gain the rewards in recognition, status, and compensation that our society accords to those who make practical contributions to the filling of people's needs.

An analysis of our economic system shows that the rewards geneally go to those who make the most direct practical contributions to achieving the long-range objectives and solving the far-reaching problems with which the president of a business and other members of its top management are concerned. If space permitted, this might be illustrated by tracing the evolution and growth in prestige of various management functions such as finance, production, engineering, sales, and research.

The president's job is to organize and integrate all functions of a business so that each makes its maximum contribution to achieving profits. Therefore, the act of bringing personnel administration closer to the president is bound to result in greater contributions by personnel men to the long-term growth, security, and profitability of their corporations.

New Interest in Human Factors

Personnel people, I am convinced, are on the threshold of an opportunity to be of much greater service to their businesses and to society as a whole. Among the directors and executives of many leading corporations there is a widespread and growing recognition that the most important factors determining the long-range success of any business are the caliber of its management personnel and the way their efforts are organized and motivated.

Moreover, the contributions made by the social sciences to our understanding of human motivations and behavior, and the results achieved by businesses that have applied these concepts, have opened the eyes of progressive managements to the enormous untapped potentialities in this area. Increasingly, hard-boiled executives are saying that the greatest opportunities for increased productivity and profits in the future will come from finding ways of releasing and directing the creative abilities and energies of people toward company goals.

Herein lies an opportunity for personnel men that is potentially as exciting as those that lie before the nuclear physicist or the organic chemist. It is an opportunity that, properly developed, not only can increase the importance of the personnel man's function but can lead him to the very top, to the presidency of the business. In all but a very few companies today, however, the development of such opportunities for personnel men has scarcely reached the "gleam in the father's eye" stage.

An Analogous Function—
Finance

Today two functions—personnel and finance—cut across all others in a business. The financial function provides the money, is responsible for its efficient utilization, and accounts for the results.

Where the opportunities inherent in this function are fully developed, the chief financial officer is the right arm of the president. Personnel people have an opportunity to play a potentially even more important role as advisers to the president on the human resources of the business, especially its management personnel. However, because the personnel function is less well established and its techniques less fully developed, in only a limited number of companies have the personnel people yet attained this status and recognition.

At the present stage in the evolution of their function, personnel people can profit from taking a look at what has happened to the financial function. Originally the financial function was concentrated in the treasurer, who was concerned with providing the necessary financial resources for the business and conserving its assets. Under him was the chief accountant or controller. As cost accounting, budgeting, and other tools of management developed, progressive controllers recognized the potential value of these tools to management and pushed them aggressively. They also analyzed the figures they produced, thus helping the president and the production men to plan and control the business and solve problems. Increasingly the more progressive controllers began looking at the problems of the business from the president's viewpoint and working on those problems of greatest concern to the president. Today controllers have attained a stature at least equal to that of their former bosses, the treasurers, because they are providing practical tools and analyses that help the president and the operating people to run the business and solve important problems. Many versatile financial men have been able to assume both responsibilities and become the president's right arm in regard to both internal and external questions. Typically, such an executive becomes financial vice-president of the organization.

Today, many personnel people stand at the crossroads. Are they going to go the way of the treasurers and confine themselves to functions that, though of great importance, are not of immediate or direct help to the president and other line executives? Such personnel functions as recruitment, salary administration, employee services and benefits, and possibly even labor relations may well be compared with the treasurer's function of providing money, safeguarding assets, and handling taxes. Or will personnel men concern themselves, in addition, with activities that, while perhaps no more important, are more directly related to the problems of the president and other line executives?

Three Top Management Problems

So much for the longer-range opportunity and challenge open to those who have the vision, courage, and ability to develop it. What are some of the things personnel people can do right now to increase the value of their function to top management? First, they can start working on personnel problems of greatest concern to the president and other top management executives.

I select only three problems that are in the forefront of the minds of progressive corporation directors and top management executives today—problems personnel people can do something about right now. They involve the top 1 percent, and even the top $^1/_{10}$ of 1 percent, of the personnel whose decisions and leadership shape the course of the business.

1. What can we do to improve the ability of our present executives? The increased size of businesses and the growing complexity and difficulty of the conditions under which they operate have contributed to the urgency of this question. Old trial-and-error and rule-of-thumb methods are no longer adequate.

2. How can we motivate and reward our management people to give them the greatest incentive for promoting the long-range profitability of the company?

3. How can we do a better job of selecting individuals of high potential and developing them so that they can assume greater responsibilities created by retirements or by growth of the business?

All three of these are problems that involve people and hence are clearly in the personnel area. On all three subjects we still are far from knowing as much as we should like to, but we know enough to make significant contributions.

All three questions are essentially interrelated. For example, good organization and management methods alone will not achieve the desired results without the right people. Combining the right people with poor organization and management methods is likely to result in friction, frustration, working at cross purposes, and loss of effectiveness. No compensation plan alone will overcome deficiencies in organization, personnel, or management methods. In fact, no compensation plan can be effectively administered without good organization and methods. Without these, any money spent on incentive compensation is probably being wasted. But, given the proper conditions, sound basic and incentive compensation can provide a real stimulus to increase the long-range profits of the business.

Recognizing the interrelation of these problems, let us touch briefly on the main considerations involved in each area, and, in so doing, try to summarize briefly some of the types of problems that even the most progressively managed companies are facing today.

Improving Managerial Effectiveness

What can the director of personnel do to help the president improve the ability of executives to deal with the complex and difficult problems of managing a business today? The approach to this problem has two phases. First, a framework of clearly defined objectives, policies, organization structure, and decision-making processes that channel executive efforts along the most productive lines must be created.

Second, methods must be sharpened so that executives can make most effective use of their time, improve the quality of their decision making, and work more effectively with people. Let us look briefly at the factors going into each of these phases.

Framework for Executive Action

Analysis of many businesses has convinced me that among the most important factors contributing to unity of purpose, teamwork, and an effective, hard-hitting organization are clearly defined objectives and policies. A clear understanding, resulting from thorough analysis of company objectives, of what the company as a whole or an individual department is trying to do, and of the principles set up to guide individual decisions, will go far to (1) make teamwork possible, (2) reduce time and effort spent unproductively, and (3) eliminate major sources of executive frustration.

Conflicting or constantly shifting objectives and policies can produce the reverse effect. For example, every company is interested in producing the maximum volume of products of acceptable quality at optimum costs. But often higher management, instead of taking a balanced approach, will alternately put extreme heat first on one and then on another of these aspects of production. When the heat is on volume, quality and costs tend to go to pieces, and vice versa. Sometimes each member of top management is driving for his own objectives without regard for those of the others. The operators, whipsawed between conflicting or shifting objectives, tend to throw up their hands in despair.

It is equally important to see that the company's organization plan enables individual executives to work together effectively as a coordinated team. Therefore, the director of personnel can profitably review his company's plan of organization in the light of questions such as the following:

1. Have all essential activities been specifically provided for?
2. Are responsibilities properly grouped to achieve the most effective results?
    a. Have activities been so classified as to facilitate their supervision by one individual?
    b. Have the responsibilities assigned to any one person become too numerous and complex for him to handle effectively?
    c. Have any functions been assigned to more than one unit in the organization?
    d. Wherever possible, does each organizational unit have responsibility for some completed unit of work?
3. Are lines of authority and communication between individuals best adapted for effective supervision, coordination, and control?
    a. Do executives have more subordinates reporting to them than they can supervise and coordinate effectively?
    b. Are the number of levels of authority kept at a minimum?
    c. Do some persons report on a line basis to more than one superior or to none? Does each member of the organization know to whom he reports and who reports to him?
    d. Has adequate provision been made for the coordination of related activities?
4. Are responsibility and authority properly assigned and defined?
    a. Has authority been delegated to the greatest extent possible, consistent with necessary controls, so that functions are coordinated and decisions made as close as possible to the point of action?
    b. Are distinctions between line and functional authority and staff work recognized?
    c. Are the responsibility and authority of each executive in his relationships with other parts of the organization clearly defined?
    d. Is responsibility matched by authority?
    e. Have the organizational plan and responsibilities, authorities, and relationships of executives been reduced to writing in an organization guide?

Such an analysis will probably disclose a number of opportunities for improvement, which the director of personnel should call to the attention of the president or the executive concerned, pointing out the problems and benefits that would result from correcting them. Thorough investigation of operations will usually supply proof in terms of measurable increases in efficiency, reduced costs, and improved profits.

What can be accomplished by the application of our knowledge of how people work most effectively is simply illustrated by the case of a very large order-processing unit that was originally set up by industrial engineers on the basis of a highly specialized division of labor. Processing time was five to eight days, errors were high, and morale and productivity were low. The activity was reorganized by a personnel man who understood how people worked most effectively. Processing time was cut to five hours, errors almost completely eliminated, and costs reduced 20 percent. While results are less easily measured in top-management organization, the same benefits can be achieved by personnel men, taking advantage of their present knowledge of what makes people work most effectively.

In fact, one of the most important things the director of personnel can do to step up the effectiveness of executive action and to improve teamwork is to persuade the president to undertake a thorough analysis of the organization, enlisting the participation of the entire group. Here are some of the benefits that can result from such a project:

Each executive can be required to think through his objectives, responsibilities, and authorities. He can then discuss these with other members of the executive group to determine how they should be assigned and integrated. Any disagreements can be resolved by the parties concerned. An organization manual can be developed that clearly defines responsibilities and offers each executive a method of getting together with his subordinates and deciding what is expected of each. This provides objective criteria on which there is mutual agreement. On the basis of these criteria an executive can review performance regularly and compare it with agreed to standards. Channels of communication can be clarified. Everyone in the organization will gain a better understanding of every other executive's responsibilities as well as his own. As a result, coordination and teamwork can be improved.

The effectiveness of executives and supervisors in achieving long-range company goals and in developing people is also greatly influenced by the company management philosophy. For example, one practice followed by some businesses—requiring executives to account for their operations in detail almost on a daily basis—tends to be self-defeating. The pressure to produce daily results often causes executives and supervisors to do things that are actually harmful in the long run. It also tends to produce a backward-looking approach to the job with the emphasis on alibies rather than on what will produce the best results in the long run. Moreover, it promotes over-supervision and the by-passing of responsible management personnel by their superiors. Higher levels of supervision become immersed in details and in the needs of the moment, and, as a result, fail to devote adequate attention to long-range planning. Lower levels of supervision feel that their superiors lack confidence in them, and this reduces their initiative. This not only produces poor results in the long run but seriously retards the development of management personnel.

Where Does the Personnel Man Fit In?

It may be asked what responsibility and authority personnel men have over these matters and what, as a practical matter, they can do about them in any case. My answer is that if the personnel man conceives his job as including responsibility for seeing that the company has provided the framework and mechanics within which people can work most effectively, these things *are* his responsibility. Certainly the responsibility of the personnel man in these areas is as great as that of the financial man in many of the areas into which he is drawn, simply because they involve money. Moreover, the most progressive personnel man—the one who has earned the right to be the president's adviser on any problems involving people—is actually entering them. True, it is not the personnel man's province to say what the objectives, policies, or organization plan should be, or what should be communicated. These are the responsibilities of other executives. However, it is clearly his job to point out the need for, and the benefits to be derived from, clarity in the definition of objectives, policies, organization, communications, and other aspects of management, and to show what problems can result from its absence. He can also assist the responsible executives in clarifying and communicating these matters.

In addition to his responsibilities for creating the framework and the mechanics within and through which the executive group as a whole can function most effectively, the director of personnel can and should assist individual executives to develop their skills in applying methods that will (1) improve the quality of their decision-making, (2) make the most effective use of their time, and (3) enable them to work most effectively with and through people.

A number of companies are making excellent progress along these lines through "executive methods round tables" and individual coaching.

Executive Compensation

The second major top-management personnel problem is how to motivate and reward our management people in order to give them the greatest incentive to increase the long-range profitability of the business.

The seriousness of this problem is highlighted by a survey of 41 leading concerns in a carefully selected cross section of industries made by Arch Patton of McKinsey & Company. Briefly, it showed that in the period between 1939 and 1950, average nonsupervisory compensation had increased 106 percent; supervisory compensation, 83 percent; middle management, 45 percent; and top management, only 35 percent. After adjusting these figures for increases in taxes and cost of living, it was found that nonsupervisory personnel had experienced a 3 percent increase in real income. On the other hand, supervisors had suffered a 13 percent decline in net real income, middle management a 40 percent decline, and top management approximately a 60 percent decline.

The implications of this condition in the motivation of the people who are responsible for providing leadership not only to our individual companies but to our profits system are obvious and do not require comment here. However, it seems fair to say that if personnel people do not consider themselves responsible for compensation of the executive group as well as those in lower pay grades, this condition represents a serious failure on their part. If they have not been responsible for executive salaries—and in most companies they are not—it is pretty clear that they should have been. In fact, management could well reproach them as a certain executive did his doctor. The executive was suffering from insomnia and appealed to his doctor for relief. The doctor informed the executive that he was unable to help him because the executive was allergic to barbiturates. Whereupon, the executive said, "How about this twilight sleep I've been hearing about?" The doctor replied, "Oh, you can't use that. That's for labor." Whereupon the executive cried in anguish, "Good grief! Haven't you got anything for management?"

This condition has caused many companies to reexamine the problem of executive financial incentives. In part, this revived interest in how to reward management for doing a good job stems from the desire to find some way out of the restrictions imposed by current tax regulations. But even more, progressive ownership and management are looking for more effective ways of attracting and motivating executives who will make their companies grow and prosper in today's competitive world.

It is an unfortunate and well-known fact that many executive incentive plans have failed. The record is full of abandoned or moribund programs. Sometimes these failures can be traced to external economic forces beyond the company's control. But even more frequently they are due to deficiencies in the management of the company, and to lack of objective, far-sighted planning before the incentive systems are put into effect. Executive incentives are no substitute for sound and clearly defined goals, policies, organization, and methods. Other causes of failure can be found in the structure or the operation of the plan itself. But those companies that have worked successfully with the financial incentives have also turned in impressive records of profit performance. In this connection, it might be pointed out that both the study just referred to and one that Arch Patton made for the American Management Associations provide considerable evidence that there is a relationship between high executive compensation—particularly incentive compensation—and a favorable profit record by the company.

The surveys have also brought to light, wide discrepancies in executive compensation levels, not only between industries but between companies in the same industry. Although these studies have made such executive compensation data available to management for the first time, in many cases little could be done to correct the inequities revealed until salary stabilization ended in February 1953. Now—with salaries decontrolled—it seems likely that there will be a wave of salary readjustments. This gives the personnel man a unique opportunity to make a contribution to executive effectiveness that will bring him closer to top management.

However, it also presents the personnel executive with problems. During the long period of the salary freeze, the relative value to a company of some jobs may have increased or decreased. Thus if salary boosts are made in the prefreeze pattern, the more important profit contributors may be under-rewarded. Experience indicates that a good deal of executive unrest can be attributed to such unbalance in compensation.

As I see it, the personnel man now has a responsibility, as well as an opportunity, to see that his company reexamines its executive incentive plan and revise it to correct the inequitable relationships that had to be tolerated during Salary Stabilization. It is also his responsibility to administer it so as to avoid the pitfalls of unsuccessful plans and profit by the thinking and experience of companies that have made their plans work. This, incidentally, is a responsibility that in too many instances has gone by default to the financial executive rather than the personnel executive.

One method of executive incentive compensation that has become increasingly popular is the stock option. This has been widely adopted, first, because it was the only form of executive incentive compensation that could be generally inaugurated under Salary Stabilization without a ruling; second, because it offers the executive a number of potential tax advantages. While this method has some drawbacks, it also has three very important merits:

1. It most closely identifies the interests of the executive with those of the stockholder.

2. It is a long-range incentive and minimizes the risk that executives may sacrifice long-range profits for today's "bird in the hand."

3. It allows executives to acquire capital gains, thus moderating the heavy burden of high tax brackets.

Management Development

The third major top management problem of concern to personnel executives is how the company can do a better job of selecting individuals with high potential, and developing them so that they can assume the greater responsibilities of positions made vacant by the retirement of senior executives or created by growth of the business.

There is widespread awareness of the causes that have contributed to this problem and of the amount of attention it is receiving today. There is hardly a company president who does not regard it as one of his major problems. Approaches vary from what appear to be rather naïve efforts to find panaceas to carefully thought-out plans that should pay real dividends in the long run. Almost every one concerned with management has contributed his two cents' worth to the discussions of this subject. I shall confine myself here to saying that, in my opinion, an important part of the answer to this question lies in the solution to the other two questions discussed in this article. A plan of organization, and management philosophy and methods that encourage men early in their careers to reach out for responsibility, make independent decisions, and profit by their mistakes, supplemented by incentive compensation that encourages competitive spirit and profit consciousness and rewards good performance, will create an environment that attracts and develops good men. There are many supplementary methods, of course, that can improve and speed the development process. All personnel men, I am sure, are familiar with these. They can make important contributions to helping other members of management to develop and apply these methods.

Getting on the Right Road

In companies where personnel people enjoy a close confidential relationship with the president, the latter is undoubtedly already aware of these problems. But how about the companies where management does not now recognize that personnel people can assist in the solution to these problems? How can personnel people get started on the road that will make them the president's advisers on all the human problems of the business? There is no single or easy answer to this. However, I believe personnel people can profit from the story of Androcles and the lion—or even the lion and the mouse! Even the operating executives who regard themselves as lords of all they survey—even the ones who roar like lions—occasionally get thorns in their paws or get caught in nets. If the personnel man demonstrates his ability to give these executives prompt and practical help in solving their problems, he will earn the opportunity to be consulted on the next problems that arise, which may be bigger ones. In this connection, it is well to start with limited objectives, relating to problems on which the line executive recognizes that the solution would bring tangible and demonstrable benefits, and work up to the broader and less tangible problems. Incidentally, executive compensation is not only a very timely problem, but it is one on which prompt attention is quite certain to receive favorable recognition from the management group. But, even more important, the personnel man must have broad enough vision to conceive of himself as the president's right arm in the handling of all human problems; he must also have the courage to seize the opportunities that will lead to making this vision a reality. He must be alert to recognize these opportunities when they arise. Busy chief executives are not going to come running to tell him about them; he must search the opportunities out for himself, and be ready to act at the proper moment.

No Easy Road

I have suggested three broad personnel problems that are of major concern to directors and top managements of forward-looking companies. None of them is susceptible of easy solution; on each we should like to know far more than we now do. But the same could have been said of the methods employed by the controller, the sales manager, the production manager, or the research director when their functions were at the same stage of development as personnel administration is today. Personnel management is a relatively new, and, I believe, a rapidly rising star. How quickly it establishes itself—as some others have already done—in the galaxy to which the president looks for light on his major problems, is up to the individual personnel man and no one else.

17

November 1956

Personnel Staff
and the
Line Organization

Louis A. Allen

WHAT is the proper role of the staff personnel department in relation to the line organization? What authority does the personnel manager have? What decisions can he make? From chief executive's office to production floor, questions such as these are at the nub of many a dispute over accountability, prerogatives, and plain "who gives orders to whom?"

When the personnel manager is asked to give his side of the story, he usually sees his job as that of determining personnel policies and plans and preparing programs to be carried out in the line departments. Also, he believes he has an obligation to inspect line operations to make sure that a good personnel job is being done. The line reaction to this point of view may range from skepticism to derision.

Consider policymaking as a case in point. In one company, the president delegated to the personnel manager responsibility [1] and

---

[1] Responsibility is the *work* assigned to a position. The term as used refers to the work itself. Work is physical or mental effort.

authority [2] to "decide and enforce personnel policies and programs." The personnel manager took this as his charter. In the wage and salary area, for instance, he developed and published companywide salary ranges for newly hired college graduates. Typical of the reaction was a vehement protest from the production vice-president. "The market for engineers is so tight we can't get half the qualified managers we need," he said. "Now our personnel people have put a ceiling of $375 on college graduates and they're sitting on it. I have a program for product expansion, but I won't be held to account if personnel won't let me hire engineers at whatever rates we have to pay to get them."

Look at another aspect of the problem—accountability [3] for personnel programs. If the management development program fails to develop managers, should this failure be laid at the door of the personnel function? The question has many implications, most of them troublesome. According to a commonly accepted principle of organization, the personnel manager *cannot* be held accountable for developing managers unless he has the requisite authority. But rare indeed is the suggestion that personnel should be given authority over line managers, even to aid management development.

The predicament of the personnel man is pointed up by one training manager who recently instituted a new training program. He was perturbed because attendance at training classes was poor. "I've designed these courses to develop management skills," he said, "and our managers need development. Plenty of it. But I rarely get as high as 40 percent attendance. If the company is laying out money for training, I feel I should have some control over attendance."

Identifying Line and Staff

Examples such as these are commonplace. Their net toll to the company is loss of efficiency, unnecessary expense, and jeopardy to effective teamwork. While the solution to the problem will vary in detail from company to company, there are certain fundamentals that apply to all situations. Basic is an understanding of how staff differs from line and the proper role of each in the company. Let us examine the line organization first. What is line? How can it be identified?

[2] Authority is the sum of the powers and rights necessary to carry out responsibility.
[3] Accountability is the obligation to carry out responsibility and exercise authority in terms of existing performance standards.

The line organization comprises the elements that are accountable for accomplishing the company's basic objectives. To identify line, you must know for what purpose the company is organized.[4] A rubber company, for example, is organized to manufacture and sell rubber products. Hence its line departments are manufacturing and marketing. In a chemical company, where research to replace obsolete products is as essential to maintaining competitive standing as the manufacture and sale of the existing product line, the line organization consists of the research, production, and sales departments. An oil company is organized to explore and develop sources of petroleum and petroleum products and to refine, transport, and market them. Here, the line functions are production, manufacturing, transportation, and marketing. By contrast, an insurance company is organized to insure against predetermined risks on a favorable basis, to sell insurance, and to pay the losses incurred by policyholders. The line functions in this case are underwriting, sales, and claims.

What do we mean by staff? Staff comprises those elements of the organization that are responsible for providing advice and service. Staff departments exist primarily to help the line accomplish the objectives of the company. Thus personnel is characteristically a staff function. We can define the role of the personnel staff as that of providing advice and service to the line organization and to other staff elements in making most effective use of the human resources within the company.

Personnel Objectives and Policies

The personnel department provides advice and service to all levels of the organization. At the top management level, it assists the chief executive in developing objectives and policies for personnel administration. Personnel *objectives* are the overall goals of the company with regard to its people, such as, for example, "To train and develop the company's personnel for improved performance and greater responsibilities within the company." Personnel *policies* are the continuing, relatively permanent decisions needed to implement personnel objectives. Thus a policy aimed at achieving the goal just stated might be, "Every manager will evaluate the performance of each of his subordinates at least once each year and counsel with him to help identify weaknesses and work toward improvement."

[4] Louis A. Allen, *Improving Staff and Line Relationships,* National Industrial Conference Board, Studies in Personnel Policy No. 153, 1956.

The chief executive of the company and the board of directors have responsibility and authority for determining objectives and policies for all aspects of the business, including personnel administration. They decide whether the company will pay equal wages for equal work, whether it will promote on the basis of seniority or performance, or both, whether it will require employees to join a union as a condition of employment, and so on. In most cases, however, neither the chief executive nor the board has the time or the specialized training to go into these matters in detail. Accordingly, responsibility for studying the company's requirements, reviewing what has been done by other companies, and consulting with line and staff managers to secure their suggestions and ideas as a basis for recommending personnel objectives and policies to the chief executive is delegated to the personnel department. The chief executive reviews the recommendations of his personnel staff, integrates them with the sometimes conflicting demands and suggestions of other functional heads, assesses the whole in terms of the long-range objectives of the company, and either arrives at a decision himself or makes appropriate recommendation to the board of directors.

Once personnel objectives and policies have been determined by top line management, the personnel staff provides advice and service in interpreting them to lower levels of the organization. In this capacity, the personnel staff frequently *does things* for the line because the appropriate line manager does not have the special skill, or the time, to do it for himself.

For example, the personnel staff develops overall personnel programs, such as wage and salary administration and management development, *for* the chief executive. After the chief executive has decided to put these programs into effect, he delegates responsibility and authority for compensating and training people to the accountable line and staff managers concerned. It is the function of personnel to provide the line organization and other staff departments with the advice and service they need to do this job; but the personnel staff itself should not be held accountable for compensating or training employees.

It follows that personnel may set and police salary ranges; it may test and interview job applicants; it may conduct contract negotiations; and it may set up training conferences and classes. In each case, however, personnel does these things because the line and other staff departments call upon it to help them carry out the chief executive's decision with respect to personnel objectives, policies, and company programs.

There is a danger here that the line will try to persuade personnel to take over work that it does not want, or finds it difficult, to do. For example, line managers frequently ask the personnel department to take over the job of appraisal and counseling. The personnel manager may welcome this opportunity because it enables him to provide an important service to the line. However, each such assumption weakens both the personnel staff department and the line organization.

Whenever possible, a program developed by the staff personnel group should be directed toward its own liquidation. Except for purely technical personnel procedures, such activities as training, compensation, labor relations, and communications should be turned over to the accountable line positions as expeditiously as possible. This helps keep personnel staff to a minimum and broadens and develops line managers. The personnel manager should not become enmeshed in the routine of repetitive operation, but should free himself to work with line managers in developing on-the-spot solutions to human relations problems and to originate and develop new activities designed to achieve more profitable operation of the company as a whole.

Personnel Controls

The personnel department also provides advice and service in the development and application of personnel controls. Control, as used here, means the evaluation of work. To be effective, it involves four steps: (1) The development of standards of performance; (2) measurement of work; (3) analysis and comparison of work completed with the standards that have been established; and (4) corrective action to bring undesirable variations into line. The personnel department assists in the development of *performance standards* for personnel activities by helping to establish objectives, policies, programs, procedures, and budgets, which are in themselves yardsticks for performance. The actual *measurement,* or determination and recording of the degree of performance, is best carried out by the position or unit doing the work. Thus the number of grievances and their handling, extent of tardiness and absenteeism, or effectiveness of job performance in comparison with position responsibilities should be determined by accountable line and staff heads.

Departmental *analysis and comparison* of control information is necessary to the effective self-control of the operating department involved. But provision should also be made for analysis and comparison on a companywide basis by the personnel staff to ensure an objective survey of all the facts and a balanced analysis of underlying or contributing causes. Where *corrective action* is indicated, however, this is invariably a line responsibility. The personnel director may suggest or recommend it; but if he *directs* that changes be made when he detects discrepancies or omissions, he is assuming the authority of his line superior and is inviting trouble.

Many personnel directors will complain that this concept, by limiting them to the function of "advice and service," belittles the part of staff and gives it an inferior role. This is no more true, however, than to say that the work of the anesthetist or pathologist is less important than that of the surgeon, or that the position of tackle or guard is inferior to that of quarterback. Each has an equally important, if different, part to play. Effective teamwork can exist only if each knows his proper role, is convinced of its importance, and is willing to play it to the hilt without overstepping the prerogatives of the rest of the team.

Basics of a Sound Relationship

It should be clear by now that the line departments, and not the personnel staff, are accountable for making the most effective use of the human resources of their own units. Each department head is responsible for selecting, training, placing, transferring, promoting, compensating, and terminating his subordinates in accordance with corporation policy. Each operating executive, manager, and supervisor who directs the work of others should be accountable for the wholehearted and effective execution of the principles of personnel administration and employee relations set forth by the company. It is the job of personnel to aid in carrying out these principles.

What are the essential components of a sound and workable relationship between the personnel department and the line organization? Of paramount importance are the delegation of carefully defined responsibility and authority to both line and personnel staff and a mutual understanding of the limits within which each may operate.

Both line and personnel staff are delegated authority to carry out their responsibilities. Both make decisions. However, the authority they exercise and the decisions they make differ as to kind and degree. As has been seen, line managers are accountable for the success of the primary activities of the company; hence, they must be delegated authority for final decisions in operating matters. To the extent that this authority is withheld, line managers cannot be made fully accountable. Personnel staff is held accountable for the effectiveness of the advice and service it provides to the appropriate elements of the line organization and to other staff departments. Convincing line managers of the need for and the practicability of his advice and service are part of the personnel manager's accountability.

Who is responsible for establishing the proper roles of line and personnel staff? In the great majority of cases, the relationship is worked out fortuitously, or through a process of strategic attack and retreat. However, if there is to be a sound relationship, responsibility for clarifying the part each is to play must be assumed by the coordinating executive with jurisdiction over both line and staff positions. On the company level, for instance, division and personnel managers report to the chief executive; in the plant, the personnel manager and the production superintendent report to the plant manager. It is the responsibility of the coordinating executive to ensure that both line and personnel staff are delegated enough authority to perform the work assigned to them, and no more. He must see to it that there is no overlap, and that both line and staff on a common reporting level recognize that neither has authority over the other. Each has a different job to do, and needs different authority to make it possible.

Some Further Questions

Should personnel stand and wait to be called or should it volunteer its services? Though in some instances personnel may find it advantageous to wait until its help is asked, it is responsible for keeping itself informed about the problems confronting the line. Hence, it should proffer advice and service where it believes it is needed and without being specifically invited. Staff is most valuable when it thinks ahead, makes constructive plans, and helps the line solve its difficult operating problems.

The question also arises whether the line is obliged to accept the programs and suggestions advanced by the personnel staff. Obviously, line should give serious consideration to all offers of advice and service by personnel. Line heads should call upon staff in all matters where it possesses wider experience and more knowledge than is available within their own units. Where there is doubt, the sole criterion for acceptance of the advice should be whether it is in the company's best interest to do so. Nevertheless, line managers should have clear authority to accept, reject, or modify the advice or service proffered by personnel staff. The only exception is in those cases where top line management, as a matter of policy, has decided that such personnel services as job evaluation, training, contract negotiation, or recruitment will be used by the line organization. This decision is binding at all levels.

Where there is disagreement as to whether staff recommendations should be followed, both line and personnel staff should have a right of appeal to higher line authority. However, when the exigencies of the operating situation so require, this right of appeal should not be permitted to supersede line's authority to make immediate decisions.

The role outlined here provides a sound basis for harmonious working relationships between line and personnel staff. While variations and modifications will always be occasioned by the personalities involved and the immediate operating situation, it may serve as a useful pattern for executives concerned with making use of all available resources in developing maximum productivity and teamwork.

New Frontiers
for Personnel
Management

Charles A. Myers

THE central fact of industrial life in the second half of the 20th century is the accelerating pace of basic scientific knowledge and its impact on technology. The revolution in information technology through the advent of the electronic computer is only one consequence. Young engineering students today are studying and doing research in fields that were hardly even known 15 years ago—fields that are just beginning to have their impact on industry. Among them, for example, are modern atomic and nuclear physics and nuclear engineering; the application of the modern computer to engineering analysis and design; computer-aided design and control of machine tools; and solid state physics and molecular engineering. There are, of course, many others, too numerous to cite here.

These rapid advances in our knowledge have, in turn, accelerated the pace of change, which today confronts management with new problems and has added new dimensions to old ones. Is the average personnel executive equipped to help management deal with these problems, or will he have to give way to the new specialists already coming to the fore—the experts in information technology, in the management of research and development, and in manpower and organization planning?

Will the personnel man be content to put out little fires and handle only peripheral personnel services, while someone else sits in on the councils of a top-executive team concerned with the more serious problems growing out of the scientific revolution? Will personnel administration actually sink to the level characterized in Peter Drucker's harsh words, "partly a file clerk's job, partly a housekeeping job, partly a social worker's job, and partly 'fire fighting' to head off union trouble or settle it"? There is an uneasiness in the minds of many personnel executives about these changes and these criticisms. What can they do about them?

I believe the personnel man's first step must be to acquaint himself with these changes, so that he can comprehend where they are leading. Next, he must determine what their specific consequences will be for management, so that he can help management anticipate and plan for these consequences insofar as they affect the people in the organization. This kind of understanding is indispensable to the advance planning needed to meet the challenge of change.

But advance knowledge of and preparation for change takes hard work and professional competence. If there are any personnel executives who still work only an eight-hour day, or are failing to keep abreast of the expanding body of knowledge about such fields as information technology or research in the behavioral sciences as they relate to the world of work, they had better face the fact that their effective days are numbered—that is, unless they are content to be what Peter Drucker said they were. If he is truly to function as an adviser to top management, the personnel executive will have to live down the stereotype of a hail-fellow-well-met trying to keep everybody happy by administering a variety of employee benefits and services. These may still be important, but they are not of first importance today.

The Central Facts of Change

It is not possible, in the space of a short article, to enlarge upon all the changes confronting management in the years ahead. Since my emphasis is on science and technology, I have to omit from my discussion such far-reaching developments as the civil rights movement, which undoubtedly presents a whole raft of challenges and problems of its own. Accordingly, I shall confine myself here to three major areas of change: (1) the changing composition of the labor force, (2) changing information technology, and (3) changing jobs and skills. Let's look at each of them in more detail.

1. *Changing composition of the labor force.* The proportion of white collar workers in our labor force exceeded that of the blue collar group as early as 1956; by 1970 there will be nearly one-third more white collar than blue collar workers. Though clerical workers still represent the largest single work group, professional and technical workers are increasing more rapidly. By 1970, they will constitute 13.3 percent of our total labor force—nearly double the percentage for 1940; in fact, there will be more professional and technical workers than either skilled workers or laborers, and nearly as many as in the semiskilled group. This prospect underscores the growing importance of science and technology in our economy, and raises doubts about the relevance today of personnel policies and procedures developed in the period when blue collar workers predominated.

By way of example, let's consider what is now one of our largest industries—aerospace. Here, production workers now represent less than two-fifths of the workforce; three-fifths are professional, technical, and clerical employees. As compared with 1950, when a workforce of 69 percent production and only 12 percent engineering employees was required to produce a DC-6, the manufacture of a Saturn S-4 rocket launch vehicle now requires 51 percent engineering and only 41 percent production employees. Here is a graphic illustration of the impact of the space age on personnel.

Moreover, by 1975, the employed labor force will be better educated than it was in 1960 or will be in 1965. Levels of educational attainment have been rising in the United States, and these will continue as the postwar baby boom hits the secondary schools and then the colleges. Better-educated people have different expectations and different aspirations than do most blue collar workers. This is particularly true of the growing number of scientists, engineers, technicians, and other people with advanced training.

A Permanent Fissure?

Meanwhile, at the other end of the scale, there is the mounting problem of those without enough education for the scientific age: the high school drop-outs and the people with even less education than that. If enough job opportunites develop in the economy, possibly even these can find jobs, or at least be trained and upgraded to fill them.

On the other hand, there is a very real danger that, as Secretary of Labor Wirtz recently said, "The confluence of surging population and driving technology is splitting the American labor force into tens of millions of 'have's' and millions of 'have not's.' " Public policies to expand educational opportunities, training programs, and retraining will be necessary to supplement all that private industry can do to avoid this permanent fissure in our society.

2. *The revolution in information technology.* In less than a decade, the electronic computer has revolutionized information technology—a revolution that is likely to have its greatest impact on management itself. According to the Diebold organization, the number of general purpose digital computers increased from fewer than 400 in 1955 to over 11,000 in 1962—more than 27-fold in seven years! And in 1962 half of these were large computers costing a million dollars or more and operating at phenomenal speeds. The literature on computer applications—its ability to provide management with more detailed and rapid information, to integrate functional areas of the business, and to eliminate the routine functions of management—is already voluminous, but it is something that no farsighted personnel man can afford to neglect.

For the first time, technical change in the form of the computer is displacing *management* personnel, and this is likely to be increasingly true at the middle levels of management. As Shultz and Whisler noted in their introduction to *Management Organization and the Computer:* "Those who previously reached comfortable conclusions about the social gains from technological change—the managers—are now the people affected. The problems are those of retraining, transferring, and—unfortunately—of layoff or severance." [1] They might have added, and "of management featherbedding." Is the personnel executive preparing himself to deal with these growing problems right in the management ranks?

3. *Changing jobs and skills.* Expectations are that these will change more rapidly over the next 25 years than they have in the past 25. In fact, it is rapidly becoming impossible now to learn a skill or a profession that will continue unchanged for a lifetime. Who would have

[1] G. P. Shultz and T. L. Whisler, eds., *Management Organization and the Computer,* The Free Press of Glencoe, New York, 1960, p. 20.

thought ten years ago that the jobs of "information technologist" or "computer programmer" would become so important as they already have, let alone how important they will be in the future? As I pointed out earlier, today's electrical engineers are a different breed from the ones turned out even a decade ago. Similarly, the "pipe fitter" now working in an atomic energy plant is a far cry from yesterday's "plumber." Not only have new jobs opened up in fields that did not even exist in the early 1950s—there has also been a marked increase in the demand for such skilled workers as mechanics and repairmen. Meanwhile, semiskilled jobs in manufacturing are being steadily eliminated by the expansion of automated production processes. These continuing shifts in the job picture obviously have profound implications for longrange manpower planning.

The Main Routes Ahead

The changes I have outlined above will affect nearly every organization during the next decade or two. How can the personnel executive help top management plan to meet them? It seems to me that he should focus his efforts on the following seven areas:

1. It must be recognized that existing personnel policies and procedures, many of which were probably developed years ago when blue collar workers predominated, are no longer adequate for a better-educated workforce with its steadily increasing proportion of professional and technical employees. Has the personnel executive kept abreast of the growing literature on the aspirations of scientific and engineering personnel, and the most effective ways of managing them?

If so, he can assist management to understand and better integrate these employees' professional goals with the goals of the organization. This understanding is especially important in the management of *creative* people, upon whose talents the forward thrust of the enterprise may well depend. Some traditional personnel policies are only too likely to dull the very qualities for which these people are hired.

2. Planning for the organization's anticipated expansion (or contraction) is an essential part of the managerial process. How many personnel executives are taking time from "putting out fires" to assist management in planning for the manpower needs of the future? Or has manpower planning taken a back seat to product planning, sales planning, and the planning of technical changes? In our recent study, *Education, Manpower and Economic Growth,* Frederick Harbison and I stressed the need for each nation to work out its individual "strategy

of human resource development." [2] I believe that each company should also have such a strategy, based on its present labor force, its projected future manpower requirements, and anticipated future labor supply at all levels.

Many-Faceted Planning

All these data then have to be related to training and internal manpower development programs, as well as to external recruiting plans. But this cannot be done effectively unless manpower planning is more closely integrated with production and sales planning than it has been in the past. Furthermore, it will have to take account of the resources of talent and potential ability among members of minority groups, particularly Negroes, who will have access to better educational opportunities than they have had hitherto.

3. Training and manpower development must be a continuing function, with emphasis on the *retraining* of present employees to meet changing job requirements. Even professional employees, as well as managers, will need midcareer training to keep them abreast of the rapidly changing body of knowledge. Is the personnel executive beginning to plan now for this increasing volume of retraining? Some of it will have to be done within the enterprise and some with the cooperation of outside organizations. The growth of executive development programs foreshadows the extension of special training programs to important groups of non-managerial personnel. Computerization, for example, requires considerable retraining of the people who have to use the new information as well as of those who process it. How can the personnel administrator be helpful here unless he also understands what computerization means? Perhaps he will have to undergo midcareer retraining too!

Retraining will also be needed for overseas assignments. With more U.S. companies investing in manufacturing and sales subsidiaries abroad, it is becoming more and more important not only to select the right people to send overseas, but also to train them to work effectively with the nationals of the countries to which they are assigned. Yet a Conference Board symposium held about a year ago concluded that many companies have hardly begun to plan in earnest for these needs.[3] It's still quite common for people to be assigned to overseas positions on short notice.

[2] F. Harbison and C. A. Myers, *Education, Manpower and Economic Growth,* McGraw-Hill Book Company, Inc., New York, 1964.
[3] H. Stieglitz, "Effective Overseas Performance," *Management Record,* Feb. 1963, pp. 2–8.

4. Someone is going to have to pay attention to the organizational structures and managerial responsibilities affected by the new information technology. Surely, this should be one of the personnel man's key functions—yet in some firms, the introduction of electronic data processing has scarcely involved the personnel department, even though it has had a tremendous impact on personnel. Thus in his recent study of 12 diverse companies Leonard Rico has concluded, "The personnel function played a sterile and inconsequential role in the management of change in the survey firms. The personnel department was not consulted, and generally had little or no idea of the organizational and manpower problems associated with computerization in their firms." Dr. Rico further found "no evidence that top management has concerned itself with anticipating changed manpower requirements under computerization." [4]

Anticipating the Computer

Now, there is normally plenty of lead time for such planning. First there are the feasibility studies, then the cost calculations, the delays in delivery due to computer manufacturers' backlogs, and the initial programming. All this takes place before the data processing center is actually in operation. Here is a prime opportunity for the personnel executive to work with the computer unit in planning for the impact of the computer on the entire workforce. Advance planning for change is often required by union agreements covering blue collar workers; it is no less necessary for changes affecting nonunion white collar, technical, and managerial personnel. In fact, the impact of computerization on some levels of middle management may be far reaching indeed, as I have already suggested. Plans must be made not only for transfers and retraining, but also possibly for earlier retirements or severance allowances.

5. The personnel executive should recognize, too, that the changes I have been discussing here all have important implications for managerial philosophy, that is, the organization's pattern of management. A question much under discussion at the present time is whether the traditional pattern of management by centralized direction and control (which Douglas McGregor has called Theory X) will work as well with the new type of labor force and the new technology as might management by integration and self-control (which

[4] L. Rico, "The Dynamics of Industrial Innovation," *Industrial Management Review*, Fall, 1963, pp. 3–4.

McGregor called Theory Y). It has been reported that information technology brings greater centralization, because the relevant data for centralized decisions are more quickly available to top management. This looks like useful ammunition for the proponents of Theory X. But if a management believes that Theory Y is really more viable, it might equally well use the new information technology to make data for self-control more readily available to the managers of its decentralized operations. In any case, here is a question with which the personnel administrator might profitably concern himself. He will need to be familiar with the findings of the behavioral sciences on the work of people in organizations, as well as with research on the management of scientific and engineering personnel, in order to advise top management on the style of managing best suited to the organization's needs.

6. More thought will have to be given to develop better ways of handling the persistent problems of labor–management relations. Many organizations, as well as whole industries, are already taking steps along these lines—for example, the human relations committees in the steel industry. It needs to be borne in mind, though, that what works well in one industry or in a particular company may not necessarily prove equally effective in another. Labor relations people must resist the temptation to seize upon a plan that has succeeded elsewhere as the answer to their own problems. As Edgar Kaiser has said, "Each management must define its own problem, work at it long enough and hard enough to formulate some policy thinking, and then sit down with its counterparts in labor, at a time when no crisis exists, and find a mutually satisfactory approach." The outcome will probably be no one single answer, but a whole series of experiments that deserve trial. The Scanlon Plan, for example, represents one approach that, in my judgment, has not been sufficiently explored by personnel and labor relations people.[5]

New Patterns Needed

Nevertheless, it is not a surefire formula for industrial harmony. My point simply is that because of the changing work environment and the changing composition of the labor force, the traditional patterns of collective bargaining and labor–management relations need a thorough reexamination.

[5] F. G. Lesieur, ed., *The Scanlon Plan: A Frontier in Labor*-Management Cooperation, The MIT Press, Inc., Cambridge, Mass., 1958.

7. The overall implication of the changes I have discussed here is that henceforth the personnel executive will have to concern himself far more than before with the impact of the *external environment* on the management of the enterprise. The changing nature of the labor force, with its need for long-range manpower planning, and increasing emphasis on training and retraining, the impact of information technology, the emerging new patterns of management, and the continuing pressures for new approaches to collective bargaining are all examples of external forces that impinge on the personnel function.

Some of these changes will inevitably involve an increasing role for government—the provision of better educational facilities, the establishment of retraining programs, better organization of the public employment service to ease the impact of automation on employment, improved unemployment compensation, area redevelopment plans, and the like. Some managements, no doubt, will still remain strongly opposed to all such "encroachments." I suspect, though, that more managements will recognize how useful certain government programs can be as supplements to the company's own attempts to adapt to the changes growing out of the scientific revolution. If I am right in this, the future personnel executive will need to know what public programs are available and how they can be used as adjuncts to the company's own manpower plans. It will be up to him, too, to persuade his management to support the efforts to improve public education (including vocational education), official retraining programs, the public employment service, and unemployment compensation, instead of maintaining negative attitudes toward these inevitable developments.

I suppose it will be objected that the personnel executive capable of shouldering all the responsibilities I have outlined here would have to be a superman. Maybe so. But no personnel man need be discouraged on that account from trying to make some progress along the lines I have indicated. There is no doubt that more will be demanded of tomorrow's personnel executive—in study, in planning, and in action. And while he cannot neglect the bread-and-butter services he has performed in the past, he can no longer afford to occupy himself with these procedures alone. If he does, he will fail in his responsibility to give top management the guidance and assistance it must have to meet the sweeping changes in the years to come.

PART IV

How're We Doing?

KEEPING score is intrinsically motivating. Most managers, however, think of keeping score only in terms of doing better than the next fellow. This *is* an important way to look at scorekeeping, but it is often as much fun to compete against your own past performance. Golfers, bowlers, and runners, for example, work to better their past scores— even if they're not in a competition. It is the same with keeping score of the performance of the human resources function.

Measurement—scorekeeping—is an essential element of professional management. And evaluation inevitably follows. So it is, too, with the human resources function. As Robert D. Gray pointed out in his 1965 article "Evaluating the Personnel Department," the issue is not whether or not to evaluate, the issue is whether the evaluation will be informal or systematic. Gray, who was a professor of economics and industrial relations at the California Institute of Technology and director of its industrial relations center at the time he wrote the article, listed six typical criteria used in evaluating personnel department performance and showed why these criteria were inadequate. Budgets, personnel ratios, turnover, unionization, grievances, and strikes are faulty criteria, he pointed out; the only sound basis for evaluation is in terms of the objectives set for the function. Many support the validity of this attitude even today.

While Gray quite properly emphasized the broadest basis for evaluation of the human resources function in his article, managers of the function must often evaluate their activity in terms of how well they are using their resources to accomplish their objectives. In small departments this is rarely difficult. As departments grow in size and become decentralized, however, systematic procedures for periodically assessing patterns of resource allocation become necessary. Stephen J. Carroll, Jr. recommended the use of a work-sampling approach to measuring resource allocation in his 1960 article "Measuring the Work of a Personnel Department." His article presents the results obtained in a project conducted by the industrial relations center of the University of Minnesota in applying the work-sampling technique to the human resources function in a division of a large Midwestern manufacturing company. Carroll was a staff member at the center at the time the research was done.

The industrial relations center at the University of Minnesota has spawned many significant innovations in the human resources management area. Dale Yoder, who was director of the center for many years, undoubtedly stimulated many of these, and some carried his byline. One useful innovation was the development of the personnel ratio approach to evaluating the overall staffing of the human resources function and the staffing of each of its specialized activities. As use of personnel ratios spread, organizations wanted more and more to be able to compare their ratios with those of other, similar organizations. To do this requires consistency of classification of human resources staff by area of activity, and to help achieve this Yoder defined reporting categories in his 1949 article "Calculating Your Personnel Ratio." Although these categories would have to be revised to be useful today, his article represents a sound beginning.

Measuring the inputs into an organization's human resources activities provides only half the equation. An evaluation of any activity requires looking at both inputs and outputs so that some judgment of productivity can be made. The 1961 article by W. C. Jackson, "The Personnel Activity Index: A New Budgeting Tool," reports an approach used by the Adams Division of LeTourneau-Westinghouse Company to measure both input in terms of staff and workload in terms of an activity index. Staff input was measured in terms of numbers of personnel by area of activity, the traditional personnel ratios. Workload was measured in terms of an index based on the sum of weighted new hires, separations, transfers, rate changes, and first-aid cases. Given a forecast of workload developed using the index, the necessary staff can be determined; given the present workload, the adequacy of present staff levels can be determined. This is a rigorous, helpful approach, even today. The last article in Part IV is of current interest primarily because it suggests a framework for analysis of human resources activity and emphasizes again the importance of relating resources to the objectives for the function. "What About Personnel Relations Payroll Costs?" by George A. Cowee, Jr. and Gordon G. Bowen, both of McKinsey & Company at the time, was published in 1949. It outlines the procedure used to conduct a special survey of how much a small group of major U.S. companies were spending for human resources management. The specific results, of course, are an interesting historical flashback, but the methodology is as useful today as it was 30 years ago.

All organizations are concerned about the productivity of their resources, and the human resources function plays the leading role in guiding an organization on how to work with its people to obtain the highest possible level of productivity. Isn't it fitting, then, that this function should lead the way by example as well as by instruction?

Evaluating the Personnel Department

Robert D. Gray

A MAN can spend 20 years in the accounting department and neither know nor care what goes on in, say, traffic or marketing. But from the moment he signs his tax withholding authorization form, and frequently long before he has even been placed on the payroll, every employee, regardless of his point of vantage in the organization, immediately qualifies as his own expert on the merits and deficiencies of the personnel department. It can safely be said that no other area of the company's operations comes under more constant and more critical scrutiny by more people, both inside and outside the organization. The fact that the overwhelming majority of these assessments are incomplete or uninformed is not too surprising. What is surprising is that so few personnel departments themselves—when they do pause to take stock of their activities—come up with evaluations that have much more validity than the snap judgments of the rest of the world.

Against what criteria and by what methods should the personnel department be evaluated? To place this problem in its proper conceptual framework we need, I think, to answer four basic questions:

1. Why is an evaluation of the department necessary?
2. Who should do the evaluating?

3. What criteria should not be used in making the evaluation?

4. On what bases and by what methods should the department be evaluated?

Let's take up these points one by one.

1. *Why is an evaluation necessary?* The currently popular—and well-founded—concept of managing by objectives suggests that one reason for evaluating a personnel department is to make sure that both immediate and long-range goals have been established for its activities. As Thomas G. Spates, professor emeritus of personnel administration at Yale University and former vice-president of General Foods, pointed out some years ago, personnel departments come into being for a variety of reasons, including imitation, fear, and economic pressure.[1] It need hardly be said that none of these last-named reasons justifies the existence of any management function, let alone one so all-pervasive and sensitive as personnel. The primary purpose of the personnel department should be to assist the rest of the organization in achieving its basic objectives. Among these will usually be found such aims as reducing costs, increasing profits, and perpetuating the organization.

In addition to these basic and long-range goals, the department will normally have more immediate ones. These, for example, may be related to the opening of a new plant, the introduction of new equipment, or the filling of vacancies due to promotion, transfers, terminations, and the like, or to the expansion of the company's operations. The first order of business, therefore, must be to determine whether immediate and long-range objectives for the department have been established or not.

A second reason for evaluating the department is to ensure that the objectives that have been established for it are consistent with reasonable assumptions about the future. Just what changes are in the offing and to what extent are they likely to modify goals laid down before these new developments were foreseen?

If the department is to function effectively, sound short- and long-range objectives consistent with reasonable assumptions for the future are not enough. The objectives must be understood by all concerned. A third reason for evaluating a personnel department, therefore, is to measure how well its objectives are understood. Only then can the ultimate purpose of an evaluation be achieved—to de-

[1] For a fuller discussion of this point, see T. G. Spates, *Human Values Where People Work,* Harper & Brothers, New York, 1960, pp. 68–70, and *The Scope of Modern Personnel Administration,* Funk & Wagnalls, New York, 1948, pp. 2–3.

termine whether objectives have, in fact, been accomplished. Finally, since there will always be some gap between objectives and results, the end product of evaluation should be plans for corrections or adjustments.

2. *Who should do the evaluating?* As I began by pointing out, the work of the personnel department is constantly being appraised by practically everyone—top management, department heads, first-line supervisors, rank-and-file employees, along with their relatives and friends, job applicants, and other personnel people and the community at large. Moreover, all these people have a right to evaluate the personnel department, because they are affected directly or indirectly by what it does.

Thus, while the formal evaluation should be made by the personnel director himself and by top management, both in making their assessment should take into account what they can learn from the other sources I enumerated above.

3. *What criteria should not be used?* I can think of at least six criteria commonly used in evaluating personnel departments, principally because they are quantitative and simple. In my opinion, all of them are dubious measures of success, though they do sometimes serve as symptoms that all is not well.

Personnel ratios. One of the objections to the widely used personnel ratio is that there is little agreement as to what activities should be assigned to the personnel department. Doubtful categories, for example, include plant guards and cafeteria employees; in a few companies even duplicating services are classified as personnel work. A further objection to the personnel ratio is that it assumes that a wage and salary administrator, a plant doctor, or a safety engineer is equal to one records clerk, and vice versa. Nevertheless, all too often one hears a personnel manager boast that he has been able to reduce his personnel ratio below one personnel man or clerk to 100 employees, blandly ignoring the nature and complexity of their work.

Turnover rate. Probably too many conclusions can be drawn from labor turnover figures; part of the difficulty arises from the fact that all such published, presumably comparable, figures are not computed with the same formula. Moreover, varying circumstances are not indicated. By way of illustration: Turnover among employees with less than one year of service is substantially higher than among longer-service employees. Thus, if a company increases its workforce, it is normal for its turnover rate to increase; conversely, after a layoff of short-service employees, the turnover rate will decline markedly. And the labor turnover rate as a whole may also reflect general business conditions.

Turnover No Criterion

It is true that an improved employment and induction procedure may reduce this rate, but on the whole, a personnel department should not take either the credit or the blame for various changes in the labor turnover rate. Indeed, if there are great variations within a company, the chances are that supervisors are more responsible than the personnel department.

Budgets. Whether the authorized budget or actual expenditures are considered, per se an increase or decrease in these amounts does not show that the personnel department is either retrogressing or improving. If cost figures are used, they must not be interpreted by themselves, or in relation to last year's expenses, or to the per capita expenses of another company. A company should give primary consideration to its total costs, which sometimes can be reduced by increasing those of the personnel department, or at other times can be increased by a decrease in the personnel department's costs.

The use of cost data is most unrealistic when limited to a specific personnel function. For example, with graduated vacation plans, a reduction in labor turnover may result in an increased cost of vacations but a decreased cost of interviewing. On the other hand, increased labor turnover may cut the costs of vacation pay but cause an even greater increase in recruitment costs. Similarly, though a training program costs money, the elimination of this cost may be more than offset by hidden training costs on the job.

Unionization. Some companies apparently evaluate their personnel department in terms of whether or not the plant has become unionized. Since employees do have the right to organize, however, unionization is not the real measure of a personnel department. Some companies may have been organized chiefly because action by the personnel department was "too little and too late," but in such cases the blame, if there is any, should be placed initially on top management or the immediate supervisors, or both. No personnel department ever swung the decision all by itself.

Number of grievances. It is impossible to determine what is a "normal" number of grievances. An increase or decrease in the number of grievances may simply reflect a union election, a change in the membership of the grievance committee, the negotiations approach, or a forthcoming union election.

What Do Grievances Mean?

A large number of grievances can be both annoying and costly; yet the absence of grievances may be counterbalanced by undetected slowdowns or may signal that the supervisors are "giving the plant away," or even may imply that the employees are being intimidated. With so many different interpretations possible, such data obviously should not be used to evaluate the work of a personnel department.

Number of strikes. The primary objective of industry is not to produce industrial peace, but rather to produce goods and services at reasonable costs and prices. It's worth recalling that Studebaker Corporation used to boast that it had operated for 100 years without a strike—and we all know what happened to Studebaker. On the other hand, General Motors, concentrating on making profits through the design, manufacture, and sale of automobiles and other commodities, has set profit records that other companies envy. A strike can be expensive, but avoiding it may be even more expensive.

Again, this is no measure of a personnel department's overall efficacy.

It is true that, as I mentioned earlier, the six factors discussed above may be symptomatic of a problem. If they are used, they must be considered in relation to many other items. The point is that of themselves they are not accurate measures of the effectiveness of the personnel function.

In short, the objectives of the personnel department should not be defined in such terms as reducing the personnel ratio, or the turnover rate, or the budget, or the number of grievances, or the number of strikes, or keeping a union out of the plant. Instead, evaluation should focus on the larger questions of how well the department is helping the company as a whole reduce total costs, increase profits, and stay in business.

4. *How should the evaluation be made?* The place to begin is to look at the principal activities assigned to the specific department. These will normally include most of the following functions:

1. Recruitment, employment, and induction
2. Training and development
3. Appraisal
4. Wage and salary administration
5. Employee benefits
6. Labor relations
7. Safety and accident prevention
8. Complaints and grievances

9. Employee services
10. Transfers, promotions, demotions, and layoffs
11. Employee records
12. Personnel research

Obviously, many of the above functions have several subfunctions. Training and development, for example, might be subdivided into apprentice training, employee training, supervisory training, professional training, executive development, and so on. Even safety and accident prevention might be subdivided into "on the job" and "off the job."

After the major functions and their principal subfunctions have been identified, the next step is to assess each activity in the light of the following questions:

□ What is the philosophy underlying the function?
□ What principles of management are being followed in carrying it out?
□ What policies have been established for this function?
□ What procedures have been established? Are they in line with the philosophy, principles, and policies?
□ Are the procedures, policies, management principles, and philosophy of each function consistent with those of other, related functions?

As an illustration, now we might evaluate wage and salary administration. First, what is the underlying philosophy of this function? It may be simply that "the squeaky wheel gets the grease." It may be a concept of paying for years of education and experience, or years of service. Better yet, it may have this definition: Each individual should be compensated, with due consideration of both internal and external relationships, in reasonable proportion to the difficulty and responsibility of his job and his competence in it.

When we move on to consider principles of management, these questions come up: How much influence does the employee's supervisor or supervisors have in determining his salary? Are recommendations initiated at one level and approved at a higher level, or are wages and salaries set by the wage and salary administrator, or by some formula, or by contract stipulation? Is there some method of recognizing real exceptions?

The policy review shows, for example, whether the company customarily pays about the same as others in the labor market, or higher or lower, whether the policy relates wages and salaries to performance, and so on.

Next come the procedures—the "hows" of defining the appropriate labor market, of finding out what salaries are being paid elsewhere, and of the supervisor's keeping track of what work is assigned to each employee and the competence of performance.

Finally, the procedures, policies, management principles, and philosophy of wage and salary administration should be compared with those of related functions. An obvious one, in this case, would be administration of employee benefits. Is length of service being recognized by some of the employee benefits provisions? If so, should there also be length-of-service increases in pay? (Do you want to pay twice for the same thing?) Another related function would be training: What procedures are available to help the employee improve his job performance and thus qualify for more pay?

I have cited only a few typical questions that should be investigated. Many others would arise, often requiring a review of actual statistics. For example, to find out whether the salary range for a position was realistic, we would have to ask: Is anyone receiving the minimum of the classification? If no one has recently been hired at the minimum, then the rate for the job may not be a true minimum. As for the maximum, if no one is getting it, it may be only a carrot dangled a mile ahead of the donkey. On the other hand, if half the employees in a classification are at the maximum, it is doubtful that salary increases are being granted primarily on the basis of performance on the job, and again the maximum is unrealistic.

After all the other internal personnel functions have similarly been dissected and scrutinized, there are still external aspects to be evaluated.

An Eye on the Labor Markets

It need hardly be mentioned that every personnel department should be constantly aware of the extent and composition of the labor markets in which it must recruit. If the company needs college graduates, personnel must become acquainted with appropriate colleges and universities and maintain a campus recruiting program. If the company needs a great many women employees, is personnel still competing for unmarried women under 35, or does it look around for various sources of stable, older employees?

Another external personnel concern that should be probed is its knowledgeability about state and federal legislation. How does the new federal income tax law affect recruitment? To what extent is group life insurance threatened by another provision of the federal income tax law? What changes in unemployment insurance and workmen's compensation are being discussed at the state capital? How does the new civil rights law affect the company?

Finally, of course, the personnel department must keep in close touch with current practices both in its industry generally and in each community where the company operates. What changes are taking place in vacation and retirement plans? What changes are taking place in hours of work? What increases in pay are being granted? What new employee benefits are being offered?

As I said before, these are only a few questions that come immediately to mind; scores more will be asked in the evaluation process—and this brings up still another: Who will be asking these questions in the formal evaluation, and how? There are at least five agents and methods to choose from, and, in fact, all or any combination may be used:

- ◻ Observation by higher management.
- ◻ Formal appraisal by higher management.
- ◻ Group discussion among "customers" of the personnel department.
- ◻ Opinion polls.
- ◻ Use of a consultant.

Briefly, I'd like to discuss these at this point.

Observation by higher management. Willy-nilly, every personnel department is probably evaluated through observation by higher management. The accuracy of these evaluations depends upon how well higher management understands personnel objectives—on whether it has helped formulate or, at the very least, concurs with the basic objectives.

Even if management has a clear picture of objectives its observations may not be accurate because of this paradox: It is difficult to observe the obvious, and it is equally difficult to notice something that is missing. When everything is running smoothly, higher management may take this gratifying situation for granted and fail to see that it's the doing of an effective personnel department. On the other hand, sometimes higher management is unaware of what's going on in the personnel world, and doesn't realize that its company may be woefully behind the times in its own personnel practices. (The limiting of conversations to other management people in the same industry contributes to this blindness.)

Formal appraisal by higher management. In a formal appraisal, higher management can ask specific questions about each of the major internal and external activities of its personnel department: What is being done? Why? How? By whom? When? Where? What are current costs? What would it cost if this activity were modified or eliminated? What results have been achieved? What are the plans for this or that specific activity?

Some personnel departments can produce voluminous factual material in answer to all of these questions except the last. When asked about the future, the personnel manager may be inclined to throw up his hands and say, "We cannot make any plans. Our situation may change at any time."

Two Broad Planning Bases

Perhaps the reason for his negative response is that he has failed to look for information on which plans can be based. Most companies have two types of information that should be made available to the personnel department for its planning. The first is forecasts of sales of specific products. The demands for employees, or, more accurately, the demands for training and skills, are often related to a particular product, so such sales forecasts can help the personnel department anticipate manpower needs.

The other company data that should be made available to the personnel department are details of the company's capital budget— what it is planning in the way of new plant and new equipment. One of the many areas in which such information can be invaluable is that of the personnel problems attributed to automation. Not infrequently these problems can be solved or even avoided altogether if personnel, knowing the details of what's been budgeted, can make a reasonable analysis of this information, recognize the personnel problems inherent in the new plant or equipment, and develop plans beforehand to meet these new or changed demands.

Group discussion among "customers" of the personnel department. The personnel department serves, and therefore may be said to have "customers," not only in top management but also among operating supervisors, employees, and even external groups; so it may be decided that a formal appraisal should be made by other customers, not just top management.

Such a group should include at least one member of top management, however, plus at least one operating man from middle management and a man at a corresponding level in a staff function other than personnel. In addition, there should be a representative of the personnel department itself, one or two first-line supervisors, and, if possible, at least two employees, one an old-timer and the other a relatively new person. In order to increase participation, it's a good idea to assign a separate group to each of the specific internal aspects to be evaluated.

At the first meeting of a group, the personnel representative should concentrate on helping the members become acquainted with each other, setting some ground rules, explaining the department's objectives, and suggesting information they may find useful. Before the second meeting, the members of the committee should be given the appropriate information.

If the members have the information they need before each meeting, the evaluation should be completed in about three sessions after the initial one. A final report can then be prepared and discussed by the members of the committee. When they feel that their appraisal is complete, they should go over it in detail with the personnel manager, and later with top management.

Opinion polls. If opinion polls are to be made among employees or management or both, detailed questions can be developed with a choice of appropriate answers. Here, however, I should like to suggest some words of caution. In the first place, opinions should not be asked about any condition that cannot or will not be changed. For example, if the company prohibits the hiring of employees' relatives, and if it will not consider any change in this policy, there is little point in finding out what people think of it.

Also, the possible answers must be constructed carefully. With few exceptions, they should not be limited to a simple *Yes* or *No,* but at the same time the choice of answers should not permit respondents to straddle the fence. Generally speaking, the responses should include two favorable ones and two unfavorable ones. It should be possible to grade most responses as very favorable, favorable, unfavorable, or very unfavorable, but usually these specific terms are not used.

In addition to questions on specific aspects of the work that can be answered by check marks, the questionnaire should also provide some space for comments, which can be stimulated by leading questions such as: What do you like best about the work of the personnel department? What do you like least about the work of the personnel department? These replies are the most revealing part of the poll, and they should be analyzed not only for what is said, but also for what is not said—what subjects draw no response. On the other hand, the analysis of the comments should not be considered a quantitative matter; a single comment may be extremely significant, and none should be ignored.

Follow-up a Must, Not File-and-Forget

The greatest pitfall in opinion polls is failure to take follow-up action. It is essential that the personnel department follow through by maintaining what seems to have met with approval and by correcting any weaknesses or omissions that the poll reveals. Higher management, too, has the responsibility of seeing that the results are not just buried in the personnel department files.

The overall results of the poll should be revealed to all who participated. Any attempt to conceal them will be interpreted as an indication that the personnel department is really less efficient than anyone thought, or has some serious faults to hide.

Of course, the comment responses will be too numerous to summarize for distribution; this is obvious enough to be accepted by the respondents, but it is not so obvious that it should not be mentioned.

Use of a consultant. If a consultant evaluates the various specific internal and external aspects of a personnel department, he will have to go through the same procedures as those of the other appraisals we have discussed here, but his work will be streamlined because he will concentrate on it exclusively, and not be interrupted by other jobs to be done.

Moreover, as an outsider he can bring a fresh approach and new techniques from his broad experience. Finally, his opinions and recommendations may carry more weight with top management than the opinions of anyone else except top management itself.

In conclusion, let me emphasize again that an evaluation of the personnel department is inevitable; the personnel director's only choice is whether the evaluation of his department shall be conducted on a formal basis or not—systematically or by chance and snap judgment.

It is true that a personnel department could be evaluated by comparing its activities with those of another personnel department, or by comparing its activities this year with the results of its program last year or ten years ago. In the first case, however, the comparison would not measure conditions peculiar to the company in question, and the second comparison would be simply living in the past.

To repeat, the work of a personnel department should rather be evaluated by comparing its results with established objectives. For this reason, I have stressed the need to set these objectives and to make them consistent with reasonable assumptions for the future. If you know where you want to go and where you are now, you can always make the corrections needed to close the gap between your objectives and your actual results.

Measuring the Work of a Personnel Department

Stephen J. Carroll, Jr.

FROM time to time, the head of a personnel department may wonder just what his people are doing all day. This is not to say, of course, that he does not know what the department's duties are. But he is likely to have only a hazy idea of the absolute and relative amounts of time his staff is spending on each of them. When a backlog piles up for no apparent reason, he may ask himself: What's our most time-consuming activity? How much time are we spending on grievances? On paper work? Do we need another manager—or another clerk?

One way to find the answer to such questions is to carry out a work-measurement study. But this is admittedly easier said than done. Most of the work-measuring techniques commonly used in industry are appropriate only for routine and standardized tasks—and though some personnel jobs do, of course, fall into this category, for the most part the department's work is confined to the discharge of managerial and higher clerical functions. Activities of this kind—highly diversified and often involving considerable interaction with many different kinds of people—are difficult and expensive to measure by conventional procedures.

Methods based on continuous observation, for example, describe only overt behavior—hardly a good indicator of the higher-level or more abstract activities and mental processes involved in the performance of managerial jobs. Moreover, continuous observation becomes tiring and expensive when applied to jobs that need more than a day or two of measurement. Interviews, because they rely heavily on the subjects' memory, are not likely to yield useful data on highly diversified jobs. The diary method, in which a log of work activities is kept, has in fact been used successfully for managerial and clerical personnel.[1] But it proves tedious over long periods of time and thus becomes increasingly less reliable as the study goes on. It also has the disadvantage of taking up a great deal of the subjects' time.

There *Is* an Effective Measurement Technique

In recent years, a number of researchers have turned to work sampling as a means of measuring the activities of higher-level personnel. Now generally accepted as a reliable, valid, and practicable technique, work sampling eliminates many disadvantages of the procedures mentioned above. It has been applied successfully to the jobs of school teachers,[2] department store buyers,[3] and foremen,[4] as well as managers.[5]

With work sampling, observations are made at random intervals of what the employee is doing. These observations then provide the basis for inferences about the various elements that comprise his total work activity. The accuracy of these inferences depends on the number of observations that are made and on the proportion of time taken up by the activities being sampled. The number of observations needed to

[1] M. Ferguson *et al.*, "Activities of Health Officers in Local Health Departments," *Public Health Service Publication No. 245*. Public Health Service, Federal Security Agency, Washington, D.C., 1952.

H. H. Rosenberg, "Can Work Measurement Be Applied to the Personnel Office?" *Public Administration Review,* Winter 1948, pp. 41–48.

[2] E. R. Barnes, *Work Sampling.* John Wiley & Sons, Inc., New York, 1956.

[3] G. Nadler, "Do You Know What Your Supervisors Do?" *Personnel Psychology,* Autumn 1953, pp. 343–354.

[4] L. A. Allen, "Making the Foreman a Manager," *Management Record,* August 1954, pp. 294–296.

[5] J. L. Lundy, "An Analysis of Work Sampling in the Study of Management Job Activity," *Dissertation Abstracts,* January 1958, pp. 107–108.

achieve a specific degree of accuracy can be determined from tables that have been worked out for this purpose.[6]

Because only a few observations are made each day, work sampling is cheaper and less time consuming than other methods of work measurement. It is also less tedious for both the observer and the subject, and, of course, it does not rely upon the subject's memory.

A Work-Sampling Study

The applicability of work sampling to the measurement of personnel work was tested in a three-week study conducted jointly by a division of a large Midwestern manufacturing company and the Management Development Laboratory of the University of Minnesota's Industrial Relations Center. While the company wanted to know which employee relations activities and what kinds of people were taking up the department's time, the laboratory researchers were interested in finding out whether a modified work-sampling procedure could be used to study managerial jobs. The study's findings throw some interesting light on both these problems.

For the company's purposes, the usual work-sampling procedures had to be somewhat modified. The observations were made not by an outsider, but by the participants themselves (five clerical workers and four departmental managers). In this way, the researchers could obtain a record of the purpose behind each activity—a necessary element in explaining all higher-level jobs—without having to question the participants in detail. This unorthodox procedure also insured easy identification of everybody who became involved in the department's activities either by calling on the telephone or by visiting the office.

Another modification of normal work-sampling procedures was employed in the study. Normally, each subject's activities are sampled separately; here, all nine participants made their observations simultaneously when a guard quickly flicked the overhead lights on and off.

Throughout the three-week study period, an observation was taken at a previously selected random time within every half-hour of the working day. Each of the participants had been given pads of observation slips dated and numbered to correspond to the half-hour periods. At the signal, he noted on the observation slip for that particular half-hour the activity he had been engaged in, the identity of any other persons involved in it, and its purpose.

[6] E. R. Barnes, *op. cit.*, pp. 27–40.

Figure 2

Percentage of Total Work Time Spent with Various Categories of Persons

Category of Person	Five Clerical Workers		Four Personnel Dept. Mgrs.		Total Staff in Department	
	No. of Obser- vations	Per- centage of Total Work Time	No. of Obser- vations	Per- centage of Total Work Time	No. of Obser- vations	Per- centage of Total Work Time
Superior (own department)	29	02%	54	06%	83	04%
Subordinate (own department)	0	00	97	10	97	05
Manager (other department)	7	01	184	19	191	09
Non-manager (other department)	48	04	111	12	159	08
Person outside company	32	03	126	13	158	07
Associate	36	03	0	00	36	02
Combination of above	10	01	84	09	94	04
None	922	81	237	25	1,159	55
Personal activities	43	04	61	06	104	05
Insufficient data	16	01	4	00	20	01
Total	1,143	100%	958	100%	2,101	100%

signed to the category "insufficient data." Because of absence or over-sight, 59 observations were missed—57 among the clerical workers and 2 among the managers. In all, 2,101 observations were made.

What the Company Learned

As may be seen from the findings (Figures 1–3), the study fur-nished several guideposts for improvements in this company's per-sonnel department. Thus the breakdown of the relative amount of time devoted to each work activity (Figure 1) shows that communica-tion activities such as conversing with others and preparing reports and letters take up almost 70 percent of the department's time—over 80 percent of the managers' time and 57 percent of the clerical work-ers' time. The two groups differ markedly, it will be noted, in the proportion of time they spend on specific types of communication

Figure 1

Percentage of Total Work Time Spent on Various Work Activities

Type of Work Activity	Five Clerical Workers		Four Personnel Dept. Mgrs.		Total Staff in Department	
	No. of Obser-vations	Per-centage of Total Work Time	No. of Obser-vations	Per-centage of Total Work Time	No. of Obser-vations	Per-centage of Total Work Time
Conversing with others in person	105	09%	578	60%	683	33%
Conversing on tele-phone	58	05	50	05	108	05
Preparing and writing reports, letters, etc.	492	43	153	16	645	31
Examining reports, letters, etc.	54	05	53	06	107	05
Inspecting products, procedures, etc.	0	00	6	01	6	00
Mathematical compu-tation	24	02	3	00	27	01
Operating equipment of all types	67	06	2	00	69	03
Thinking and reflection	0	00	0	00	0	00
Minor clerical jobs (fil-ing, delivering, etc.)	161	14	52	05	213	10
Personal activities	43	04	61	06	104	05
Marking, recording, or sorting	134	12	0	00	134	06
Insufficient data	5	00	0	00	5	00
Total:	1,143	100%	958	99	2,101	99

A participant who was out of the office when the signal was given described on his return the activity he had been engaged in. If he could not precisely remember what he had been doing, or had been engaged in several different activities while away, he simply made a notation to this effect. Participants could tell that they had missed signals if they saw that the observation slips corresponding to past half-hour periods were blank.

At the conclusion of the study, the information recorded on each observation slip was classified under three categories: work activity, type of person involved in the activity, and departmental area of responsibility. Observations that could not be thus classified were as-

Figure 3

Percentage of Total Work Time Spent on Various Employee Relations Functions

Type of Function	Five Clerical Workers		Four Personnel Dept. Mgrs.		Total Staff in Department	
	No. of Observations	Percentage of total Work Time	No. of Observations	Percentage of total Work Time	No. of Observations	Percentage of total Work Time
Administration of the department	60	05%	214	22%	274	13%
Staffing	88	08	196	20	284	14
Training	0	00	5	01	5	00
Labor relations	72	06	122	13	194	09
Wage and salary administration	117	10	46	05	163	08
Benefits and services	490	43	257	27	747	36
Research, audit, and review	76	07	35	04	111	05
Personal activities	43	04	61	06	104	05
Insufficient data *	197	17	22	02	219	10
Total	1,143	100%	958	100%	2,101	100%

* These observations could not be classified because two participants failed to explain adequately the purpose of some of their activities.

activities. Conversing directly with others, for instance, takes up 65 percent of the managers' time and only 14 percent of the clerical workers' time. Of all the department's activities, then, communications is probably the most deserving of further analysis. At all events, a reduction in the number of communication activities could conceivably save the department considerable time and expense.

Figure 2, which shows the proportion of total work time spent by the staff with various types of persons inside and outside the organization, corroborates the findings given in Figure 1. Here we see that the managers spend only 25 percent of their work time alone; the clerical workers, 81 percent. This table shows that the managers spend more time with managers from other departments than with the members of their own department. These findings have implications for selection, for they suggest that the ability to communicate effectively with higher-level personnel on a face-to-face basis is an important asset in a personnel department manager. On the other hand, this ability does not seem relevant to the work of the clerical employees.

Figure 3 shows the relative amount of time the members of the department spend on each of the various employee relations functions. They expend little time on training, for instance, but a great deal of time on benefits and services and, in particular, on administering the company's insurance program. These findings suggest not only that efforts might be made to improve the administration of the benefits and services program but also that management might well investigate extending the use of equipment for processing insurance claims. Here again, certain implications for selection can be drawn from the findings—managers who have taken courses in insurance and clerical workers with previous experience in insurance companies would seem to be especially desirable candidates for this particular department.

Toward a More Effective Sampling Procedure

In general, the study shows that modified work-sampling procedures can be used to measure the work of the personnel department. In the three-week study period, no signals were missed by any participant actually present at the time they were given; and, since the staff usually left the office only for some specific purpose, very few out-of-the-office activities escaped tabulation.

As has been pointed out, a prime advantage of work sampling is that it is less expensive and less tedious than other work measurement methods. This advantage could be further strengthened by changes in the procedure adopted in this study. The most time-consuming stage of the study was the classifying of responses under the categories listed in Figures 1, 2, and 3. Time could be saved by using a checklist of these categories rather than open-end observation slips—and even more time could be saved in analyzing the data if the checklist were initially set by for IBM processing.

By using a finer breakdown of categories, it would also be possible to compute the cost of labor expended on certain activities. For example, if counseling were used as a subcategory of benefits and services, the proportion of time spent by each member of the staff in counseling during the period of the study could easily be computed. These percentages could then be applied to staff members' salaries for this period to determine the total amount spent by the company on counseling. Dividing this sum by the number of persons counseled during the study period would indicate how much, on the average, it costs to counsel an individual employee. This kind of analysis is, of course, equally applicable to other work activities in which the work unit can be identified.

In addition to furnishing the answers to such questions as have been discussed here, a systematic attempt to measure the work of a personnel department can improve its administration in other ways. It can show where duplication of effort occurs and can thus enable the department head to assign time-consuming activities to the lowest-paid employees able to handle them. By providing an analysis of the tasks themselves, it can serve as a basis for more efficient planning and, as has been suggested, for better selecting and training. In a multiplant company, a work measurement study can help management increase its control and set reasonable standards of performance by comparing the amounts and kinds of work done at the several personnel offices. Finally, work measurement can provide an answer to the most basic question of all—how well the personnel department's objectives are being accomplished.

21

Calculating Your Personnel Ratio

Dale Yoder

THE personnel ratio is a crude but convenient measure of the range or extent of industrial relations management in an agency or firm. It describes the proportionate numbers of personnel workers as compared with all other employees. Most frequently, it is stated as the number of personnel workers per hundred of the total working force. It thus suggests the level of interest in personnel work, the degree of concern management feels in such matters, and the extent to which an inclusive personnel or industrial relations program has been developed.

The ratio permits a quick comparison of programs from one company or one agency to another or at different dates. It provides an overall or generalized measure, comparable in the range of its usefulness to refined labor turnover rates. The personnel ratio is and must be a crude measure. For it relates numbers of personnel workers to numbers of employees. But the number of employees is only a rough approximation of the volume of personnel work to be done. If turnover is heavy, so that the number of personnel transactions is increased, that fact may necessitate more personnel workers than if employment were stable, with few separations and accessions. Hence the ratio must be regarded as a crude measure.

Some Studies on Current Ratios

Crude as it is, the ratio is widely used. Most research and information agencies can attest the frequent inquiries that seek to discover what may be regarded as a proper ratio. Three comparatively recent published reports may be cited as indicating both the tendency to place significance on the ratio and the need for additional uniformity in definition and usage.

In his "Survey of Personnel Department Costs," [1] W. C. Jackson reported on "personnel staff per 100 employees" for ten metal manufacturers, twelve miscellaneous manufacturers, and eight service and retail establishments. He described ratios ranging from 0.53 to 2.0 in metal manufacturing, with an average ratio of 1.14. In miscellaneous manufacturing, ratios ranged from 0.44 to 2.0, with an average of 0.87. In the service industries, the range is from 0.12 to 1.73, with an average of 0.82. The author concludes that "it would also seem to be a good rule to have the size of the personnel staff equivalent to one per 100 employees."

A study of salaries of personnel workers reported in *Industrial Relations* [2] provides additional information on current ratios. Although ratios were not calculated, numbers of those engaged in personnel work, together with the total number of employees for each firm, are reported. From these data, ratios may be compiled for some 44 plants. They range from 0.43 to 1.79. The median ratio is 0.50.

The author of this article has reported on personnel ratios for some 200 firms that participated in a survey of industrial relations salaries in late 1947. [3] No industrial classification was made. The average personnel ratio for all firms was 0.81. Ratios were higher in very small firms (the average was 1.06 for firms having fewer than 500 employees) and lower in firms having 1,000 or more employees (0.59 for firms of from 1,000 to 5,000 and 0.67 for those with more than 5,000). Ratios ranged from 0.20 to 3.6.

[1] *Personnel Journal,* Vol. 26, No. 7, January 1948, pp. 244–247.
[2] "A Survey of Industrial Relations Salaries in Plants with over 1,000 Employees," Vol. 6, No. 7, November 1948, pp. 9, 10 ff.
[3] Dale Yoder, "Salaries in Manpower Management," *Modern Management,* Vol. 8, No. 4, May 1948, pp. 4–6.

Defining our Terms

There are difficult problems in the use of this personnel ratio—
problems that arise particularly out of the determination as to what
employees are to be regarded as personnel workers. Are secretaries
and stenographers in personnel offices to be so regarded? How about
cooks and waitresses in cafeterias? What managerial functions may
properly be considered as personnel functions? Shall safety engineers, time study specialists, training directors, collective bargaining
negotiators, and wage and salary administrators be included? If the
ratio is to be useful and at all reliable, these questions must be answered in a consistent manner by those who report and compile the
indexes.

A somewhat similar problem arises in connection with the definition of the *total working force*, with which numbers of personnel workers are to be compared. Does it include all employees, regardless of
status and assignment, from the president or board chairman to the
lowest-skilled employee? Is it the maximum total employment for a
year or a month for which the ratio is to be calculated, or is it an
average number for some such period?

Because references to the personnel ratio are increasing and the
measure seems to serve a useful purpose, it may be of value to consider advantages and disadvantages of various definitions and thus
suggest a basis for uniform accounting.

The base of the ratio is total employment. Since the force of personnel workers is generally not adjusted from month to month, there
would seem to be little point to such a short-term base as employment
within a single month. Most personnel workers are salaried
employees—a fact that would suggest the fiscal year as the logical
base. If a monthly rate is desirable for some purposes, there may be
advantage in following the usual practice in calculations of labor
turnover, in which the base is the average of employment on the first
and last working days of the month.

For the more commonly useful annual rate, possibly the most
satisfactory base would be average monthly employment for the most
recent fiscal year. Some firms, notably, for example, in the canning
industry, have peak months in which employment is multiplied several times over that which prevails in other months throughout the
year. It may be argued that numbers of personnel workers should be
adequate to maintain whatever level of program is regarded as desirable through these peak months. To appraise this adequacy, the base
should represent peak employment. A strong case can be made for

this procedure. But for purposes of comparison among companies and agencies, the average figure appears to present a sounder, more realistic base.

Who Should Be Counted as Personnel Workers?

Definition of the term *personnel worker* presents at least as difficult problems. In terms of the purpose for which the ratio is calculated, it should certainly include all those whose major or primary responsibility is to maintain and improve manpower management. It may be and has frequently been argued, however, that manpower management is the major business and principal responsibility of every supervisor, that all managers are primarily manpower managers. Should all foremen, supervisors, superintendents, and executives be included, for this reason, in the total of personnel workers?

This question may be answered in the negative, for the reason that the primary function of supervisors is defined by the line as distinguished from the staff organization. Personnel workers are staff. The manpower management functions of line supervisors are incidental to their general management responsibilities.

A slightly different but less satisfactory approach to this particular question has been suggested, in which the lines of responsibility running to each job are considered. All jobs whose lines flow into personnel or industrial relations offices are then assumed to be filled with personnel workers. Here, however, there is the fact that organizational structures vary and that the concept of personnel management as a staff function is not too clearly understood in all quarters. As a result, many personnel functions—of a staff nature—may be operating out of a controller's office or that of a production superintendent or some other line official. Job analysis, wage and salary administration, collective bargaining and contract administration, counseling, employment, and many other functions that fall well within the general area of personnel administration are frequently attached—for reasons of convenience or tradition or otherwise—to offices other than those of the industrial relations or personnel administrator.

Another and perhaps more searching test that might be applied would ask the question: Who is employed in functions that evidence the interest and activity of management in industrial relations? All those who are occupied in such jobs should presumably be counted in the enumeration of personnel workers. The major types of activities to be considered are well recognized. They include, as major functions, job analysis and the preparation of job descriptions; selection,

recruitment, induction, and placement; training; providing service
ratings; wage and salary administration; safety and health activities;
counseling; collective bargaining and contract administration; provision of employee services of all kinds; maintenance of personnel records; and personnel research. There are others that appear less frequently, including, for example, the direction of recreational activities, editing and publishing employee handbooks and magazines,
and others. The range of jobs that are regularly included to perform
these functions is even broader.[4]

All those who are engaged in these activities should be counted,
including the secretaries, stenographers and clerical workers who assist in these programs.

[4] See "Jobs in Industrial Relations," *Bulletin* 3, University of Minnesota Industrial
Relations Center, 1947.

The Personnel
Activity Index:
A New Budgeting Tool

W. C. Jackson

THE continuing pressure to reduce overhead is forcing many an
industrial relations director these days to take a hard look at the
staffing of his department. Are all these people really necessary? And
even if they are, how can he prove it? What yardstick can he use that
will tell him what his budgeted strength should be to keep the department operating with maximum economy and efficiency?

In recent years, the most commonly accepted index for answering
questions of this kind has been the personnel ratio, that is, the
number of people on the personnel staff per 100 employees. The
Industrial Relations Center of The University of Minnesota has been
surveying personnel ratios in a wide cross section of American industry since 1948. These surveys, which have been regularly published in
Personnel,[1] have revealed a number of variations from the traditional
ratio of 1.00.

[1] The findings of the 1960 survey, which has been extensively revised and expanded over the surveys of previous years, appear in the November–December issue of
Personnel, pp. 18–28.

Though the Minnesota surveys have been continually refined, and their findings are now carefully broken down by company size and type, as well as by industry category, many companies have found them of somewhat limited value as a budgetary control tool. The main reason for this is that the optimum ratio for a particular personnel staff is obviously dependent on the department's level of activity. At times of accelerated hiring or layoff, for instance, the workload on the personnel department increases, and more people are needed to handle it. When employment remains stable, the workload is less and the department can operate with a smaller staff. The average personnel ratio prevailing throughout industry in general, or even in comparable companies, affords only a rough guide, therefore, to the personnel department head who wants to know what his budgeted payroll should be at any particular time.

What is really needed is a yardstick that will indicate the amount of staff needed to perform a specific workload. There are, in fact, some indices already in standard use that at first glance suggest themselves as being suitable for this purpose—for example, the turnover rate, calculated as a separation rate and sometimes also as a hiring or acquisition rate. Together, these two show the movements into and out of the company's workforce.

But these movements, of course, account for only a part of the personnel department's many activities, so that turnover rate alone is not an adequate measure of its workload.

In search of a more practical, but more accurate, measure whereby we could gauge the number of people needed to carry out the personnel department's responsibilities, we at LeTourneau-Westinghouse decided to construct an index supplementing our turnover rate with other yardsticks that could be readily obtained from the department's records. As will be seen, the index we devised is not a hard-and-fast formula, and any company that decided to adopt the same procedure would have to start by deciding on its own components first. But it seems to be a workable measuring tool, and the particular units we used can probably serve as helpful guidelines for other companies working out their own formulas.

We looked for statistics that could measure other departmental activities, and found data readily available on three major responsibilities: rate changes, transfers, and the processing of first-aid cases.

When these activities were considered along with separations and accessions, a reasonably complete picture of the department's work emerged. This is not to say that the department performs only these five functions. The remaining ones, however, for which statistical records are seldom maintained, usually vary with the level of employment; thus their omission did not seriously distort our proposed index. The choice of activities to be measured is, however, an individual matter, and each personnel director must decide for himself which sets of figures will be truly indicative of his department's workload.

These, then, were the measures we adopted as forming the basis of our Personnel Activity Index (PAI):

1. Hiring rate. (No. of hires ÷ average employment.)
2. Separation rate. (No. of separations ÷ average employment.)
3. Transfer rate. (No. of transfers ÷ average employment.)
4. Rate-change rate. (No. of individual rate changes ÷ average employment.)
5. First-aid rate. (No. of first-aid cases reported ÷ average employment.)

The period of average employment to be used to obtain the above rates was set at one month.

Though we could have computed an index of sorts by adding these five rates together, this procedure would have overlooked the fact that considerably more work is involved in hiring a man than in separating one. Similarly, it takes more time and effort to complete a transfer than to process a rate change. Obviously, the elements had to be assigned different weights in proportion to the amount of work they entail.

Through discussion with several members of the department, we finally decided to adopt the weights listed on page 288. (It should be emphasized that these, of course, are not necessarily valid for other companies.)

With our components thus weighted, we were able to arrive at a Personnel Activity Index for each month in two steps: (1) adding together six times the number of accessions, twice the number of separations, twice the number of transfers, and the number of rate changes and first-aid cases; and (2) dividing the total by our average employment for the month.

Not only was this formula a simple one but, as has been indicated, it was easy to assemble the necessary data, since most of it was customarily kept on file for other reasons.

Now, of course, we had to find out what—if anything—the PAI

Activity	*Weight*
Hiring—including requisitions, advertising, or other means of recruiting, interviewing, handling correspondence, testing, selection:	6
Separating—including analysis of reasons, discussions with department head and union, clearing up records, issuing checks:	2
Transfers—discussion of job assignments, clearing with various department heads:	2
Rate changes—processing, correcting records, analyzing consistency:	1
First-aid cases—reports to first-aid department, treating, recording:	1

actually meant as a personnel budgeting tool. Clearly, it had no practical significance unless we could establish that it was, in fact, a reasonably accurate indicator of the department's workload at any given moment. In addition, we needed to relate this workload index to the manpower of the department. This we could do through the personnel ratio.

Our only way of ascertaining this was to work backward and apply the index to past experience. We were aware, of course, of the inherent defects of such an approach. Our past experience might have been wrong all along and any conclusions based on it would therefore serve only to perpetuate former errors. But this objection is actually more theoretical than real. As a matter of practical experience we knew that there had been times in the past when the department was clearly overworked and others when there was not enough work to go around. We also knew that there had been periods when our departmental strength had appeared to be just about right for the workload at the time. If the same variations appeared when our new index was matched against past staffing ratios, we had reasonable assurance that the PAI could henceforth tell us how many staff members would be needed to perform a particular workload.

We began, therefore, by plotting our overall employment level and our varying personnel ratio for the years 1947–1960. From the curves that resulted (Figure 1), it can be seen that several major fluctuations in our employment level occurred over this period and that the PR tended to rise at times of falling employment—indicating that the staff remained constant though there was presumably less work to do. But the relation between the curves is not very clear and, of course, does not show whether, at any given moment, the personnel ratio was above or below what it should have been or whether it was just right.

Next, we computed our activity index for the same period. While most of the necessary monthly figures were available in reports of one sort or another, some early data—on rate changes and transfers, for instance—had to be reconstructed. Incidentally, the weighting originally devised for the PAI was not used throughout, since the department had taken on additional medical and safety activities in 1955. Because these new duties increased our first-aid activities, the weight of this element was accordingly raised from 1 to 1.5 in our calculations from that year on.

When we added the PAI curve to the other two curves (Figure 2), certain consistencies and deviations became evident. To determine what these meant, we applied statistical analysis to the data covering a ten-year span. Our normal activity level, this analysis showed, was 0.65; the normal personnel ratio, 1.00. Using these two figures as equivalent values and taking into account the standard deviation of the PAI, which we found to be 0.20, and the normal fluctuations in the personnel ratio, we developed the following table of correlations:

PAI	PR
1.15	1.25
1.05	1.20
.95	1.15
.85	1.10
.75	1.05
.65	1.00
.55	.95
.45	.90
.35	.85
.25	.80

In other words, for our department, an activity level of 0.65 necessitates a personnel ratio of 1.00, an activity level of 0.75 a PR of 1.05, and so forth. Needless to say, these correlations would not be applicable to any other company.

Applying these correlations to the curves shown in Figure 2, it will now be seen that at certain times the department's staffing was apparently more or less than what it should have been. Thus, in periods of accelerated turnover, when the PAI rose to 0.85 and higher, the PR

Figure 1. Employment Level and Personnel Ratio Curves

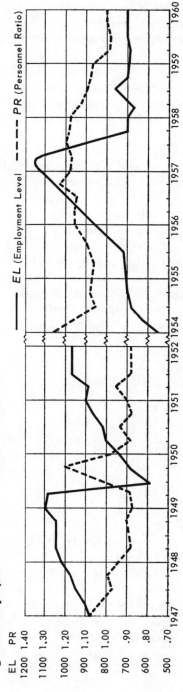

Figure 2. Employment Level, Personnel Ratio, and Personnel Activity Index Curves

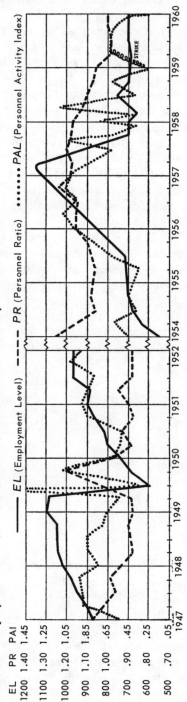

was 1.1 to 1.2; but when employment became more stable, and the PAI dropped to a maintenance level of 0.45, the PR was 0.90 or less.

On the other hand, the curves also show that, if our strength was just about right at these times, then it was not sufficient for the workload during the 1947–48 and again in 1951. This actually was the case— the department was, in fact, understaffed at those times and its work fell behind as a result.

Here, then, was confirmation from past experience that both our PAI formula and our table of correlations could serve as a usable budgeting tool. Perhaps it should be reemphasized here that neither the formula nor the correlations were taken directly from past experience: they were based initially on our judgment of the situation. It was necessary, however, to check the values used against past experience to determine how sound our reasoning had been.

It should also be noted that it would be impractical to expect an exact correspondence at all times between the PAI and the PR, since the employment level and the other factors affecting the workload usually fluctuate more rapidly than departmental strength can be increased or cut back. When there is a sudden change in the employment level, for example, the PR is bound to be out of line, as it was in our case in the middle of 1949 when, as the chart shows, employment (and the PAI) dropped rapidly while the PR rose. Though the department was then evidently overstaffed, the suddenness of the change made this unavoidable. Such inevitable discrepancies do not, however, seriously detract from the usefulness of the PAI under a company's normal operating conditions.

Incidentally, the use of this index need not be confined to the personnel department, for the staffing of other indirect departments is probably amenable to the same kind of analysis. Whatever the application, the following sequence of steps should be observed:

1. Establish a formula for calculating an activity level or workload index.
2. Apply this index to past experience and see how it compares with past staffing ratios.
3. Determine the correlations between workload and departmental strength.
4. Conduct periodic checks on the formula and the table of correlations so that they may be adjusted to any major changes in the company's operations.

Though it may be necessary to revise the index from time to time, such adjustments are not very difficult to work out and do not require any extensive gathering of data. The PAI, in short, appears to be a practical tool by means of which a department can determine its own changing staff needs and thereby achieve more flexible, more individual, and hence more economical, personnel planning.

What About Personnel Relations Payroll Costs?

George A. Cowee, Jr. and Gordon G. Bowen [1]

AS management tightens its belt and digs in for the long competitive pull, every operation contributing to overhead will come in for close scrutiny. How will the personnel relations function come out under this appraisal? And what type of questions should the director of personnel relations be prepared to answer in justifying his program?

Last fall one of the major oil companies asked us to obtain the following information from a number of large industrial companies outside the petroleum industry:

1. Relative number of employees engaged in specific personnel relations activities.
2. Relative payroll costs for these employees.

[1] The authors wish to express their appreciation for the time and effort expended by the executives of participating companies who provided the data, summaries of which are presented in this article.

To obtain this information, we worked with 24 leading companies.[2] In the process, a number of additional questions turned up.
For example:

> 3. What tangible contributions to net profits result from person-
>   nel relations activities?
> 4. When are personnel relations costs too high? Too low?

This article reports the results of this study. It also defines the
problem ahead in measuring the tangible contributions of the personnel relations function.

Nature of Activities Included in Survey

The personnel relations or industrial relations function includes a
broad range of activities that vary widely, both by industry and individual company. Final selections of the specific activities included in
this survey were made on the basis of prevailing industrial practice.
For example, salary administration, which is occasionally the responsibility of a department other than personnel relations, was included
because it is generally recognized to be a personnel relations activity.
On the other hand, activities such as the cafeteria, library, incentive
rate-setting, plant protection, and so on, were excluded because they
are frequently the responsibility of some other department and less
generally recognized to be primarily personnel relations activities.

Because of such variations, it was decided to limit the survey to
personnel engaged in the following basic activities, whether or not
they were a definite part of the personnel relations organization in
individual participating companies:

> 1. General personnel administration
> 2. Employment
> 3. Training
> 4. Wage and salary administration
> 5. Health and safety
> 6. Medical and first aid
> 7. Employees' services and benefits
> 8. Labor relations
> 9. Public personnel relations
> 10. Personnel records
> 11. Personnel research

In addition, activities of questionable allocation were listed under

---

[2] Each employs 10,000 or more people and each has multiplant operations.

a miscellaneous heading so that they could be examined separately. Wherever possible, these were reallocated to one of the 11 basic classifications. Definitions of each classification, together with the reporting instructions, are included as an Appendix to this article to assist those who want to compare their personnel payroll costs with those of participants.

Gathering and Refining Data

The data were gathered for the most part by personal interviews with the top personnel relations executives of participating companies. These discussions, in turn, were supplemented by letters and telephone calls to clarify the data received.

All data shown have been expressed in *relative* terms, such as annual personnel relations payroll costs per company employee. This was done to facilitate comparison and to prevent disclosure of data sources. No *absolute* figures, such as total employment or total payroll, are shown.

To aid in comparing the data, while still preserving anonymity, participating companies have been classified in broad industrial categories such as light manufacturing, heavy processing, and so forth.

Survey Findings

The results of this survey, in terms of the relative number and payroll costs of employees engaged in *all* personnel relations activities, are shown in Figure 1.

It is readily evident that there are wide variations in the relative size of participants' personnel relations organizations. The largest number of personnel relations employees per 1,000 employees is approximately five times the smallest. And the greatest annual personnel relations payroll cost per company employee is approximately ten times the least. Both the mean and median number of personnel relations employees per 1,000 company employees closely approximate eight, or, expressed differently, one personnel relations employee for each 125 company employees. It is interesting to note that this figure does not vary too greatly from the figure of one per 100 reported by W. C. Jackson in his survey of personnel department costs of firms in Indianapolis.[3]

---

[3] *Personnel Journal*, Vol. 26, No. 7, January 1948, pp. 244–247.

Figure 1

Comparison of the Relative Number and Payroll Costs of Employees Engaged in All Personnel Relations Activities of 24 Large Industrial Companies

Company Classification	No. of Pers. Rel. Employees per 1,000 Employees	Annual Pers. Rel. Payroll Cost per Company Employee
Heavy process. & light mfg.	14.05	$57.69
Light processing & mfg.	13.68	58.34
Heavy process. & light mfg.	12.87	69.73
Heavy process. & light mfg.	11.37	36.91
Light manufacturing	11.12	41.72
Heavy process. & light mfg.	10.87	48.16
Heavy process. & light mfg.	10.23	38.84
Heavy process. & light mfg.	9.92	42.76
Light manufacturing	9.70	39.02
Heavy manufacturing	9.14	29.57
Heavy processing	8.43	40.42
Heavy processing	8.11	30.54
Heavy manufacturing	7.70	28.97
Light manufacturing	6.59	20.00
Heavy processing	6.57	33.75
Light processing & mfg.	6.46	30.58
Light manufacturing	6.26	24.76
Heavy manufacturing	6.18	22.10
Heavy processing	5.24	21.02
Heavy processing	5.10	22.87
Light manufacturing	4.76	16.55
Light processing & mfg.	4.46	15.26
Light processing & mfg.	3.07	9.17
Light manufacturing	2.70	7.08
Mean	8.11	$32.74
Median	7.91	$30.56

Summary breakdowns by the reporting classifications are shown in Figures 2 and 3. Figure 2 shows the number of employees engaged in each personnel relations activity per 1,000 company employees. Figure 3 shows the annual personnel relations payroll costs of specific personnel relations activities per company employee.

Here again, while extremely wide variations exist in the ranges for participating companies, the mean and median figures are reasonably close. In examining these tables, it should be noted that the data

Figure 2

Summary of Number of Employees Engaged in Each Personnel Relations Activity Per 1,000 Company Employees

| Classification | Number of Companies Reporting * | Number of Personnel Relations Employees per 1,000 Company Employees | | | |
| | | Range | | | |
		From	To	Mean	Median
Gen'l. personnel administration	24	0.14	4.13	1.24	1.03
Employment	24	0.04	2.20	0.88	0.95
Training	23	0.04	2.27	0.44	0.26
Wage and salary administration	21	0.06	1.84	0.67	0.49
Health and safety	20	0.10	1.54	0.67	0.68
Medical and first aid	23 **	0.59	3.28	1.83	1.79
Employee services and benefits	21	0.15	3.42	1.12	0.88
Labor relations	22	0.08	0.92	0.35	0.27
Public personnel relations	10	0.01	0.41	0.14	0.11
Personnel records	24	0.07	2.65	1.04	1.02
Personnel research	12	0.02	0.71	0.19	0.18
Combined activities (incl. "misc." activities)	24	2.70	14.05	8.11	7.91

* Participants classifying employees in the activitiy indicated.
** One company excluded from data calculations because its medical and first-aid services are provided by insurance policies and contracts with physicians' associations; the cost is paid for entirely by employee contributions.

presented cover only those employees who could be allocated to the specific survey activity classifications. In some instances, where individual plant personnel relations staffs are quite small and individuals are engaged in several activities, it was not always feasible to distribute their costs over more than one classification. Such employees, therefore, have been included under the classification *general personnel administration*. This, of course, tends to weight this classification slightly.

Cautions in Using Survey Findings

As stated earlier, the purpose of this survey was to determine the relative numbers and payroll costs of employees engaged in personnel relations activities in large industrial companies. It did not seek to appraise either the personnel relations staffing requirements, or their effectiveness, in participating companies. Therefore, we cannot know specifically the reasons for such wide variations among individual companies. Some of the probable reasons, however, include differences in:

1. Company philosophy and policy
2. Type of manufacturing operations
3. Number, size, and location of plants
4. Nature of labor markets
5. Community practices
6. Provisions of local and industry collective bargaining agreements
7. History of company employee relations

The authors strongly urge that no attempt be made by readers to judge the effectiveness of individual activities or the total personnel relations function in their companies by comparing their payroll costs with the survey data. For example, one participant, a company well known to the authors, reported the fewest people engaged in *health and safety* per 1,000 employees. Yet this same company consistently wins both national and local safety awards for its industry classification.

However, the findings should be useful in suggesting personnel relations activities in your company that could bear study. If the costs of any activity are relatively high, are you receiving full value? If they are relatively low, should you expand the activity? More important, what tangible contributions to net profits result from each personnel relations activity?

The Problem Ahead

Before management can answer such questions as these, better measurements of the value of individual personnel relations activities must be developed. Because of the difficulty in justifying its expenditures profitwise, the personnel relations function is likely to be one of the first to be attacked. The prospect of reduced profits in the future already has focused top management attention on general cost reduction. Despite this, however, the chief personnel executive is still for the most part without adequate means of determining which personnel activities should be reduced, eliminated, or expanded, and to what extent. Staff-size standards based on workloads have not been de-

Figure 3
**Summary of Annual Personnel Relations Payroll Costs of Specific
Personnel Relations Activities Per Company Employee**

Classification	Number of Companies Reporting *	Annual Personnel Relations Payroll Costs per Company Employee			
		Range		Mean	Median
		From	To		
Gen'l. personnel administration	24	$ 0.93	$22.56	$ 7.19	$ 6.02
Employment	24	0.18	6.88	2.98	2.77
Training	23	0.18	11.36	2.04	1.13
Wage and salary administration	21	0.21	8.48	2.87	1.91
Health and safety	20	0.46	5.72	2.69	2.47
Medical and first aid	23 **	2.49	13.39	7.04	7.70
Employee services and benefits	21	0.53	9.51	3.71	2.99
Labor relations	22	0.33	6.53	2.12	1.63
Public personnel relations	10	0.05	2.09	0.67	0.46
Personnel records	24	0.15	6.62	2.64	2.35
Personnel research	12	0.10	2.94	0.83	0.58
Combined activities (incl. "misc." activities)	24	$ 7.08	$69.73	$32.74	$30.56

* Participants classifying employees in activities indicated.
** One company excluded from data calculations because its medical and first-aid services are provided by insurance policies and contracts with physicians' associations; the cost is paid for entirely by employee contributions.

veloped widely, either for specific industries or individual companies. Some research in this field has been undertaken by one or two government agencies.[4] However, knowledge of how much work should be accomplished by how many people still would only partially answer the basic question of how much the activity contributes to net profits.

Because the benefits of the personnel relations function are often intangible and difficult to isolate, it may never be possible to isolate their total contribution to net profits. Still, much can be accomplished outside of the realm of sheer crystal-ball gazing.

Defining Personnel Relations Objectives

Certainly the first step in seeking to measure the effectiveness of

[4] Cecil E. Goode, "Controlling Personnel Office Costs," *Personnel*, March 1949, pp. 320–331.

the personnel relations function should be to prepare a clear statement of the company's personnel relations objectives. While many companies have prepared excellent statements of overall personnel relations policy, few have defined the specific objectives of each activity. Only when management knows clearly what it is seeking to accomplish can it hope to evaluate its progress in attaining its personnel relations objectives.

Some Practical Yardsticks

After the objectives of each activity have been clearly defined, management is then in a position to develop practical yardsticks for measuring the effectiveness of the activities. The first step is to determine what tangible data are required for appraising how well each objective is being attained. Such data should be compiled on a continuous basis and analyzed to disclose significant trends. Some areas which might well bear study are:

1. *Worker productivity.* At what percentage of efficiency are employees working? Has it increased? Fallen off? Are new employees reaching performance standards faster? What has been the effect upon direct labor costs? What has been the trend in hiring and training costs?

2. *Costs of grievances.* Number and nature? How long do they take to settle? At what levels are they settled? What salary and wage expenses are involved in processing grievances? What are the costs of settlement awards?

3. *Turnover.* What is the turnover rate? What is the trend? How much does it cost? (Very few companies have attempted to determine realistically what it costs them to lose a man at varying levels in the organization.)

4. *Absenteeism.* What is normal absenteeism for your industry? Are you above or below? What is the deviation in terms of increased costs or savings?

5. *Accidents.* What is your frequency rate? Severity rate? What are your medical costs? Hospitalization costs? Compensation costs?

6. *Suggestions.* How widespread is employee participation? What tangible savings result from adopting employee suggestions? What is the cost of operation of the program?

7. *Wage and salary expense.* To what extent has orderly classification of jobs provided a more effective control of direct labor expense? Indirect labor expense? Has it reduced grievances? Increased productivity? Made the employment task easier? Improved selection? Facilitated labor contract negotiations?

These are just a few of the areas in which factual measurements of the effectiveness of various personnel relations activities can be obtained.

Some Subjective Appraisals

In addition to such objective measurements, there are a number of subjective appraisals that might be advantageously employed. For example, many companies conduct periodic surveys to determine employee attitudes bearing on the effectiveness of the company's personnel relations policies and programs. Exit interviews will frequently reveal significant employee attitudes toward employment conditions. The extent to which it is necessary to go outside for competent personnel can also be compared with past experience as a measure of the effectiveness of personnel planning and development. These are but a few of the possible subjective appraisals of personnel relations activities.

Role of Personnel Relations

In developing bases for appraising the contributions of the personnel relations function, its relationship to the line organization should always be borne in mind. Personnel relations is, of course, a staff department. As such, it is responsible for assisting the line organization in achieving its objectives.

Naturally, where the personnel relations department does not assist the line organization in carrying out a specific activity, it should receive no credit. However, where the personnel relations department does participate in a specific activity, it is not necessary to divide the credit between the personnel relations department and the line organization. It is enough to know that the personnel relations department is assisting the line organization in achieving its objectives.

Conclusion

In summary, mere knowledge of how your personnel relations costs compare with those of leading companies will not by itself satisfy the chief executive. Too many variables exist to make such comparisons of real value. If personnel relations departments are to be permitted budgets that will enable them to provide effective service to the line organization, they must be able to demonstrate realistically the value of their services. Otherwise, they will be one of the most vulnerable departments in a companywide cost reduction program.

Appendix
Classification Definitions and Reporting Procedure

Following are the definitions of the survey classifications:

1. *General personnel administration.* Includes supervisory and clerical personnel at headquarters and plants who are engaged in the personnel relations function *generally*, rather than in a *specific* personnel relations activity. Examples are the director of personnel relations, regional personnel directors, their secretaries, and any administrative assistants that they may have.

2. *Employment.* Includes recruitment, selection, placement, testing, and related activities. Employee records, however, are covered under *Personnel records.*

3. *Training.* Includes personnel development work, such as apprenticeship, operator, foremen or supervisory, and executive development programs. Part-time instructors were reported in the same way as part-time doctors, as explained below under *medical and first aid.*

4. *Wage and salary administration.* Includes job and position descriptions, analysis, and measurement; also progress review and wage and salary control programs. Excludes time study and production rate-setting, as being industrial engineering rather than personnel relations activities.

5. *Health and safety.* Includes safety engineers and inspectors even though organizationally they may have reported elsewhere. Recreational activities are classified below under *employee services and benefits.*

6. *Medical and first aid.* Includes doctors, nurses and technicians, and clerical staff. Doctors or other professionals employed part-time, or whose services are engaged only as cases arise or by contract, were converted to an equivalent number of full-time employees and reported as such, together with the actual fees for such services.

7. *Employee services and benefits.* Includes welfare and recreational activities; also, administration of such service activities as group and hospitalization insurance, pensions, mutual benefit associations, and credit unions. It specifically includes the suggestion system and house organ, and specifically excludes the cafeteria (or lunchroom) and the library.

8. *Labor relations.* Includes labor relations director and staff. Also includes legal services in connection with collective bargaining and settlement of grievances in the same way as in doctors' services, outlined above.

9. *Public personnel relations.* Includes public relations activities that are *directly* concerned with personnel relations. For example, personnel engaged in working with civic agencies on plant and community recreational projects.

10. *Personnel records.* Includes personnel concerned with maintenance of central personnel records.

11. *Personnel research.* Includes personnel engaged in projects of a research nature. While all companies do not segregate this activity, it was requested that rough allocations of personnel and payrolls be made for the sake of uniformity.

12. *Miscellaneous.* Includes those activities not allocated to one of the 11

preceding classifications and not specifically excluded for reporting purposes.

Participating companies were requested to observe the following procedures in reporting their data:

1. Count an *employee* as a personnel relations worker if he devotes *most* of his time to personnel relations activities; otherwise do not count him. For example, in a plant too small for a personnel relations department, an administrative assistant to the works manager might spend three-fourths of his time on personnel relations matters. He should then be counted in this survey as a personnel relations worker. If, on the other hand, he spends only a quarter of his time on such activities, he should be disregarded in this survey. Note, however, that this rule does not apply in the case of part-time *non-employees* such as doctors, instructors, and lawyers engaged in personnel relations activities.

2. Allocate fractions of the count for an employee (and corresponding payroll costs) in cases where he is regularly engaged in two or more of the ten specific activity classifications, numbers 2 to 11 inclusive, used in this survey.

3. Report as payroll costs direct charges for salaries, wages, and fees for personal services. Include overtime payments, bonuses, and other supplementary compensation. Exclude any charges for materials and supplies or for indirect overhead items, such as housekeeping, rental value, heat, and the like.

PART V

Employee Attitudes and Work Climate— The Critical Measure of Success

THE human resources function serves the needs of the organization. Its objectives are the organization's objectives. An organization, however, is more than its trustees or its owners or its management—it is also its customers, its suppliers, its community, and, as important as any and more important than most, its employees. So the human resources function serves the organization by serving its employees. For that reason, employee attitudes are the critical measure of the success of the function. This was true yesterday, is true today, and will be true tomorrow.

To give this orientation to the function does not relieve it of its responsibility to contribute to the short- and long-term financial success or effectiveness of the organization. Nor is it meant to suggest an emphasis on paternalistic welfare-type programs. Rather, an effective human resources function focuses on relating the needs of its employees to the needs of the organization and strives to satisfy both sets of needs.

To work to satisfy employee needs requires that they be known. Many techniques are used to learn what employees want and expect from their employment, none more productive than face-to-face conversations between a supervisor and an employee. Given the size of many organizations, however, such personal methods are often difficult to apply. Attitude surveys are a useful—but partial—substitute.

That the use of attitude surveys has a long history is supported by the first article in this part, Arthur W. Kornhauser's "The Technique of Measuring Employee Attitudes." Kornhauser wrote this article in 1933, while he was an associate professor of psychology at the University of Chicago, and it was based on many years of prior research on the subject by him and other psychologists, such as L. L. Thurstone. Although there have been developments in attitude-surveying methodology since that time—the scaling technique of Rensis Likert is one example and the unidimensional scaling technique of Louis Guttman is another—everything Kornhauser said in his article is still relevant today. Fifty-five years ago he emphasized the importance of the attitudes of workers in establishing work climate and productivity—and as an end in themselves. (He wrote that the attitudes of the workforce, that is, the job satisfaction of employees, are important in themselves, thereby anticipating by many years those who now speak of the importance of the quality of work life.) In addition he identified the main measurements methods and described the problems in their use in attitude measurement. Most important, he pointed out the desirability, the necessity, of putting in place a continuing program of attitude measurement.

The article by Louis A. Allen takes up where Kornhauser's article leaves off; it provides a detailed outline of how to go about making an attitude survey in an organization. "Action-Oriented Attitude Surveys" was written by Allen in 1952, while he was manager of personnel administration and training at Koppers Company, Inc. This step-by-step guide to developing, implementing, and acting on an attitude survey is as useful today as the day it was written.

The next article, "Factors Influencing Industrial Morale," shows what kinds of information can be obtained when attitude research methodologies are put to work. Although this article by Mason Haire and Josephine S. Gottsdanker was published in 1951 while they were at the University of California at Berkeley and at Santa Barbara, respectively, the study was done under the auspices of the industrial relations section of the Massachusetts Institute of Technology. The findings of this study are as relevant today as when first reported; the methodology, too.

David Sirota took the use of attitude surveys in a slightly different direction in his 1974 article "Opinion Surveys: The Results Are In—What Do We Do with Them?" He prescribed the use of surveys as a cure for the high-priest complex that many behavioral scientists bring to organizations, which leads them to recommend action based on their wisdom rather than on facts. The article points out that workers will tell you exactly what they want if you only ask them. Such survey data are more helpful than expert prescriptions. As a specialist in this field and president of his own consulting firm, his words have weight.

The last article in Part V presents a concept for the 1980s. Although written in 1969, Melvin Sorcher and Selig Danzig's article "Charting and Changing the Organizational Climate" is as current as today's newspaper. At the time the article was written, Sorcher was a psychologist in General Electric's behavioral research service and Danzig a consulting planner in organization and manpower for GE's Aircraft Equipment Division. The study they reported in the article was done at GE and indicated that organizational climate is a major determinant of productivity and, if measured and the measurements used as a basis for revisions in management practices, significant favorable changes in climate and results can be produced. A fitting—and timely—note on which to close.

24

The Technique
of Measuring
Employee Attitudes

Arthur W. Kornhauser

MANAGEMENT'S interest in employee attitudes arises from the belief that attitudes are important determinants of efficiency. That belief is amply supported by casual observations as well as by the more careful attitude studies of recent years. Favorable feelings make for efficiency; antagonistic attitudes lead to unnecessary waste, friction in getting work done, poor quality workmanship, withheld effort, increased costs. This relationship is a foundation principle of industrial personnel philosophy. Improvement of attitudes—heightening of morale—constitutes a prime objective of personnel management. It is not, however, that favorable attitudes are the ultimate goal; they are prized because they mean effective work and reduced labor costs.

Employee attitudes have direct human significance, however, along with their implications for production. Viewed socially, industry is to be judged not only by the skyscrapers, loaves of bread, and profits it produces but also by what it does to its working people. Workers' attitudes, though never listed in our census of manufac-

tures, constitute a most significant industrial product. Students of
labor can ill afford to neglect the question: What does work bring in
the way of personal adjustment and feeling of well-being? What does
it mean in units of satisfaction or of discontent? Studies of employee
attitudes have these questions to answer as well as the ones of more
immediate practical concern to management.

An immense part of our industrial discontent is unnecessary. If
management knows what its employees are really thinking and feeling, the sources of trouble can usually be greatly reduced in seriousness. Too often the workers' attitudes are guessed at—or ignored—or
damned.

During the past few years a number of studies of employees' attitudes have shown how this guess work may be eliminated. The
studies take a significant step beyond ordinary casual observations
and off-hand impressions. They attempt to analyze and measure attitudes by specially planned interview and testing techniques. The
studies have ranged from an intensive investigation in a Philadelphia
railroad shop to large-scale inquiries at the Western Electric Company
and in a number of important public utilities; from problems concerning women workers in a Wisconsin factory to employees of a metal-
working plant in western Pennsylvania. The organizations studied
include one of the largest soap factories, several machine shops, textile mills, and a metropolitan bank.

These studies have contributed both to our knowledge of how to
measure attitudes and to our understanding of important causes and
effects of employees' feelings. It has become clear that good and bad
attitudes reflect the whole tangled network of industrial conditions on
the one hand, and the varying amount of emotional stability, temper-
ament, and intellectual equipment of workers on the other. Especially
outstanding are such influences as insecurity of employment; the personalities and methods of supervisors; the intensity and routine
character of the job; improper placement of workers; wages, hours,
working conditions, and labor policies; home conditions and personal
problems. Often one or two dominant sources of irritation color attitudes toward the entire work relationship. Workers may complain of
bad working conditions when the real trouble is bad supervision.

How well are actual attitudes revealed in these studies? Can we
measure how people really feel about their jobs? Certainly the obstacles are formidable. Skilled, sympathetic, sincere interviewing is required if employees are to talk frankly. The interviews and question
blanks must be planned with extreme care and must eliminate per-

sonal bias as far as is humanly possible. Employees' statements must be interpreted in relation to one another and with reference to underlying causes of unrest. Moreover, employees must be fully convinced that the inquiry is honest, is in their own interests, and will harm none of them. Feelings of suspicion make the study worthless. Accordingly, few concerns—especially in these days of stress—can be advised to conduct such inquiries.

Under favorable conditions, however, studies of employee attitudes do perform valuable services, among them the following:

1. They give management a measure of how well it is doing its job of leadership, how well morale is being maintained. It is a rating of management's efficiency in personnel matters.

2. Attention is called to specific problems and sources of irritation that need attention—conditions of work, supervision, personal problems, and so on. Often the employees have specific constructive suggestions to offer.

3. Workers are given an opportunity to unburden themselves—to get things off their chests and to feel that the company is really interested in them and their problems. The mere talking makes them feel better.

4. A mine of specific concrete cases is opened, to be used—anonymously—in instructing supervisors in better methods of dealing with their men.

Our particular interest here is with the techniques of analyzing and measuring attitudes. The term "attitude" is conveniently vague. The very fact that it has no clear-cut psychological definition lets it serve usefully to designate the varied reaction tendencies of a person—his readiness to respond in one direction or another. Thus we speak of attitudes of friendliness, resentment, or antagonism; a critical attitude; a broad-minded attitude; or a capitalistic attitude. The attitudes may refer to particular persons and objects, or they may have less specific reference, for example, an attitude of friendliness toward all change, or an attitude of opposition to all incentive wage plans. In each instance, the attitude implies a predisposition toward action of a somewhat definite, but not highly specific, character. The pugnacious attitude is a tendency to fight or respond aggressively—but by means of a variety of specific actions. There is simply a "set" or direction for the behavior to follow. Usually, but not always, the attitude is charged with emotion; it is a matter of feelings. Moreover, the attitudes are for or against, with corresponding favorable or unfavorable feelings. When we speak of measuring attitudes, it is the degree of this positiveness or negativeness that we are seeking to determine. How strongly do employees favor a pension plan? How intensely do they resent the methods employed by their foreman? Is their attitude for or against the rate-setting department? Or, more generally, how high is morale in different departments or plants? How great is unrest or dissatisfaction?

There are many ways of trying to get at employee attitudes. And there are many and serious difficulties. We shall look at the several methods that have been used in industrial investigations and then raise some critical questions concerning these techniques.

All the methods for studying attitudes must perforce start with what people do and say. Attitudes themselves are not objectively observed facts; they are inferences, interpretations. Sometimes the inference is entirely safe. But there is usually considerable doubt. The results of an attitudes study are likely to depend largely on the methods of the investigation.

The first method to consider is the use of objective records. Why not go directly to the attitude effects with which management is concerned? That is, why not analyze labor turnover figures, output records, and behavior on the job? The answer is that we should. However, these studies will take us only a short way. High turnover figures, poor quality records, low output may indeed indicate unfavorable attitudes. But these are gross results. We must go back of them to learn how far causes other than attitudes are involved and just what sorts of dissatisfaction are operative. To stop with objective records would be like taking mortality statistics and nothing more in studying problems of health.

In addition, one encounters serious difficulties in an attempt to find usable measures of individual output and job behavior. For vast numbers of jobs, measurements of performance are impossible; in many other instances records have not been kept adequately. The figures are not readily comparable from job to job. Usually dozens of disturbing influences must be considered in interpreting the records when they are available. Nevertheless, studies of attitudes, to be of greatest value, should always utilize statistics of work performance and observations of behavior along with evidence collected by the usual procedures of attitude investigations.

The usual methods of surveying attitudes are verbal. They make use of what employees say or write. I shall break them into five classes.

1. *The impressionistic method.* This method is admirably illustrated by the work of Whiting Williams. It arrives at its interpretations on the basis of a thousand incidental observations of what men say, how they

say it, what they do not say, how they look, how they work, and how they play. The method is not "scientific." It is subjective and informal; it tries to see things as a whole; to understand sympathetically; to get at the deeper feelings of men. Of course, we all use these scattered impressions and flashes of insight as a partial basis for attitude interpretations. The method, in that sense, is an indispensable supplement to all the more formal methods.

2. *The unguided interview.* This method is also somewhat informal. It is the method stressed by the psychoanalysts. In the industrial field it is most associated with the name of Elton Mayo and with the Western Electric Company's investigation. The essential spirit is: Let the employee talk. The interviewer is there to listen. What is wanted is anything that the worker feels is important. The interviewer asks no questions, does no guiding beyond encouraging the employee to continue with whatever is on his mind. Written notes are kept of everything of any consequence at all.

3. *The guided interview.* All degrees of guidance are possible, from none to the rigid following of a list of questions. The usual guided interview is intermediate. The interviewer may have a set of topics or questions to be covered, but in no regular order, with no set form of questioning, and with free opportunity for the employee to branch off into anything he pleases. Thus, for example, in a study made in the Kimberly-Clark Corporation a list of about 50 questions was compiled to serve as aids or reminders to the interviewer of what to look for. Full notes are kept in this method, including what the interviewer says and what the employee contributes even where this is not related to any questions on the list. More formal interview procedures are illustrated in J. David Houser's investigation in several public utility companies and in B. V. Moore's study of attitudes of a group of textile workers toward an employment guarantee plan. The latter asked 15 set questions, many of them answerable by yes or no. The former devised a system for grading the responses into five levels of favorableness or unfavorableness.

4. *Question blanks.* This method owes most to the work of Houser and his associates. It has also been used in a number of later studies. Usually the blank contains simple questions that can be answered yes or no in a way to reveal the employees' opinion about specific points. The questionnaires are given to groups of workers, with oral explanations, and are answered and returned at the time. Such blanks yield simple quantitative data showing the number of people declaring themselves satisfied or dissatisfied about various conditions and relationships. Responses to a number of questions bearing on one subject,

such as supervision, may be combined to give a rating of favorableness of attitude. Simple lists of items to be checked are also included in some of the question blanks—for example, a list of job characteristics in which the employee indicates which he likes and which he dislikes. There are many other variations in form of question; some are ingenious and useful.

5. *Scales for the measuring of particular attitudes.* The development of this technique is the special contribution of L. L. Thurstone. Application of his scaling methods in an industrial study has been made recently by R. S. Uhrbrock. A scale is constructed for attitudes toward one specified object—say, attitude toward the job. The scale consists of a number of statements of opinion—20 or 30 perhaps—ranging from ones extremely favorable to others extremely unfavorable. In measuring attitudes a person is merely asked to check the statements with which he agrees. From these responses a rating or score is readily computed that shows how fully the person stands for or against the matter in question. The refined techniques in scaling come in the statistical procedures for placing the statements along the scale like the inch marks on a yardstick. The use of an attitude scale enables us to secure an accurate record of one attitude, such as favorableness of feeling toward the job as a whole. If we are interested in a number of more specific attitudes, separate scales are required. The scales are somewhat expensive to construct and a large set of them would be cumbersome to administer. But much may be said for the use of one scale, or two or three, supplemented by the more ordinary questionnaire and interview.

What are the problems and difficulties in the use of these methods? Five questions arise that call attention to certain of the problems and needs:

First of all, will employees cooperate? Will they talk? Unless they will, the attitude study had better stop before it begins. Without a favorable setting, no amount of refined and subtle technique will go far. Above everything else in the study of workers' attitudes, I would emphasize the necessity for creating and maintaining conditions that make for frank and willing expression, with no fears of reprisals and no doubts that personal confidences will be absolutely respected. It is no less essential that the goodwill of supervisors and managers be maintained.

The investigators themselves can do much to reinforce the employees' willingness and confidence. Every detail of interview and questionnaire procedure should be considered from this standpoint. One important problem, here, is whether the study can be made by persons already in the organization and identified with management. Research students from outside seem to me to have a tremendous advantage. Another question is whether interviews and question blanks must be kept anonymous. While this procedure has usually been followed, I believe names can be secured with proper precautions. This was done at Kimberly-Clark. The great advantage is that attitudes can be correlated with personal data.

In this connection, a question is also often raised whether attitude studies are not likely to stir up trouble, to make employees think about things to criticize. How true is that criticism? My experience indicates that people need no extra stimulation to develop grievances. In fact there is considerable support for a view quite the opposite. When people can talk freely they are less likely to store up and exaggerate their troubles. Hence, a well-conducted attitude study should have direct therapeutic value as a by-product.

The general answer to our first question is that in many fortunate industrial situations, employees will cooperate. Even in places where they are less willing, skilled interviewers can accomplish a great deal—especially by informal or impressionistic methods. What, then, shall we do about attitude measurements in less favorable settings—where they are probably most needed? I leave that question to you.

The second question is: Even where employees cooperate fully, how well are they able to reveal their attitudes? The problem is partly one of language limitations. Can workers put into words any save the simple and familiar feelings? Or, where questions are used, do the words mean what they do to the investigator? Apparently the only solution is to use utmost care in avoiding ambiguities, to adapt one's language to the persons dealt with, and to judge the attitude in terms of many statements or answers which check one another. Here, too, arise the difficulties created by rationalizing or self-defense tendencies on the part of the people studied. A demoted employee, for example, declares his new job is splendid; he likes it better than any other work he has done. Now this may be only his surface attitude, what he is trying to make himself believe to save his face. He would probably seize an opportunity to be reinstated in the old job. Question blanks miss the deeper attitudes in such cases; so also do interviewers who are not highly skilled. This is one sample of the whole question of how far verbal attitudes and the attitudes that determine behavior agree. This entire problem of how well people are able to reveal their attitudes seems to me to point to the desirability of informal and skilled interviewing instead of, or in addition to, questionnaire and scale methods for studying attitudes. It also suggests certain values of the guided as against the unguided interview.

The third set of issues centers in the question: How well can the investigator report and interpret attitudes? What training should interviewers have? How seriously do their biases, expectations, and pet theories color their findings? How do their own emotional attitudes affect what they are looking for and are prepared to see? Answers to these questions are fragmentary, but a little disquieting. Great differences are sometimes reported from different interviewers. In one study, for example, an interviewer with a prohibition bias reported that 34 percent of the men in a destitute group gave liquor as the cause of their condition, while another interviewer in the same inquiry found that only 11 percent blamed liquor. Thorough preparation of interviewers is a most important need in attitude studies, both on the side of skill in conducting the interview and in recognizing and allowing for their own prejudices. Formal question blanks and scales have a decided advantage in this matter of objectivity. In all methods save the unguided interview, however, there is great danger of suggestive questions. Constant care is needed to avoid asking questions in a way that will bring the expected reply.

Fourth, do our attitude measurements give us a rounded or complete picture? In the case of unguided interviews, do employees actually mention all their important attitudes—or only those that for one reason or another are at the surface? Are they not especially prone to stress the recent objects of feelings, things that are changing or that have created new strains or new good feelings? In other words, are the matters that are uppermost in our thinking necessarily the ones important in the long run? Do we not readily overlook deep-seated attitudes to which we have become accustomed? The trusted and admired head of a concern may be the outstanding influence affecting the morale of employees. Yet he may not be mentioned by them. He is taken for granted; he is not an object of present attention. New lockers or a safety slogan contest loom larger for the moment. In some instances the deeper motivations may never have been clearly recognized. These considerations are serious difficulties of the unguided interview method.

In the case of questionnaires, scales, and guided interviews, the problem is to plan broadly enough to cover everything that may be significant. We have an unlimited number of attitudes, of which certain dominant ones are particularly worth inquiring into. An important part of attitude studies is the preliminary gathering of points to be inquired into, the survey of possibly significant attitudes. Impressionistic methods are probably best in this preliminary stage. As an aid, however, a comprehensive psychological classification of attitudes in terms of "dependable motives" or needs is of value. What about the question of whether the job satisfies or interferes with self-assertive impulses? Workmanship tendencies? Sex and family motivations? What things in this industrial situation arouse anger or fear? I believe there is much to be derived from closer tie-ups of our attitude inquiries with our psychological theories of motivation along such lines as these. On the side of technique, it means that our question blanks would be planned more fully to cover the field of workers' feelings. We would secure a more rounded and better balanced picture. Single attitude scales clearly cannot meet this need.

Finally, our fifth set of questions. Do our attitude measurements give us a realistic view? This question applies particularly to the use of formal question blanks and scales. The very conception, in fact, of measuring attitudes carries with it some necessary abstracting from the complexity of the actual attitudes. Attitudes as they occur in the natural state have most complicated interconnections. What we call one attitude is usually one aspect of a tangled network. What we get in our measurements is a one-dimension description—simply an index of how favorable or unfavorable the feeling is toward an object. For practical purposes we usually want to know far more. Take, for example, employees' attitudes with respect to economizing or eliminating waste. These attitudes are all tied up with attitudes toward the boss, toward wage policies and fairness of treatment, toward the wealth of the company and what happens to profits, toward what the management itself is doing to eliminate waste, toward security of employment, toward thrift and the sinfulness of waste in general. If something is to be done about the problem of waste, we want to know these attitudes in something of their actual richness and relatedness. To know that the attitude is unfavorable takes us only a short way. A negative attitude may reflect fear or anger or disgust or lowered self-esteem. It is important to know which. When we force people's attitudes into a form to fit our measuring stick, let us remember what it is we have measured.

The conclusion is that employee attitude studies for practical purposes should always depend less on formal measurements than on informal, more realistic interview and question-blank methods.

I fear that my recital of difficulties and criticisms may seem to indicate that my attitude toward attitude studies is a negative one. If I have given that impression, it merely illustrates anew how easily attitudes are misinterpreted. I believe so heartily in the value of having employees express their feelings, in fact, that I should go far beyond an occasional survey. We need provisions for continuous expression. Sound personnel planning will not be content with morale stocktaking once a year or once in several years. What is needed is a perpetual inventory. Especially is this true since the inventory functions at the same time to maintain goodwill and relieve tense feelings.

The continuous flow of employee attitudes to management may occur through three principal channels—through the regular line organization, through employees' representatives—either labor union or company organization—and through the personnel office or some member of management functioning in a personnel capacity. While it is not appropriate to go into details on these matters here, we should at least be clearly aware of the close tie-up of special attitude measurement work with the broader problem of fostering adequate means of communication and understanding between workers and management. The job of knowing employee attitudes is a day-by-day responsibility of management. Special attitude studies and measurement techniques are aids and supplements in the performance of this task. Few personnel functions are more deserving of attention.

25

Action-Oriented Attitude Surveys

Louis A. Allen

PERSONNEL programs are frequently installed without much knowledge of whether they will really help increase efficiency or improve employee relations. Do people in the plant need and want a different kind of wage and salary program? Are all supervisors as inadequate as some are pictured to be? Have the poster campaigns been paying off? Is there a real need for more or better communications? Unless an answer is secured to such questions as these, considerable amounts of money may be expended like buckshot, with little certainty that the activities they support are hitting the mark. What is needed is a rifle-bullet approach: some means of determining what needs employees actually have and what can be done to satisfy those needs.

Role of the Attitude Survey

Several methods have been developed for getting factual, objective reports of what employees think about their jobs, their supervisors, and their working conditions and what they feel is unsatisfactory about them. One of the most useful ways to get this information is the employee attitude survey, or opinion poll, administered in questionnaire form and followed up by personal interviews where necessary.

What It Is

The attitude survey or opinion poll is a list of carefully prepared, written questions about the work situation that employees are asked to answer on a completely anonymous basis. If properly administered, tabulated, and interpreted, these responses will give a valid picture of what employees think about the areas covered by the survey questions. The survey responses thus become a report of employee opinion. In picturing the conditions that exist, the responses are colored by the same bias, misinformation, and unsound conclusions as would be the case if you were to eavesdrop on the same people during a conversation. However, since these responses represent what employees really think, they reflect attitudes that must be taken into account in developing effective personnel programs.

What It Can Do

The employee attitude survey is a special tool for a particular purpose. It can do certain things, but the limitations of the technique must be kept in mind if it is to be of real value under operating conditions.

The attitude survey is best adapted to telling *what* is wrong. It can be used successfully to point to friction areas where trouble may develop. Although it is not as effective in providing reasons *why* things are wrong or *how* they should be corrected, when properly used it can be useful in giving at least partial answers to these questions.

It should be emphasized that the questionnaire-type attitude survey does not draw fine lines. It is a finger that points to areas that require further investigation; only rarely can it be used as a detailed guide for specific corrective action.

In addition to its value as a barometer to register the high and low points of morale, the survey also has a cathartic value. At any given time many small gripes and complaints exist in every plant. Unless the immediate supervisor is able to encourage the unburdening of these real and fancied complaints, they frequently grow into grievances that require money and time to handle. However, if each employee is periodically presented with an anonymous ear into which to pour his woes, and if he sees some action taking place as a result, he is likely to feel both relieved and satisfied.

The attitude survey or opinion poll has two primary uses in common industrial practice. It can be used for the evaluation of employee response to a broad selection of questions for the purpose of determining the overall attitudes that exist with regard to a related set of things, conditions, or situations. This might include everything from working conditions to pay.

A second, more narrowly restricted use of the technique consists of asking one or more questions to determine what the people in the plant think about one specific subject. The difference here is in quantity, not in kind. This type of survey might be restricted to finding out whether the job evaluation system is understood or what supervisors think about the basic economics meetings in the supervisory conference program.

The purpose of drawing this distinction is to point up the fact that the survey technique can be used for purposes in the plant other than the usual broad survey of employee attitudes. Since employee opinion is likely to be the make or break factor in the long-run success of personnel programs, the opinion poll can be used periodically to find out what employees actually think about programs in which they are participating.

To cite an example, a companywide conference-type supervisory training program was introduced in one plant without any specific attempt to tailor the program to the needs of the departments participating. An opinion poll at the end of six months revealed that the program required too many "reports" and "minutes" to serve the needs of the small groups concerned; it involved too much time away from the job on the part of the supervisors; and, finally, no advance notice was being given of the subject matter to be discussed. These matters were corrected, and it was made clear to the supervisors concerned that the action had been taken as a result of their suggestions. A second opinion poll taken at the end of another six months showed vastly improved supervisory acceptance of the program.

As a further example of the use of the questionnaire to determine reaction to a specific subject, supervisors were asked what title they wanted to apply to their supervisory conference program. In spite of the commonly accepted idea that the word "training" is taboo and should not be used, in a group of 1,100 supervisors, 36 percent checked Supervisory Training Program as their preference in a list of six choices given. This was the highest response. Management Development Program, with 20 percent, was next highest.

Some Fallacies About Attitude Surveys

More credence is sometimes placed in survey responses than is warranted without very careful interpretation in the light of all the pertinent factors. In such cases, remedial action may be initiated upon false premises.

The "Halo" Response

It is unfortunate that the attitude survey returns lend themselves so readily to generalities and ambiguity. Without proper explanation, percentages attached to a particular statement can be inferred to mean many things. If the percentage happens to be high and is characterized as favorable, it is easily accepted as a *carte blanche* endorsement when, in actual fact, the favorable point may be a minor item among others that are either definitely unfavorable or unidentified.

For example, perhaps an attitude survey is being used to find out how much good a poster campaign is accomplishing. Typical of the questions asked might be these: "Do you like the poster service?" and "Do you look at the posters on the bulletin board?"

Since the pictures on the posters are generally dramatic and colorful, there is no reason for the average person to dislike them. Consequently the 95 or 98 percent favorable response that results from such a poll is advanced as glowing proof of the effectiveness of the poster campaign. In actual fact, of course, it is nothing of the sort. Further evidence is required to show that the posters are changing attitudes or initiating the kind of action desired.

Another example of the same sort of thing occurs when an opinion poll is used to measure the effectiveness of a particular training program. A common practice is to select a homogeneous group from one plant level and to administer a questionnaire within a few days of the completion of the training course. Power questions are included to find out how many of the key points are remembered. With a group of average memory and intelligence, there is very good recall at the end of such a short period of time. This response is then publicized to show how effective the program has been. Such a statement, of course, overlooks the fact that periods of less than one week are *not* the important forgetting periods. Only follow-up surveys at the end of one, three, and perhaps six months can give the true picture of what the training course has accomplished.

Acceptance of this type of "halo" response is one good reason for the remark that is often heard to the effect that "surveys can be used to prove anything." The situation can be corrected by using surveys for the purposes for which they are best suited and by objective evaluation and analysis of the results that are obtained.

Overmeasurement

The attitude survey is not a measuring instrument that is capable of recording small differences. There is little purpose in using fine comparisons based on the survey responses when only gross comparisons can be considered valid. For instance, perhaps we want to use the response to the question, "How do you feel about the company you now work for?" as a general morale index. We find that three departments are grouped closely together; four percentage points cover the difference in their responses. The tendency is to say that Department A, with an 86 percent response, is better than Department B, with 84 percent, or Department C, with 82 percent. In actual fact, this kind of differentiation will not stand up. For all practical purposes, Departments A, B, and C can be said to have the same response to this question.

Conducting the Attitude Survey

In the discussion that follows, the points developed apply particularly to the broad type of survey that is being used to gauge plantwide attitudes on all topics of current significance. The same principles, with appropriate modification, apply to the more restricted type of opinion poll that also has been described. Five steps that are basic to a successful program are outlined:

1. The survey should be approved and thoroughly endorsed by each responsible executive who will be expected to take action on the results.

2. The questionnaire should be properly prepared and administered.

3. The survey responses and written comments should be tabulated and interpreted to point out clearly specific friction areas in which action is indicated.

4. The results of the survey should be made known to those who participated in it.

5. Action should be taken where indicated by the survey results.

1. Approval and Endorsement by Responsible Executives

Since the attitude survey is conducted for the purpose of producing action that will correct unsatisfactory conditions, it is important for top management, department heads, and operating superintendents to understand the purpose of the survey, to approve the questions asked, and to be prepared to take action based on the survey responses.

This approval and endorsement must start from the top. Perhaps the personnel man has received the go-ahead from the top executive, who is fully cognizant of the values and shortcomings of the survey techniques. Quite probably the aims and objectives of the survey are appreciated by the executive group. However, the personnel man should make sure also that each member of the policymaking group understands that he is committing himself to the possibility of far-reaching action when he approves the administration of the survey in his organization. Each executive should be acquainted with the general procedures to be used in conducting the survey. He should personally read and approve the wording of the survey questions. This participation should extend to operating superintendents and department heads.

2. Proper Preparation and Administration

The questions must be so worded that they will be easily understood by the people who will be expected to answer them. Areas that are to be covered should be determined to fit organizational needs. The mechanics of administration should be worked out carefully beforehand to assure anonymity and a large percentage of valid responses.

Areas to Be Covered. It is sometimes difficult, particularly with a first survey, to determine what general areas are giving rise to employee dissatisfaction or unrest. In some cases, supervisors and executives can give helpful advice in regard to what areas to probe. Production records and such personnel data as statistics on absenteeism, exit interview reports, and grievance records can be helpful. In the case of a first survey, it is often wise to use a set of questions that will cover all probable areas of unrest. After responses from the first survey of this type have been evaluated, it is generally possible on the next survey to pick out those areas that need a series of questions and those in which a single question will prove adequate to determine that a favorable situation is remaining so.

Periodic Surveys. By itself, the first attitude survey can be helpful. But to take advantage of the intrinsic values of the survey procedure, the process should be repeated on a periodic basis. Many factors, some of which may be temporary, can have a profound effect on the responses obtained. For instance, if a wage "freeze" is operative in several departments during the period in which the first survey is conducted, most of the responses concerning wage and salary are likely to be on the low side. When the "freeze" is lifted, however, considerable variation in response between departments will be shown. This gives us an opportunity to isolate such factors as poor merit-rating procedures, inapproachability of supervisors on pay questions, and lack of understanding of the job evaluation system. After surveys have been conducted once every year or two for a period of years, trends will be established that will give an accurate picture of basic questions.

Control Questions. Since the final objective of the survey is corrective action, it is highly desirable to localize areas of dissatisfaction as much as possible. If working conditions are bad only in one department, once this fact is determined there is no point in conducting interviews or investigations for nonexistent troubles in the other departments. Perhaps a change in pay policy is displeasing only to employees who have been with the company since 1949, because that was the year in which the new system went into effect. Relative newcomers, who have no recollection of the old policy, accept the change without comment. If such be the case, it is important to know what group is affected before widespread and expensive changes are advocated.

A simple method of singling out the major areas in which complaints are centered is to ask a set of control questions at the beginning of the questionnaire. These might cover department, years of service, sex, age, and other pertinent factors. To facilitate tabulation, the control questions are better set up in multiple-choice form, rather than as write-ins. For example, to get information concerning length of service, the question might be worded thus:

How many years have you worked for this company?

1. _____ Less than 1 year
2. _____ Over 1 but less than 3 years
3. _____ Over 3 but less than 5 years
4. _____ Over 5 but less than 10 years
5. _____ More than 10 years

By use of statistical accounting machines, it is relatively simple, in this example, to find out the responses of people who have been with the company a short time and to compare these with the old-timers'. If the comments are properly numbered when being transcribed, it is also possible to find out by which group the most meaningful comments were offered. Although these additional breakdowns add to the expense of the survey, they are worthwhile if they point up or localize the need for action.

The Questionnaire Proper. The questions used in the body of the survey must meet certain criteria. Most important, ask questions only about matters concerning which effective action seems possible. For instance, if the personnel man is trying to promote a program that has not yet gained executive acceptance, there is a great temptation to ask employees such questions as whether they are in favor of bonus plans, whether they like the present cafeteria system, or whether they think the method by which their pay is determined is fair. A favorable survey response would be a good selling point. But unless the policymaking executive is aware of the implications of such questions and is willing to approve action if it is indicated, they should be avoided. A good criterion for every question is this: Can effective action be taken or a satisfactory answer be given explaining why action is not possible in answer to the response that can be anticipated from this question?

Wording of Questions. Employees answer questions as *they* understand them, not in terms of what the survey administr: tor thinks they mean. This matter of semantics is difficult to overcome, for frequently the personnel man, the executive, and the employee being polled will each have a different way of wording the same question. Further than this, people in different parts of the plant or, if there are a number of plants, employees in different sections of the country will read different meanings from the same words.

While there is no foolproof method for eliminating all the "bugs" from the wording of the questions, there are some things that can be done to help. The best insurance is to have the questions checked by the people who are being asked to answer them. To do this, pretest your questionnaires with small but representative groups of the employees being polled. Tell these people why they are being called together. Then instruct them to go through the questionnaire, answering each question in full. Ask them to circle any word or phrase that they do not understand or that they feel could be better worded. After you have discussed your proposed questions with several of these pretest groups, you will find that the wording of many questions is changed. You can be sure that the new phraseology is most nearly correct for the people who will complete the questionnaire.

After the questionnaires have undergone this preliminary trial by fire, they should be submitted for approval to each executive who will be responsible for later action. A summary of the remarks and suggestions obtained from the pretest groups can be submitted at the same time to give the executive an idea of what kind of responses he is likely to be confronted with when the survey is completed.

The Questionnaire Form. The questions should be printed in an attractive, easily read form that lends itself to the mechanics of tabulation. Instructions should be printed on the first or cover page. Since some employees will object to the arbitrary presentation in the multiple-choice type of question, space should be provided for free comments at the end of each question, plus one or two blank pages at the end of the survey form for any general comments respondents wish to make. At first glance, this would seem to entail a great amount of additional clerical expense in transcribing comments. However, this procedure gives everybody the opportunity to add whatever gripes or complaints the question may evoke. As has been noted, this catharsis in itself is of considerable value.

Publicity. After the questions have been finally approved and the questionnaire has been printed, there comes the problem of working out a procedure that will convince employees that their participation in the survey will be of advantage to them and that the anonymity of their responses is guaranteed. This is important. It will be successful if certain details are observed.

A general story describing the questionnaire and its purpose should be published in the plant paper and on bulletin boards in advance of the date on which the survey will be conducted. If a supervisory conference training program is in progress, the survey may very profitably be made a subject for discussion. Through these meetings foremen and supervisors can be given an opportunity to anticipate some of the action that may be required of them as a result of the survey. This sense of participation in itself is certain to contribute to the success of whatever course of action finally results. If unionized employees are being polled, the program should be discussed beforehand with the union officials. Shortly before the scheduled date, more detailed stories should be published announcing meeting rooms, the date and hour, and other pertinent details.

Survey Groups. Supervisory, salaried nonsupervisory, and hourly employees should be divided into separate groups. Each group should meet separately to complete the appropriate questionnaire. Desks or tables should be so placed as to discourage collaboration. No employee should be able to see another's questionnaire easily.

The Survey Supervisor. A survey supervisor should be appointed to present and explain the survey. The survey supervisor should know in advance the number of employees scheduled for each meeting so that all are present before he begins. When everybody is present and seated, the survey supervisor briefly describes the questionnaire and the procedure that will be used to complete it.

The Filling-in Procedure. The questionnaire blanks should be passed out by volunteers from the group. After the forms have been distributed, the survey supervisor should read aloud the introductory statement on the front page of the questionnaire. He should state that the questionnaires will be transcribed and tabulated by an outside agency and that nobody inside the company will have access to them once they leave the employees' hands. When the employees begin filling in their forms, the survey supervisor should not move about the room or manifest interest in what any employee is writing. After the questionnaires are completed, the individual may either seal his copy in a blank envelope or simply drop it in a large box with a slot in the top. After everybody is finished, volunteers are asked to seal the box and mail it to the outside agency.

This procedure will help insure anonymity. However, if employee relations have not been particularly good in the past, there is every likelihood that the first questionnaire will be met with some degree of skepticism. This in turn may distort the responses, for the employee who feels that his questionnaire may be identified is very likely to answer the questions the way he thinks the company wants them answered. This, of course, will result in an abnormally high percentage of favorable responses. If employee confidence is maintained throughout the first survey administered, with no cases of broken anonymity occurring, the response in succeeding surveys will be increasingly frank.

3. Tabulation and Interpretation of Results

Editing and tabulating the survey responses is most easily handled by an outside machine-tabulating agency, which is set up for this type of work. The sealed boxes containing the survey forms are returned from the plant to this agency. There the questionnaires are edited, the comments transcribed, and the questions tabulated.

Method of Tabulation. To be most meaningful, the survey responses should first be tabulated, and percentages calculated, to show the total response to each question item. This will give the overall picture for the entire organization. The totals should then be broken down for the next larger organizational grouping, and, finally, breakdowns should be made to give the picture in the smallest organizational units.

Caution should be exercised in making separate tabulations for units in which fewer than 25 or 30 persons answer the questionnaire. Statistical treatment of such returns becomes progressively more questionable with the decrease in number. For example, if only five people participate in a survey, each person's response has a weight of 1/5. In this case, a very negative reaction by one person, occasioned perhaps by a few sharp words with the boss that morning, would give a definite coloring to the percentage results. On the other hand, if 30 people are included in a group return, each person's response is weighted by only 1/30. The danger of incorrect interpretation increases as the group size grows smaller.

Delineating Friction Areas. After the returns are in, there comes the important step of defining the friction areas clearly. If the data available are handled properly, this can be helped by the use of a few simple charts.

The easiest way to point a bold finger to the areas in which action is required is to compare the strong or weak points of one unit of the organization against the others. Thus the most significant differences will exist in proportion as the response of a specific unit varies from the highest or lowest response in that area. So far as action is concerned, the further below average a unit stands in its survey responses, the more immediate and vigorous is the action indicated.

A profile chart of the survey responses is most useful in reporting the comparative showing of each unit. Bar graphs (see illustration) are used to indicate the deviation from the mean on each response. Since responses are grouped in representative categories, the profile formed in this manner gives a clear and readily understood picture of attitudes in the unit covered by the report.

The basic profile charts show the response of the unit as compared to the company average. Perhaps it will be helpful to compare the response of a smaller organizational unit against that of a larger unit and both, in turn, against the company average. For example, we may want to compare the response in a department to that of the plant and then compare both to that of the company.

This can be done easily in one chart simply by showing the bar graphs of the smallest unit in red. The red bars are superimposed in printing over the black bars, which represent the larger unit. Since both are represented as deviations from the company average, the three-way comparison is made obvious at a glance.

The Written Report. Using graphs to show the survey results gets your point across clearly and quickly. To hammer the conclusions home, it is a good idea to provide a brief, pointed analysis of the areas that require corrective action, as indicated by the charts. Do this in numbered steps, starting with a statement of the outstanding friction area and proceeding with those of decreasing importance.

Conclusions from Comments. Make particular mention in your report of the conclusions you draw from the written comments. A statement as to the frequency of comments covering specific areas is helpful, but appropriate caution should be exercised in making the analysis. Ten favorable comments do not necessarily balance out ten unfavorable ones. Far from it. It seems that people who are satisfied are less inclined to comment about it, while the dissatisfied are likely to be the more voluble. For instance, perhaps 80 percent of the people in a unit give favorable responses on the subject of external equity so far as pay is concerned. Only 12 percent may express real dissatisfaction. How-

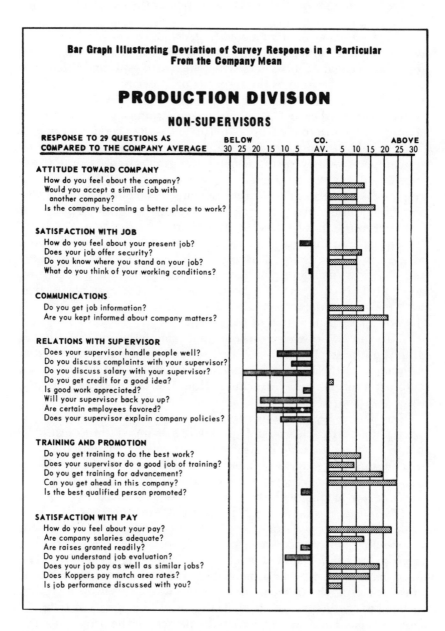

Bar Graph Illustrating Deviation of Survey Response in a Particular From the Company Mean

PRODUCTION DIVISION

NON-SUPERVISORS

RESPONSE TO 29 QUESTIONS AS COMPARED TO THE COMPANY AVERAGE

BELOW   CO.   ABOVE
30 25 20 15 10 5   AV.   5 10 15 20 25 30

ATTITUDE TOWARD COMPANY
How do you feel about the company?
Would you accept a similar job with another company?
Is the company becoming a better place to work?

SATISFACTION WITH JOB
How do you feel about your present job?
Does your job offer security?
Do you know where you stand on your job?
What do you think of your working conditions?

COMMUNICATIONS
Do you get job information?
Are you kept informed about company matters?

RELATIONS WITH SUPERVISOR
Does your supervisor handle people well?
Do you discuss complaints with your supervisor?
Do you discuss salary with your supervisor?
Do you get credit for a good idea?
Is good work appreciated?
Will your supervisor back you up?
Are certain employees favored?
Does your supervisor explain company policies?

TRAINING AND PROMOTION
Do you get training to do the best work?
Does your supervisor do a good job of training?
Do you get training for advancement?
Can you get ahead in this company?
Is the best qualified person promoted?

SATISFACTION WITH PAY
How do you feel about your pay?
Are company salaries adequate?
Are raises granted readily?
Do you understand job evaluation?
Does your job pay as well as similar jobs?
Does Koppers pay match area rates?
Is job performance discussed with you?

ever, it is entirely possible that over 50 percent of the written comments will indicate a belief that the company pays less than other companies in the area.

Dissatisfaction on most items seems to start with certain people in the group and spread from them to others. If these "thought leaders" are dissatisfied, it is quite probable that their influence will soon affect the attitudes of the whole group. These natural leaders are often the most ready to express themselves in the written comments. From this point of view, the unfavorable comments are significant. If a specific complaint is repeated several times, it merits attention. The more frequently people go to the trouble of writing about it, the more it demands careful investigation.

Personal Interviews. Many times complaints about one item actually refer to real trouble that lies somewhere else. For this reason, if you want to find out *why* a certain response is low, it is often a good idea to go to the people concerned and ask them. This entails conducting personal interviews with the individuals in the group under investigation. The information obtained in this way can be used to bolster the survey conclusions.

Since word of the interviews gets out quickly, every precaution should be taken to keep them completely confidential. It is generally best to interview every member of the group, so that none will feel that he has been passed up. Depending on the quality of employee relations in the plant, members of the plant staff may do the interviewing or an outside agency may be called in. There seems to be no good reason why the plant personnel staff cannot get a detailed and authentic set of interviews if the people who are doing the job know how to interview and if the personnel department has won the confidence of the people in the plant. If properly done, there should be no more question of validity concerning this type of personal interview than would be the case with effective exit interviews or employment or counseling interviews.

When personal interviews are conducted, they provide a detailed and well-documented statement of why certain conditions exist. If anonymity is maintained and disclosure of the results is handled with the utmost discretion, these interviews can be a most valuable factor in determining the proper course of action to remedy an unfavorable situation.

4. Making the Results Known

Confidence in the attitude survey program can be maintained only if the results are publicized within a reasonable time after the questionnaire is administered. Very definite obstacles may arise to block this important step. Some of the following difficulties may crop up:

The survey results are not favorable. Quite frequently the response on certain questions will be so poor as to be very embarrassing or even incriminating. The problem then is whether to wash the dirty linen in public. Generally the decision as to what should be publicized and what held back must be made by the management concerned. If certain items must be held back, it is best to do so without apology or explanation. This has become confidential information and is of constructive value only to the management people who are in a position to do something about it.

So much time elapses in processing the questionnaires that the results are stale when published. Since the opinion survey reflects the attitudes that existed on the day and hour the questionnaires were administered, the compilation of results becomes less meaningful with every day that passes. In the nature of things, situations that give rise to unsatisfactory attitudes generally change rather slowly. Results can be considered as fairly accurate reflectors of the plant picture for perhaps a month after the survey is completed. Events that will change the situation materially during that period are usually of such magnitude as to be readily noted. If such a thing as a new vacation policy is put into effect, or a new supervisor is appointed, these events can be accredited their proper influence in the interpretations of survey results.

Tabulation, preparation of graphical presentations, categorizing of comments, and interpretation of responses and comments are laborious and time consuming. However, the time necessary to accomplish these procedures can be materially decreased by adequate prior planning. For instance, most printed materials can be laid out well in advance. The art work on graphic profiles of comparative results by organizational units can be prepared except for the final placement of graph bars and the imprinting of percentages. A dummy copy can be prepared well beforehand for use as a guide in preparation of the final report.

Since the whole point of the attitude survey is to bring about necessary changes in situations that employees consider unsatisfactory, it is good dollar sense to let people know as soon as possible about changes that are brought about as a result of the survey. It is quite possible that the people who complained about poor ventilation and excessive heat on a survey questionnaire one summer will fail to associate their remarks with the air-conditioning equipment that is installed the summer following. Or, just as possibly, they may give credit for it to some other agency and thus deprive management of the pearls that rightfully belong in its crown.

If the survey results are properly publicized, follow-up letters to employees or articles in the plant paper can be used effectively to bring home to everybody the fact that concrete action was taken and that this action was the direct result of the employees' own recommendations. At the same time, if certain action contemplated proves impossible to carry out, an appropriate explanation in the same letter or article will prove satisfactory to anybody who is at all inclined to be reasonable and fair-minded about the situation.

5. Action Where Indicated

It is safe to assume that action cannot be taken on each and every individual recommendation that is brought forth by the attitude survey. Some complaints are bound to be out-and-out "sour grapes"; others will be found to be based on misinformation; yet more will refer to situations that it is economically or organizationally impractical to change. The best approach seems to be to take immediate action on those things that can be handled conveniently at the local level and make appropriate explanations regarding further consultation or approval required to carry out other suggestions.

How to Engineer the Action. There are two ways to approach the action involved. One is to have the executive concerned indicate what action he wants taken. The other is to place the survey recommendations before the supervisory group that will actually have to carry out the action and let the members develop their own approach.

The latter method seems to offer the best returns. If supervisors are given a chance to be heard in planning the action that is required, they will generally come up with suggestions that most closely fit actual operating requirements and the needs of all the people involved. In the nature of things, a large part of the remedial action necessary can be carried out by the supervisors themselves. If the problem-solving conference approach is used, the group can spell out its own plan of action and put it into effect. Those matters that require approval or action on a higher management level can be forwarded for consideration as the recommendation of the group.

Use of Group Censorship. Attitude surveys have a particular tendency to put supervisors on the spot. The reason is quite obvious when we consider the fact that most of the direct operating responsibility is placed in the hands of the supervisory group. As an example of how the survey may place the burden where it belongs, perhaps spot checking of one questionnaire return through comments shows an employee who expresses an unfavorable opinion of his own pay, the job evaluation system, and internal equity. At first glance this would seem to indicate that the fault lies with the wage and salary administration program. But investigation shows that the plant is definitely above the average for the area and that the department in question is in line with the rest of the plant. A clue comes on the question, "How often does your supervisor discuss your job performance with you?" Here we find this illuminating comment: "Mostly during the annual review—and he tries to find fault as an excuse for holding off a raise."

This begins to delineate one of the factors which has contributed to the unfavorable attitude toward pay in this particular department. Further analysis of the returns indicates that poor merit-rating procedures by supervisors are at the root of the trouble. Several approaches are possible if this shortcoming is to be corrected. An intensive campaign aimed at improving merit rating by supervisors can be initiated through talks given by the wage and salary administration staff. But perhaps this has been done many times in the past. It has not been very successful.

Very likely the same thing holds true in many other situations involving interrelationships of people on the job. Edicts and exhortation are not very effective in changing attitudes or initiating action. One method that works is to present the situation in detail to the entire group of supervisors. Through a combination of case discussion and role playing, the censorship of the group can be instrumental in changing attitudes and also in giving individual supervisors an opportunity to practice the right kind of approach away from the pressures of job situations. If this results in proper action on the part of the individual, the attitude survey—which was primarily responsible—has begun to pay for itself.

*   *   *

Since they actually report what people in the plant are thinking and saying, attitude surveys can be useful when planning and developing personnel programs. Properly used, they can point out conditions that are having an unfavorable effect on morale and productivity. They can help to outline specific areas that require further investigation through personal interviews. If the survey results are graphically and clearly presented, they can be a most potent force for initiating action from the highest to the lowest levels of the organization. As such, they can be a valuable tool of the personnel administrator.

Factors Influencing Industrial Morale

Mason Haire and Josephine S. Gottsdanker

PSYCHOLOGISTS and industrial relations research workers are producing more and more reports on industrial morale and on the attitudes of workers in factories. The literature [1] is increasing so fast that it threatens to overwhelm us.

It is no wonder that more and more attention is being directed toward the attitudes of workers. It is impossible to work in the industrial situation and to worry about productivity without getting the strong feeling that the workers' attitudes toward management, their confidence in the company, their feeling toward the job and toward their own security are of primary importance among the determinants of the productivity and stability of a workforce. To be sure, as soon as we get into the problem we find that it is somewhat circular, for just as morale may lead to high production, high production may lead to good morale. Nevertheless, there is a continuing pressure for more information about the attitudes of workers and the relation of these attitudes to industrial productivity.

Much recent research in morale and industrial relations has been in the direction of a search for factors in morale. We have many

[1] An excellent bibiography appears biannually in the journal, *Occupations.*

studies comparing the importance, for instance, of wages and working conditions, of supervision and getting along with associates, of one's chance for advancement and one's autonomy at work, and the like. We have gone a long way in the attempt to identify factors, and the natural next step has been to try to rank order the factors in terms of their importance in morale. It is unnecessary to give references that will include rank orders of factors. Almost half the research reports on morale will include some such rank ordering of the factors involved. It is to this problem of the rank orders of factors in morale that the present paper is directed. At the risk of overburdening an already weighty bibliography of factors in morale, this paper presents another rank ordering of factors, along with a discussion of what the list means, and a general discussion of the problems involved in rank ordering the factors in morale.

The Study

The data which are reported here were gathered as part of a larger study which had two major aims. The first of these was an attempt to define, in as much detail as possible, the perceptual field of the worker—that is, to investigate the way in which he saw his job, his boss, and his company, to try to find what barriers, threats, goals, and paths to goals he saw in his work situation. The other major aim of the overall study from which these data are drawn was to investigate the relative efficacy of various techniques for attitude sampling in the accomplishment of this definition of the perceptual field.

The sample that is reported here consists of 40 retail grocery store workers. They work in four different retail grocery stores that are part of a large chain. Their physical working conditions were quite similar and, of course, they shared the same company policies on economic benefits, job security, and the like. There was some variation in productivity among the stores, but all the stores are grouped together here. It should be pointed out, in defining the sample, that these people were well satisfied with their jobs.[2]

Moreover, they have, relatively speaking, good jobs. The average

[2] In response to a direct question, about 90 percent of these people reported themselves to be generally satisfied with their jobs. It is a curious anomaly along morale surveys that a percentage on this order is not unusually high. Most of us would probably feel, from our everyday experience with people, that somewhat less than 90 percent of them were generally satisfied with their jobs. However, on the basis of the way such percentages run in morale surveys, if an employer finds that his percentage drops, say, below 80 percent, it is probably a sign of a more or less serious defection in the organization. Sufficient experience with these percentages gives us a rule-of-thumb way to handle them. Nevertheless, the figures are certainly spuriously high. This distortion must surely mean that we are not getting a perfectly clear measure of the employee's attitude toward his job.

worker in this sample was about 35 years old, had worked for the company for seven years, and was earning in the neighborhood of $55 for a 44-hour week. Relative to the industry and the neighborhood, this is a very good wage for a retail clerk. The company has an excellent reputation for its general treatment of employees, and has made a considerable investment in the interest of producing "one big, happy family." These objective facts about the nature of the jobs seem to be of vital importance in considering the attitudes expressed, since these attitudes are at least partly a function of the situation in which the workers find themselves. In order to understand the attitudes, we must know something about the objective situation in which the people are imbedded.

Each subject was approached through an interview and two projective techniques, in separate sessions. The interview was open-ended, under the most permissive conditions possible, in which the respondent was encouraged to take whatever tack he liked and go on as long as he liked, followed by a series of objective questions of the sort that has characterized morale surveys in the past. The third technique was an adaptation of projective techniques that involved story completion, and the fourth involved interpretation of T.A.T. type pictures.[3] The stories and pictures were specially selected for this purpose, and were designed to parallel the content that was brought out in each of the two interview techniques.

Interview Results

In all, three specific questions and two story completions were used that approached the general problem of the factors in industrial morale. The following three questions were used in the interview:

1. What do you think of your job? What are the things you like about it?
2. If you were going to take another job, what are the things you'd look for?
3. Which of these things we've been talking about means the most to you in how well you like your job? [4]

[3] For a description of the Thematic Apperception Test, see "Executive Personality and Job Success," by William E. Henry, *AMA Personnel Series No, 120.*—Ed.
[4] This question was presented at the conclusion of about 40 minutes of interviewing, during which time various aspects of the job had been discussed. It came immediately after a question in which the respondent was asked specifically how fairly he thought he was treated, his opportunity for autonomy, opportunity for advancement, the amount of work expected of him, salary, and working conditions. In terms of the responses, it seemed clear that the respondents did not interpret the phrase "which of these things"

Figure 1
Factors Leading to Job Satisfaction
(% of mentions)

	Interview Questions			Story Completions	
	Why he likes his job	*Things you'd look for in a desirable job*	*Most important single factor in present job*	*Why man likes job*	*Why man dislikes job*
Interesting job	19%	11%	5%	19%	30%
Likes associates	17	3	22	15	9
Contact with customers	12	3	5	3	0
Working conditions	12	15	3	10	14
Wages	9	24	3	17	17
Fits well with habits of life and work	7	10	3	12	0
Easy work	6	6	0	2	5
Fair company	5	2	5	2	0
Job security	5	6	3	5	0
Supervision	3	3	22	7	15
Future advancement	2	7	29	5	10
Autonomy	2	7	0	2	0
Union protection	1	3	0	1	0
Total	100%	100%	100%	100%	100%
N = (no. of mentions)	89	115	40	107	86

In addition to the three direct questions, the respondent was asked to complete the following two stories:

1. While riding home on the bus one night, a couple of men were talking with each other about their work. One of them said, "It sure would take a lot to make me change my job, be- cause. . . ." What else did he say?
2. The other fellow said he'd be ready to quit *his* job any time, and added, "I'd be glad to give the first decent job that comes along a try, because. . . ." Then, what else did he say?

The responses to these stories and questions were coded, and it was found that they fell into 13 categories. The responses to the

as having specific reference either to the question which immediately preceded his answer or to the first question listed above. The response was usually in answer to the (unasked) general question, "What is the most important single determinant of job satisfaction?"

different questions, and the percentages with which different factors are mentioned are shown in Figure 1.

There are several points of interest in Figure 1. Perhaps the most striking thing is the radical shift in the importance that is ascribed to various factors by the employee when he is asked different questions that get at the same thing. It is quite clear that the relative importance of the factors is to a large extent a function of the way he is questioned and the things he is thinking about when he answers. This kind of relativity is something that we will have to go into in more detail later.

"Like" versus "Dislike"

It will be seen in Figure 1 that the factors that a man chooses as his reasons for liking a job are not at all the inverse of those which he chooses for disliking it. In making this comparison, we can either compare the two projective stories that ask indirectly why a man likes and dislikes his job, or compare the projective story on dislikes with the response to the direct question about why he likes his present job. In neither case is the "like" the opposite side of the coin from the "dislike." This lack of symmetry agrees with the findings of Reynolds and Shister in their book *Job Horizons* (6) (see Bibliography), and it is not a particularly startling fact in human motivation to realize that we cannot produce an exhaustive or coherent collection of positively cathected objects by assembling a group of negative ones and reversing their meaning. For some reason, there seems to be a great temptation, in considering the factors in industrial morale, to assume that just this sort of symmetry exists, and hence it is worthwhile to underline the fact that it is not necessarily true.

"Interesting" Work

The category of *interesting job* deserves some special attention. It will be noted from Figure 1 that this category includes more responses (19 percent) than any other single category when the respondent defines why he likes his present job. It receives the third most responses (11 percent) when he describes the things that he would look for in looking for a new job. It also receives the most responses of any single category in both the projective stories (19 percent and 30 percent). To some extent this category is a catchall; to some extent, however, it is not. It includes all the responses that say, "The job is interesting, it is varied, I like the activity in it, there is always something new happening," and the like. It is apt to include the respondent's first somewhat vague statement as he gropes for a way to take hold of the answer to the question. In this sense the category *is* a catchall.

However, the question of the characteristics of work as being interesting, varied, and of compelling attention to itself as work, is something that is returned to so often and so explicitly by many subjects that characteristics seem to include a very real aspect of the job, as well as a catchall. This factor of interesting work has been pointed out before in morale studies, among them that of Lindahl (4). There seems to be no questioning that it includes an important factor but, equally, it seems clear that we do not understand exactly what is included under this heading of interesting work.

Associates

The category *associates* includes all the respondent's statements that his contacts with fellow workers were important to him, and general references to the importance of a "good group" at work. This category receives a large bulk of the responses in our study. In the description of why the employee likes his present job, it received 17 percent of all the responses, and among the most important determinants in liking a job in general, it received 22 percent. Similarly, in the projective story on reasons for liking a job, it received 16 percent. In general, this stress on the importance of interpersonal relationships among employees parallels closely the important role that was given to it by Whyte (7) in his excellent study of the restaurant industry, and also by Reynolds and Shister in the book referred to previously.

Wages

The role of wages among the factors influencing industrial morale is of considerable interest. A good deal of the importance that has been attached to nonfinancial incentives has come from just such studies of morale that have shown that wages are relatively unimportant determinants of the employees' attitudes. Similarly, in this case, only 9 percent of all the things mentioned as reasons why the employee likes his present job fell into the category of wages. In picking the most important determinant of a good job, wages come off even worse—only 3 percent of the people pick wages as the most important determiner of a good job. It is worth noting, however, that when the question is asked, "If you were looking for a job, what aspects would you look for?" the wages come out very much higher. In looking for a job, 24 percent of all the factors mentioned fell in the category of *good wages*. The question about looking for a new job asks both (1) what are the desirable characteristics in a good job, and (2) which ones can you see. Pay is one of the easiest things to ascertain in looking for a job. This, no doubt, accounts for some of the increase in percentage when we ask "what would you look for in looking for a new job." There is some reason to believe, however, that the importance of wages is underestimated in other questions because there is a cultural inhibition against talking about them—in a sense it isn't nice to say that you like your job because you get good pay. In this connection it is interesting to notice that wages are mentioned 9 percent of the time when an employee describes why he likes his own job; when he describes why some other fellow likes *his* job, the wages jump to 17 percent in importance. Still another factor, and perhaps the most important in accounting for the possible underestimation of the role of wages, is the fact that the wages are apt to be taken for granted. These people have good jobs. They get good pay. Wages are a *sine qua non.* They are taken for granted to such an extent that it isn't even worthwhile mentioning them. If the foreman used a blacksnake whip to keep production up, that would certainly be one of the major determinants in disliking the job. The fact that he doesn't is not mentioned. It is taken for granted that the behavior of the supervisor will vary within certain limits, and it is not necessary to point out, in explaining why you like your job, that his behavior does not go outside these limits. Similarly, it is taken for granted that wages must be up to a certain level. It is not necessary to point out, in explaining why you like your job, that they are at least that high.

Supervision

The role of the foreman in determining industrial morale is interesting in these data. When an employee describes why he likes his job, only 3 percent of them mention the supervision. However, when the same employee describes why a hypothetical man dislikes his job, 15 percent of them blame it on the supervision. Similarly, in describing the most important determiners of a good job, 22 percent of these people refer to the foreman. This pattern puts a very peculiar pressure on first-line supervision. These people like their jobs, but the foreman is not the reason why they like them; on the other hand, they see the foreman in a role that makes it very easy for him to control the desirability of the job, and as having an important part in making a worker dislike his job. The impression is that the foreman works largely in the negative range. He can account for a considerable dislike of the job, and, if he works properly, he can bring the job up to a sort of zero level—a point from which the job can either be good or bad depending on a host of other factors. His main function, human relationswise, is to keep the job from being undesirable; after that, other things will make it desirable.

Before we have the implications of these data, it is interesting to notice the number of factors in the list that are associated with on-the-job need satisfactions. Most of the things that are mentioned as important here are things that the employee can enjoy on his job—interesting work, contact with associates and with customers, good working conditions, good supervision, and the like. Only in the area of wages, chance for advancement, and future job security do we get much emphasis placed on the kinds of need satisfactions that are primarily enjoyed off the job. We have become quite accustomed, in thinking about the motivations of industrial workers, to divide the incentives into financial and nonfinancial incentives. In view of the tremendous weight that is placed, in this and other morale studies, on need satisfactions that occur on the job, it seems possible that we should give more attention to the distinction between on-the-job and off-the-job satisfactions as incentives and motivators. When we want to increase productivity, we customarily increase the off-the-job satisfactions—we raise pay, provide benefits in terms of retirement, vacations, pension plans, and the like. It seems worthwhile asking whether we cannot provide more work-relevant incentives, in the area of factors that provide need satisfactions that can be enjoyed on the job.[5]

The Problem of Relativity

Presenting lists of the rank order of factors mentioned in industrial morale surveys is open to serious question as a way to lead us to an understanding of the nature of and the components of industrial morale. Asking the question, "What is the rank order of factors in need satisfactions at work?" seems to imply two things: (1) relatively fixed amounts of (2) relatively independent things. The question gives the impression that the situation is parallel to an analysis of the chemical content of a rock. What are the relative amounts of iron, silica, magnesium, and the like? It leads us to the belief that we can tease out and identify the separate components, estimate their relative magnitudes, and in this way understand the sum of the parts. There also seems to be, in this view, some implication that we can change the amount of one of the components without changing anything but its place in the rank order.

In practice the situation seems to be quite different. The factors involved in the attitude of industrial workers seem to be highly interdependent and fluctuating in intensity in response to changes in the individual or in the environment. The importance of opportunities for advancement must surely grow partly as a simple function

[5] We are indebted to Dr. Douglas M. MacGregor, in unpublished statements, for pointing out to us this distinction between on-the-job and off-the-job returns.

of time; the role of security in the job must be seriously influenced by the employee's perception of the whole national and international situation; and it seems quite possible that his response to supervision will be in some measure connected with his interpersonal relationships off the job and at home. The components are not fixed and inflexible. They are fluctuating and probably highly specific to the particular situation in which they are measured. Moreover, they are probably complexly interdetermined, so that an attempt to raise or lower one of them will not only change its rank order in the list, but will vigorously influence the others. For instance, in the areas in which unemployment is rising sharply and offering a serious threat to future job security, this factor (job security) no doubt increases greatly in importance, but at the same time the foreman takes a very different role, and the somewhat peripheral factors, such as working conditions and interest in work, probably lose some of their absolute as well as relative value.

In addition to their interdependence and fluctuating character, the things that we customarily list as factors in industrial morale seem to have a hierarchical character.[6] Some of them are more basic than others, and the less basic ones become real demands only after the more basic ones have been satisfied. When a man is crossing the desert, his thirst becomes so great that a host of other things that we would ordinarily list as important factors in his adjustment to living drop out because of the dominance of the single need. Once he has reestablished his equilibrium with respect to the need for water, some of the other "higher" needs may make an appearance. Similarly, in the industrial situation, if wages fall below a certain point, or job security is threatened, some of the "higher" factors may drop out of the picture altogether.

The other side of this coin may lead to a paradoxical picture. When the "basic" needs are satisfied, the demand for satisfaction of "higher" needs may become greater, rather than less. In more specific terms, this may mean that when pay and job security are high. It puts even more importance on the human relations aspect of the job than before rather than vice versa. To some extent there seems to have been a tendency to think that the various factors were substitutive: if we pay enough, we don't need to worry so much about the other factors. On the contrary, it seems quite possible that if we pay enough and pay it surely enough, it provides an opportunity for the other factors to become even more important. The history of industrial relations and personnel practices over the last few years illustrates the

---

[6] This point draws heavily on the theoretical work of A. H. Maslow (5). A. Kornhauser also raises somewhat the same question (2).

point. As we got into a period of full employment, with wages high and job security relatively good, more and more importance began to be demanded and placed on "human relations in industrial management." The reverse is true in a period of economic retrenchment. As unemployment mounts, there is a noticeable tendency on the part of employers to devalue the role of the "higher" need satisfactions in the area of human relations. This is generally explained as a cost problem—employers can no longer afford the luxury of a human relations program. It is, perhaps, also an implication of the hierarchical character of need satisfaction. A threat to basic need satisfaction activates defense mechanisms with respect to those basic needs which may make the satisfaction of "higher" needs temporarily less important.

If it is true that these patterns in industrial morale have the three characteristics that have been discussed here: (1) high interdependence, (2) relative flexibility in level, and (3) a hierarchical character, there are several important implications for our thinking in this area. Maslow points out ". . . a good way to obscure 'higher' motivations and to get a lopsided view of human capacities and human nature, is to make the organism extremely and chronically hungry or thirsty. . . . It is quite true that man lives by bread alone—when there is no bread. But what happens to man's desires when there *is* plenty of bread and when his belly is chronically filled?" Conversely, to obscure the importance of "basic" needs, we should study the situation where they are relatively well-satisfied, and relatively less detectable as behavioral determinants.

Much of the experimental work on motivation has been done on rats. The easiest things to control about rats' motivations are the basic need satisfactions. We have primarily tested them under extreme conditions of hunger and thirst. The theoretical development that has followed this work has perhaps overemphasized the role of basic drives and emergency functions. Industrial morale studies may have gone to the opposite end of the scale. They are customarily done in situations where the basic needs are relatively well satisfied. Very few workers in this country have wages so low that their actual eating is threatened, and we have almost no studies from the most marginal industries where this has in the past been true on occasion.[7] For this reason, we have to some extent the reverse result of the studies of

[7] In a recently completed but unpublished study of workers in a New England city who were threatened with very serious local unemployment, Drs. Charles A. Myers and George P. Shultz of M.I.T. point out that as their subjects lost job security, job security became much more important in their responses when they are asked why they like their present jobs and what they are seeking in jobs.

motivation in rats. We have probably grossly underestimated the role of basic needs, and hence of the economic factors associated with basic needs, and this situation may have led, to some extent, to the very considerable emphasis that has recently been placed on nonfinancial incentives. Nonfinancial incentives may appear primarily in situations where the financial incentive, and the consequent guarantee of basic need satisfactions, is so secure that it no longer appears as a primary and obvious behavior determinant, but is something that is taken for granted. In this connection we might notice again what happens to the percentages on the economic factors as determinants of morale in our study. In answering why he liked his job, or in describing the most important determinant of liking for the job, the economic factor gets very little weight. However, when we put the employee in the hypothetical situation of looking for a job—when he has no job, when he has no wages, when his basic needs are conjecturally threatened— the role of the economic factor goes up considerably in his responses. If he were actually in the situation that we have described hypothetically—if he were looking for a job in a less-than-full employment economy—would this factor rise even more in importance?

This concept of the hierarchical and relative character of the need satisfactions involved in morale influences the consequences of satisfaction and deprivation. It may be (and there is some experimental evidence in this direction) that those individuals whose basic needs have been satisfied in the past are best able to tolerate deprivation. We might, for example, think that a work group that had been accustomed to certain high levels of satisfaction would be more seriously threatened by a reduction in those levels than a group for which the level of satisfaction in the past had been lower or less reliable. This may not, however, be exactly the case. It is quite possible that the former group will prove to be more stable in tolerating present deprivations than the latter. It is not necessarily true that the way to learn frustration tolerance is to be frustrated.

It should be pointed out, in this connection, however, that money may be a special case in the deprivation of basic needs. It may be generally true that individuals who have been well satisfied in the past may tolerate present deprivations, but high wages as a means of obtaining basic need satisfaction produce a standard of living that becomes functionally autonomous and independent of its basic physiological counterpart. Under these circumstances, money may have a more rigid role in basic need satisfaction than, for instance, the provision of food and water to the hungry or thirsty rat would have.

The Problem of Context

It is a truism today that the way in which questions are asked is very important in interviewing. It needs to be reemphasized in the area of industrial morale, however, because it has special weight here. Questions about jobs and about the need satisfactions obtained at work are answered against a background of a certain level of need satisfaction that the employee is currently receiving, and the expectation of a certain level in the future. We cannot ask the same question of two employees in radically different work situations. There seems to be little doubt that the employees reported here who answered our questions about wages, for instance, were to a large extent determined by their relatively high wages and their relatively secure jobs. If we asked the same questions of migratory workers, we would no doubt get very, very different answers. Not only is the wording of the question important, but the background against which the questions are answered may change their meaning so much that they are very little comparable from one situation to another.

Many questions in morale studies are conjectural. "If you were going to do so and so, what would you want?" "If the situation were so and so, what would you do?" They evoke different organizations of the (conjectural) environment, and hence include different expectations of levels of need satisfaction and emphasize threats that may not be currently present in the work situation. To some extent all our conjectural questions are projective tests, and they need to be interpreted in this light. The organism dominated by a need changes its whole view of the world, and its evaluation of the future and of the things that are good and bad. The need shapes the picture of the environment. Conversely, when we ask about certain specified environments, we rouse certain needs. The picture of the environment shapes the need. In many cases we may not be tapping needs that are present in the current situation or, at best, we may be tapping complex compound results of needs generated by the present situation and those evoked by the conjectural environment specified in oour question. Such a situation may be extremely valuable if we interpret the response in the way in which we would interpret a projective test protocol. It may give us a valuable insight into the characteristics of the individual, but it may or may not reflect the situation in which he presently finds himself, or which we may be interested in studying.

In our study it seems probable that we ask three very different questions of the worker.

They are very different questions, and the answers to them are very different. The answer to the first question (What do you like about your present job?) is probably highly specific to the particular work situation in which these employees find themselves. It puts 60 percent of the weight on three factors: interesting, varied work; contact with people; and working conditions. The answer to the second question (When would you leave?) is still different. Five factors took in 85 percent of the responses: interesting work, working conditions, pay, supervision, and future promotion. Still another answer appears in terms of what an employee would look for in a new job: 60 percent of the weight falls on pay, working conditions, interesting work, and fitting the habits of living and working which employees presently have.

We have asked very different questions and got very different answers. If we are to go on and ask the question "Which of these answers tells us the factors that are important in morale?" the response is not at all clear. It may be all of them or none of them. It is difficult to know what remedial action to take. From the point of view of doing something about morale, we have raised very different issues to guide the employer:

1. How to keep employees liking their jobs.
2. How to keep them from leaving.
3. How to attract new workers.

The answers that we get from each specific area may be a guide to the employer in terms of practices that will accomplish each specific end. But by no means is this necessarily assurance that we have put our finger on the connection between morale and productivity, nor does it mean that practices based on these answers will insure good morale in another particular plant.

The Problem of Validity

In few other places in psychological research do we have so many measurements of "what's out there" with so little theoretical connectedness and so little detailed observation of change in criterial measures as we have in morale studies. To be sure, in some cases we do have measurements of changes in productivity, absenteeism, grievances, and the like, which provide a certain amount of measurement to validate observed levels of morale. However, even in these cases there is very little attempt to show any necessity in the relationship between the morale measure and the criterion.

Part of the reason for this lack of validation is our considerable poverty in an adequate theory of motivation in general and the theory of the specific motivational problem in industrial situations in particular. Still another part of the reason for the lack of validation lies in the fact that many of the research studies in the problem of industrial morale have their origin more in the commercial interest of an employer than in the interest of "pure" research. Very often this means that the problem is satisfactorily answered at the level of raw empiricism, and a statement of "what's out there" is all that the employer requires. Regardless of the reasons, the fact remains that we have little adequate validation to bolster our analyses of industrial morale, and the chief defect in this area seems to be a lack of a thorough-going theoretical formulation.

Lewin's formulation (3) has led us a long way in the direction of a theoretical formulation of the problem of what may happen if x force is changed. His theory has the advantage of affording us an opportunity to deal with motives and factors influencing morale in terms of dynamic patterning of the factors, and in addition it has the virtue of generating implications. An example of the kinds of implications that can be drawn from Lewin's formulation to the industrial situation can be found in the excellent article on factors influencing productivity by Coch and French in *Human Relations* (1).

While Lewin's statement does lead us some ways in the direction of being able to handle some of the problems of group behavior in the industrial situation, it does not at all answer the question of the internal patterning of needs within an individual, or the problem of relativity and the hierarchical character of needs within these patterns. We still find ourselves in the position where our most pressing demand is for an adequate theory of motivation that will allow us to make sense of the mass of data that has been accumulated in the area of industrial morale.

Bibliography

1. Coch, L. and French, J., "Overcoming Resistance to Change," *Human Relations*, 1948, 1, 4, 512–532.

2. Kornhauser, A., "Psychological Studies of Employee Attitudes," *Personnel*, November 1944, 21, 3, 1944, 170–189.

3. Lewin, K., "Frontiers in Group Dynamics," *Human Relations*, 1947, 1, 1, 5–41.

4. Lindahl, Lawrence G., "What Makes a Good Job?" *Personnel*, January 1949, 25, 4, 263–266.

5. Maslow, A. H., "A Theory of Human Motivation," in *Twentieth Century Psychology*, ed., P. L. Harriman, Philosophical Library, 1946.

6. Reynolds, Lloyd, and Shister, Joseph, "Job Horizons," *Harpers*, 1949.

7. Whyte, William, *Human Relations in the Restaurant Industry*, McGraw-Hill Book Company, Inc., New York, 1949.

Opinion Surveys:
The Results Are In—
What Do We Do with Them?

David Sirota

PEOPLE problems, particularly those that occur in the workplace, require pragmatic rather than what can be termed "religious" approaches. Pragmatism means simply determining what problems there are before attempting to solve them, whereas religious approaches define problems in doctrinaire fashion and then apply doctrinaire solutions. Because it is characterized by predefinition of problems, the religious approach rarely takes account of existing evidence. Generally, those who adhere to such approaches rely on a priestly class of "experts" to define problems and prescribe their solutions. In today's climate, for example, the high priests of the social sciences are prone to see boredom as the pervasive demon of the workplace; the cure, they claim, is an exorcism conducted with generous doses of job enrichment. But managements cannot afford to go along with faith healers for long. After a while, infatuation with terms such as "motivators," "hygiene factors," "consultative management," or whatever jargon they have been fed passes, as the nitty-gritty questions have to be answered: What is all this costing? What is it accomplishing? This is the real day of judgment.

One way to survive that day of judgment is to ensure that the right solutions are applied to the right problems. Organizations are complex; each has its own particular problems, based on variables such as its particular marketplace and product conditions and its management style. Something as ephemeral as the personality of an organization's top man, for example, can have an enormous influence as it translates itself into the personality of an organization. But individual peculiarities aside, it still holds true that any organization must find out what its problems are before it can solve them. Thus the first real step in chasing the corporate demons is to define the problems through sound diagnostic techniques.

As simple as it may seem, the soundest diagnostic technique consists of going directly to an organization's employees and asking them what's bothering them. More than once it has happened that what was bothering an assembly-line worker was nothing more than having inadequate equipment. But questions can also be as "complex" as: What do you think of your boss? The answers to these kinds of questions are readily attainable through opinion surveys and they can provide an accurate basis for beginning to address employee problems.

The case of a North Carolina textile plant illustrates the point. One of the company's plant managers was seeking outside help in job enrichment in his plant, which he believed was needed because employees were complaining about their pay. This plant manager had been told by a psychologist that when employees complain about their pay they are really providing subtle clues to the problems that *really* annoy them. Perhaps they are, but it's unlikely. Nearly everyone knows that when people complain about money, they are not being at all subtle. When a person contends that the cost of living has risen more than his salary and that as a result he has taken a pay cut, we don't need an inkblot test or a psychoanalyst's couch to figure out what he means. He means he has taken a pay cut.

The Distorting Effect of Built-in Bias

This example illustrates another danger of the religious approach—the tendency among those who follow it to lean toward what is in their own best interests. Too much amateur psychologizing produces a variety of hidden meanings to explain problems. Not surprisingly, these hidden meanings are frequently designed to serve the apparent ends òf those who think them up. Isn't it in the plant manager's interest to make people so happy with their work that they forget about asking for more money? It's tempting to think so, but more than likely, the company's self-interest would be better served by some healthy gains in productivity or by a lowering of turnover rates that would come from attention to real, rather than imagined, problems.

It cannot be emphasized enough that prejudging problems almost never works. The cases of a bank and of an engineering company illustrate the point. Both businesses had the same problem— employee turnover. The bank thought it was losing analysts because the content of the work was essentially boring; the engineering firm had no idea why it had such a high turnover rate among its engineers.

The people who had left the firms were asked, through questionnaires, to explain why they had done so. The people who stayed were also asked a variety of questions designed to determine whether they were planning to leave and why. (Data from these and other case studies indicate that questioning present employees is a more reliable method of predicting turnover than the usual studying of last year's statistics.) Some of the information obtained from both organizations was nearly identical. The employees who had left both firms said they did so for the same reasons that employees who stayed gave for planning to leave. In other respects, however, the companies differed markedly.

In the engineering company, the problem was one of job content and underutilization of people. It stemmed primarily from an old practice that continues to plague many engineering managers—their propensity to hire engineers when they really need technicians. The bank's data were different. There the problem was simply money; the highly trained trust analysts enjoyed their work, but were leaving for better pay.

In a review of the data with the bank's president and staff, the personnel director immediately took out his employee manual and noted that the salary ranges of the trust analyst positions were "competitive" with other institutions. But the basic objection to looking at salary ranges is that employees don't shop with them. As it turned out, the average actual pay of 50 percent of the employees who had left the bank was below the minimum of the range. (Ironically, by the most conservative estimate the bank's turnover was costing four times as much in recruiting and training expenses than what it would cost to raise salaries to the point where people were willing to stay.)

What's the best way to determine proper salary levels? Here again, the direct approach is best. Asking employees exactly how much money it would take to keep them provided the best figure. In this case, the bank took corrective measures and its turnover rate dropped 18 percent in just three months. This kind of result shows what can happen when solutions are based on empirical definitions of problems rather than on guesswork, however educated the guesswork may be.

The "Magic" of Job Enrichment

Of course, job enrichment is sometimes a valid solution to an employee problem. But when it is, managers must be careful not to approach job enrichment (the solution) any more doctrinarily than they approached boring work (the problem). If managers aren't cautious, the religious approach can take over at any stage of the problem-solving game.

At Company Y, where a great deal of enrichment work was done, it was found that the best approach to job enrichment was, simply, the one with which people felt the most comfortable. In many instances, AT&T's famous brainstorming techniques were used. In a number of cases, employees participated in the process; in other cases they did not. As yet, there simply isn't enough information to be sure which approach works best. It seems sensible enough to assume, however, that the Company Y yardstick of what people are most comfortable with is a good one.

Flexibility and a willingness to set aside common assumptions are keys to the successful application of techniques such as job enrichment; this holds true even in deciding who should do the job enriching. Those who take religious approaches to corporate problems insist that handling an organization's people problems requires special "priests," who are generally ordained with various degrees and who have been thoroughly schooled in the rituals of the behavioral sciences. At Company Y, however, it became apparent that the best way to introduce job enrichment was to develop internal company resources and get the experts out of the picture as quickly as possible.

There are capable, conscientious, and respected people in any office or plant. With a minimum of training (generally no more than about four or five days), these people (whether they are engineers, production men, or clerks) turn out to be ideal job enrichers. It took a lot of trial and-error at Company Y to arrive at these astoundingly simple conclusions. But trial and error is better than preordained ritual, because managers eventually pin down exactly what techniques produce the best results *for them.*

"Magic" Substantiating—and Revealing—Solid Facts

In fairness, it must be noted that not all diagnoses produce startling revelations that are completely at odds with management's initial impressions. Diagnostic work just completed at a large insurance organization is an illustration, because here, management's prior diagnoses of the need for job enrichment held up.

The accompanying figure shows the results of a survey in which white collar workers within the organization were asked to respond to statements such as: "My job makes good use of my skills and abilities." Sixty-one percent of the supervisors agreed that their skills and abilities were well used, but 70 percent of the employees disagreed. Such data clearly, even dramatically, indicate problems for which job enrichment is an appropriate remedy. But, despite its accuracy, it still could have been costly for management to follow its a priori diagnosis. Other questions asked of this group of white collar workers (in all, about 140 questions were asked) identified a range of other significant problems, as well as some organizational strengths.

As it turned out, job content was only one of the problems. Another was workload. Clearly, giving additional responsibilities to employees who already see themselves as overworked can exacerbate dissatisfaction rather than ameliorate it. The point about job enrichment—and any other formalized technique, for that matter—is that it can solve one problem but seriously aggravate another, if the total context of the problem is not comprehended.

Job enrichment can also be dangerous when it is applied to people who have salary grievances. If employees believe they are underpaid, and the discrepancy between what they are giving and what they are getting is increased, the result is trouble. Some managers have the foolish notion that interesting work is a substitute for good pay. And job enrichment is also of dubious validity if applied to employees who will continue to work under close supervision. In such instances, employees are likely to view the redesign of their jobs as just another management gimmick. And they will be right.

In the insurance organization where job enrichment training was begun, the broad organizational context did receive consideration.

Employee Opinion Survey Results
from a Government Agency:
Job Content Questions and Answers in Percentages

Q. My job makes good use of my skills and abilities.

	Agree	*Neither*	*Disagree*
Supervisors	61	23	16
Employees	12	19	70

Q. Most of my work could be handled by a person with *less* experience or training.

	Agree	*Neither*	*Disagree*
Supervisors	51	26	23
Employees	22	11	67

Q. My work is interesting.

	Agree	*Neither*	*Disagree*
Supervisors	68	23	9
Employees	14	18	68

Q. My job gives me a feeling of worthwhile accomplishment.

	Agree	*Neither*	*Disagree*
Supervisors	48	32	20
Employees	10	17	72

Five or six units were designated for enrichment to be carried out and five or six control groups were selected. The organization devised its own means of training, which included heavy emphasis on changing supervisor behavior, along with content of jobs. Supervisors and employees worked together as enrichment teams. The evaluation of this project is not yet complete, but early indications are that it is working well.

When it is successful, job enrichment is a dynamic and beneficial way to go. An 8 percent improvement in productivity after one Company Y enrichment experiment saved the company $150,000 on the cost of manufacturing an electronic component. But as impressive as such statistics are (and they abound), managers must not allow themselves to be tempted by the pie-in-the-sky dreams to which such statistics lend themselves. Managers must seek out from employee opinion surveys hard evidence and take nothing on faith or on clever admixtures of various opinions on various subjects. Again, the point is best put simply: Find out what the problem is before butting in—and find out from the horse's mouth.

Charting and Changing the Organizational Climate

Melvin Sorcher and Selig Danzig

IT is almost a truism that the continued growth of a business organization is largely dependent upon the resourcefulness and energy of its managers, its technical employees, and its administrative staff, yet there is disappointingly little effort directed at stimulating and sustaining the highest possible creative and energetic performance. There are, of course, many programs and techniques that presumably "develop" managers and others for improved performance, but the lasting value of their application has not been demonstrated in critical evaluations.

Managerial example is not often discussed or even thought of as part of the development process or as a motivational activator, but managerial behavior can certainly influence the development of subordinates and also, by example, set the tone of the *climate* within the organization, which is management's "silent partner." Indeed, it is the manager who exerts a major influence on organizational climate, and therefore on the individuals within it. He should play a crucial and active role in stimulating his subordinates and in helping them grow, but many managers are not fully aware of the impact of their behavior or style.

Lost in the Crowd

In a small company, the performance of each professional employee is visible and usually important, but in large, complex corporations the very size and multilayered management contribute to the relative invisibility of individual performance. Many of these individuals see their efforts as miniscule, and in many cases they are right.

Part of the problem is that under these circumstances there is no incentive for the professional employee to do anything beyond the minimum required to keep his job as a jumping-off point for one in which he dreams of becoming a vital and dynamic element. Another part of the problem is that, in their current positions, too many of these employees are not motivated to self-initiated action. They dawdle at their jobs and are unconcerned about organizational and business problems. They are not goal oriented, but instead handle things on a day-to-day basis and see little relationship between their own work and the goals or products of their company.

These conditions have been informally discussed by the authors, who believe that many professionals are not working at all close to the extent of their capabilities, and who arrived at a basic question about the inhibiting elements in work environments: Can we motivate professional people to the limit of their capability by changing organizational climate?

Components of Climate

To find answers to this question, a study was undertaken at one of General Electric's Syracuse, N.Y. plants. The study focused on the perspectives of individuals toward various elements of their work situation that were treated in research by Herbert H. Meyer and George Litwin. They identified several variables as components, or dimensions, of organizational climate:

Constraining conformity. Feelings of employees about constraints that they think stifle motivation.

Responsibility. How much responsibility employees think they are given to run the job without having to check with the boss about every decision, and how much risk management is willing to take in running the business.

Standards. How much emphasis employees think is placed on doing a good job; the degree to which challenging goals are set and pressure is exerted to improve individual and group performance.

Reward. Employees' opinions about being fairly rewarded for good work, rather than only being disciplined when something goes wrong.

Organizational clarity. Employees' impressions that things are pretty well organized, rather than disorderly, confused, or chaotic.

Cohesiveness. The degree to which employees feel that management and fellow employees are warm and trusting and that the organization is one to identify with and be proud to belong to.

Pay and promotional opportunity. Opinions about the pay and promotional opportunities available.

Recognition and support. How well other people, especially managers, can identify employees' contributions and the extent to which these accomplishments are acknowledged.

Questionnaire Approach

The study described here started with a questionnaire that was designed to determine the existing organizational climate and was given again six months later to obtain data for evaluating change. The questions asked related to each of the eight climate variables listed above, with the score on each variable based on weights assigned to four possible responses to each question.

The section managers of the participating operational functions asked their subordinates to cooperate in this project, and the subsection or unit manager of each group that participated was requested to identify the criteria of organizational effectiveness that he believed were appropriate to measure his own group. This information was to be used later as a crosscheck on the direction and magnitude of change in organizational climate indicated by the questionnaire data.

The groups participating in this research included engineering, marketing, and finance operations in the same organization. After they had scored the initial questionnaires, the authors averaged the questionnaire responses of the individual members of each group so that the final score was an arithmetical mean. With few exceptions, the distribution of scores clustered closely about the mean—a particularly important consideration here, because the number of individuals in most groups was small.

Then the research team met with each of the groups to describe their scores and ask them about the kinds of attitudes, viewpoints, and concerns that had dictated the group's averaged response to the questionnaire. (The functional manager was not present during these feedback sessions.) This information was evaluated together with the questionnaire data and reported to the manager of each group.

The Researcher's Report

This report treated each of the climate variables separately, noting relationships between them when appropriate, and included the research team's observations and recommendations. The recommendations were intentionally implicit; they were not put in directive terms because it was expected that a manager's responsiveness would depend a great deal on how much leeway he thought he had in deciding the mechanics of change and in implementing action plans.

Although the managers' action plans differed in detail, they did have points in common. For example, several plans resulted in a manager's meeting with his group and with them reviewing his responsibilities and the kinds of knowledge and information he would need for sound decision making and adequate control in various situations. The manager and his group then worked out ways for the group members to share in some of these responsibilities and to make some of these decisions.

In other aspects of the plans there were similarities, too. Some managers met with their groups to discuss what preparation the employees needed to be considered for promotion. Previously, employees had had little idea of what was expected of them and had often felt adrift in the organization, with little control over their futures. The clarifying discussions were expected to provide meaningful guidelines with foreseeable goal points for these employees.

Other managers decided, as a part of their attempt to improve employee perceptions of climate, to clearly define the relationships between individuals within the group and with people outside their group, on the assumption that an awareness of personal roles in an organization is essential to effective group performance.

It was apparent that the managers' actions were directed at the specific factors in organization climate where they felt improvement was called for. Thus, to correct what seemed to be a lack of responsibility, they sought ways to give subordinates more responsibility; to overcome subordinates' perceptions of being unappreciated or unnecessary, they introduced indications of recognition and support.

Effecting Change

With the needed changes in organizational climate fairly well established, the authors then tried to determine what procedure would be most effective in bringing about the recommended changes. Three different conditions were compared:

1. The group manager was asked to develop written action plans based on the researchers' report of observations and recommendations.

2. The group manager was not asked to develop *written* plans, but was asked to take action.

3. The group manager was only given feedback; he was *not* asked to do anything.

All the managers in the first two situations responded in action terms to the team's report, both with and without written plans. Four group managers were in the third situation; two took action on their own initiative to respond to the report of recommendations, but the other two did not.

The Second Time Around

About three months after the managers in situations 1 and 2 had submitted or discussed their action plans with the employee relations representative on the research team, the questionnaire was given again. It would have been desirable to allow more time for the full impact of change to be felt, but a major reorganization was about to take place, and it was necessary to remeasure the groups before they were reshuffled. As it was, some of the groups that began the study were no longer available, and the overall sample size was thereby reduced. Nevertheless, some clear findings and implications emerged when the questionnaire rerun was analyzed.

All the groups whose managers had been in situations 1 and 2 appeared to reflect their managers' actions to change the organizational climate, because there was a significant "before-after" difference in perceptions of climate—a difference not at all likely to be accounted for on the basis of casual or chance variation. It is particularly interesting to note that in situation 3, two managers had not been asked to take action but had anyway, and a significant change in perception of organizational climate was found in their groups, too. On the other hand, groups headed by the situation 3 managers who did not respond to the researchers' report registered no change in their perception of the climate.

These differences in results did not seem to be related to organizational function or component—engineering, marketing, finance—nor to the initial level of perceived climate, but rather to factors associated with the experimental conditions. The value of requiring a manager to write down his *commitment* to respond to the need for change in organizational climate was not established, but apparently an actual response on the part of a manager along specific, recommended lines was instrumental in changing employees' perceptions.

Implications for the Future

These findings suggest that a manager can control the climate of his group and, therefore, that an instrument to assess climate can be very useful. Rather than guessing at what sorts of situations and conditions will best motivate each of the individuals who report to him, the manager would find it much less time-consuming and certainly more fruitful to learn first how his subordinates perceive the climate in specified dimensions. This information should give a manager well-defined guidance in planning how and where to change the climate.

This study, by a feedback process, forced the managers to think about their organizational climate and its components, and how their people reacted to working in that environment. However, the most significant aspect of the study had to do with the action plans undertaken by the managers as a consequence of the data presented. It was suggested to the managers that they might develop plans to effect change in the areas indicated, but the actual plans came from them. (The employee relations representatives assigned to each functional area did, however, help the managers develop their plans and track the progress being made.)

Changing organizational climate seems to be feasible, but follow-up study is needed, with closer controls, carefully equated groups, and larger sample sizes. Also, it is important to identify outside criteria of climate change, such as performance standards. In future studies, each manager should determine what are reliable gauges of his group's effectiveness in order to validate observed changes in questionnaire replies.

We hope that this approach to the study and change of organizational climate will be confirmed by subsequent studies. There is an urgent need to bring the reality of organizational climate into line with the expectations of individuals who work in that climate; otherwise, many organizations will find that they have lost their best contributors and are left with a slow-moving, unimaginative, and uninterested collection of employees.